D1569251

More Praise for
Signs of Success

"Great minds think alike, and therein lies the problem. If you approach business (or life) from the same perspective as everyone else, success becomes that much more difficult to achieve. . . . With *Signs of Success*, Steve Weiss provides another tool for your management quiver—one that others are not likely to consider. Bad for them. Good for you."

—Paul B. Brown, business columnist and coauthor
of the international bestseller *Customers for Life*

"*Signs of Success* has put a new tool in my toolbox. Steve Weiss is a learned, insightful, savvy, and fearless explorer of places less traveled yet rich in resources. It is fascinating, provocative, and brilliantly written . . . an instant classic."

—Louis Patler, coauthor of *If It Ain't Broke . . . Break It!;*
and President, B.I.T. Consulting Group

SIGNS OF SUCCESS

THE REMARKABLE POWER OF
BUSINESS ASTROLOGY

STEVEN MARK WEISS

AMACOM

American Management Association
New York • Atlanta • Brussels • Chicago • Mexico City • San Francisco
Shanghai • Tokyo • Toronto • Washington, D.C.

Special discounts on bulk quantities of AMACOM books are
available to corporations, professional associations, and other
organizations. For details, contact Special Sales Department,
AMACOM, a division of American Management Association,
1601 Broadway, New York, NY 10019.
Tel.: 212-903-8316.   Fax: 212-903-8083.
E-mail: specialsls@amanet.org
Website: www.amacombooks.org/go/specialsales
To view all AMACOM titles go to: www.amacombooks.org

This publication is designed to provide accurate and authoritative
information in regard to the subject matter covered. It is sold with the
understanding that the publisher is not engaged in rendering legal, accounting, or other professional service. If legal advice or other expert
assistance is required, the services of a competent professional person
should be sought.

Library of Congress Cataloging-in-Publication Data

Weiss, Steve M.
    Signs of success : the remarkable power of business astrology / Steven Mark Weiss.
        p.   cm.
    Includes bibliographical references and index.
    ISBN-13: 978-0-8144-7441-9
    ISBN-10: 0-8144-7441-1
    1. Astrology and business.   I. Title.

BF1729.B8W45   2008
133.5'865—dc22

2007043424

Printing number
10 9 8 7 6 5 4 3 2 1

To Ann and Jesse

who, both blessed with Libra Moon and Jupiter in Cancer,
have so graciously and loyally put up with the household alien

contents

pARt tHRee: Business Beyond Sun Signs

PReface

It's been my experience that most (not all) astrologers tend to have an emotional guardedness about them and perhaps it's just as well. Fixated upon the heavens, playing at omniscience, protecting their odd turf from the uninitiated, astrologers make a vocational commitment that really tends to benefit from a vague personal focus. Or maybe it's as you've always suspected and they are just camouflaging the sad and ambitionless lives of overly credulous losers.

So help me, it's what I thought myself at one time. As my own early interest in astrology started to grow some roots, I came to realize that I didn't mind that astrologers were potentially quite crazy. What killed me was that these cosmic vagabonds were so immodest about what they claimed to know. Who could believe that these among all God's creatures, these people whom you would not want to invite to the dance, were given the gift of special sight?

This view has been chastened and much softened over my years of exposure to astrology and astrologers, but its acuteness in my early years of fascination with the subject left two indelible realizations: The first of these was that there would likely never be much social or financial upside in becoming a practicing astrologer and that, as a professional path, astrology should be avoided at all costs. The second, a bit more subtle but no less personally profound, was that if I wanted to believe anything that astrology had to offer, I would have to study it for myself and embrace its knowledge firsthand.

So where did interest actually begin? Like so many of the truly valuable things in one's life, for me it started with romance. The year was 1970, I was a senior in college, and I had fallen for a girl whose birthday was almost exactly the same as my own and who had an interest in astrology.

When I craftily expressed some interest in her interest, the target of my affections presented me with three books on the subject, all published in the late 1960's. These were: Linda Goodman's *Sun Signs* (New York: Taplinger, 1969); Joan Quigley's *Astrology for Adults* (New York: Holt, Rinehart and Winston, 1969); and Dane Rudhyar's *An Astrological Triptych* (New York: ASI, 1968). So many years and books later, I have come to realize that these three works still form the literary pillars of my appreciation for the subject of astrology.

It is hard to find someone with even the most superficial of astrological interests who did not first come to that interest through Linda Goodman's work. Her enduring popularity as an astrological author is signified by the fact that there are now some 100 million copies of her books in print. While the intellectual and astrological elite may turn up their noses (in envy, I might argue) at her populist presentation of astrology, the enormous conceptual epiphany of a universe working in concert with different personality types has more often than not taken place with a copy of Goodman's delightfully accessible work in one's hands.

Although the title may seem a bit patronizing, Joan Quigley's thoughtful work fully opened up for me the awareness that astrology was not merely concerned with twelve general types of personalities. Remarkable for both its breadth of insight and its literary efficiency, *Astrology for Adults* presents the knowledge that not only the Sun but also all the other bodies in the solar system are linked with human attributes that are colored by the bodies' specific positions in the heavens at the moment's of one birth. Astrology, Quigley first taught me, does not deny human beings a complexity that stretches vastly beyond the sun sign horoscopes on the newspaper comic pages.

(As a brief aside, when *People* magazine in 1988 covered the publication of a former presidential chief of staff's memoirs that "outed" Nancy and Ronald Reagan for an ongoing consultative relationship with an astrologer, that astrologer was identified as Joan Quigley. Some people were appalled that the most powerful couple on Earth was inclined towards metaphysics, but personally I was relieved. "Don't worry," I enjoyed telling people at the time, "she's an excellent astrologer.")

As for Dane Rudhyar, one confronts perhaps the most enlightened astrological thinker of the twentieth century, the field's Einstein. His enormous intelligence and spirit stamp astrology with a particular nobility of thought and purpose, managing an enlightened and evolutionary understanding of human potential and purpose as expressed through the patterns and cycles of astrological thinking. It is without shame that I report not being able to understand Rudhyar at all for a long time, but this author was immediately someone who appealed to the humanities student within, the one who occasionally believed that wise men existed and would be worth the effort of diligent apprehension.

As already indicated, all of this work first appeared in the late 1960s, and none of these authors might have made such an impression, girlfriend prospects notwithstanding, if the times had not been so right for this sort of material. Today it has become fashionable to dismiss the 1960s as a lame festival of drug-addled hippies and peaceniks, but that is an overstatement and a judgment rather than an understanding of the culture. Even to the extent that the "flower power" assessment is not completely off base, some of us who were there and freely participated in the liberation of consciousness feel better about ourselves than you may think.

Astrology was just one avenue of many at that time that let an admittedly self-involved and self-glorifying (but not inherently evil)
generation search for personal identity on a grand theatrical (not a
dirty word) scale. As children of the Cold War and nuclear arms proliferation, and as young adults threatened by the daily reality of con-
scription and the Vietnam war, you would think we might get a little
more credit for so enthusiastically celebrating life and for so sincerely
entertaining non-nihilistic scenarios regarding the purpose of existence. And ultimately, if our parents did not want us to embrace the
likes of astrology they should never have sent us off to liberal arts colleges where mind-altering substances were plentiful and freshmen
English included the mythology-infested works of the great classical
tragedians and epic poets.

Anyway, the late 1960s and 1970s became an enormously rich
period for the evolution of a quasi-psychological, quasi-transcendental
strain of astrology. Authors such as Stephen Arroyo, Liz Greene,
Robert Hand, Robert Pelletier, Noel Tyl, John Townley, and Marc
Roberts—really, there are too many to mention—took the root of
an ancient art and began expressing it in terms that were simultaneously relevant to modern character and timeless in their appeal to
whatever it is in us that responds to the appeal of universal cycles and
connections. Many of the works produced in this era also somewhat
counter-intuitively had a didactic textbook quality, and that coupled
with the early astrological programs written for the likes of the
Tandy TRS-80 computer, made it possible for an interested "everyman" to learn how to "do" astrology.

For me, this was hobby material rather than a vocational calling. By the mid-1970s I had earned an English degree and a culinary school degree, and I had taken a job as the food and wine
editor for a leading national restaurant business publication based in
Chicago. Professionally, I was eagerly tracking the trends of a na-

tional dining-out industry that was just entering into its era of most explosive growth.

It was simply good fortune that the place where my career began to flourish is also the place where I became vested in the practice of astrology. The name David Horbovetz will be recalled with fondness by anyone in Chicago's astrological community during this period, as his Halsted Street business, The Astrologers' Medium, became an important center for astrological instruction and metaphysical bonding at this time. It was David, a classically trained violinist, from whom I received much of the how-to knowledge of horoscope casting and interpretation, and from whom I bought my first computer, one of those landmark TRS-80s.

From this point the story is one of fairly straightforward career evolution, with astrology lurking as a touchstone in the background. As hospitality-industry journalism was joined by hospitality-industry consulting, and as that morphed into a larger interest in demographic research and broad consumer trends, astrology became like an old college friend I could call on when I wanted to relax and have a good think about something. Occasionally, and usually unexpectedly, it would come to visit in the world of everyday affairs.

Generally, the precipitant would be the casual discovery that a client was to some degree a fellow traveler. Once, as an example, upon discovering our mutual interest in the field over an after-hours cocktail, the executive vice president of a multibillion-dollar corporation paid me to visit his astrologer so that I could render an opinion about that astrologer's ability. On another occasion, the owner of a regional chain of restaurants asked me to help select an auspicious moment for a restaurant opening and then later blamed me (astrologers get this a lot) when I could find no good moment in the preselected window of opportunity and accurately predicted that the physical plant had severe hidden problems that would erupt after the opening.

The most marked intrusion of astrology into my normal professional affairs came as a result of some research I conducted in preparation for a speech at a National Restaurant Association convention in the mid-1980s. Upon that occasion I polled over a hundred food experts on their culinary preferences and, almost as an afterthought, asked them to reveal their dates of birth. The consonance of answers among those of the same astrological sun signs, buffered with the polling results of a few hundred more respondents, led to a book, *Signs of Taste* (Portland, Oreg.: Breitenbush, 1988), that explores astrology-based culinary insight much as this book addresses leadership and general business insight.

During the release of *Signs of Taste*, a few clients and professional associations were gracious enough to give me an audience for my astrology-based findings. What I learned from that experience is that there is a very warm empathy for this sort of material provided one is not too dogmatic in the delivery and one cheerfully allows for the differences between open and closed minds. And as I suspected at the outset, an honest allowance for fallibility keeps all but the most strident of critics from throwing real stones.

Ultimately though, whatever its systemic utility or empirical veracity, astrology has earned a place in my own life as a goad to thought and a source of delightful epiphanies that I would be hard pressed to duplicate with other tools. Whether it's a personal change of fortune, the quirk of a companion, or a "lucky guess" about trends, astrology generally has an explanation that is no less rich for being mysteriously derived. It is a constantly amusing companion.

And even before that girl in college, there was a little boy who used to go to the New York's Hayden Planetarium and marvel at the ceiling full of stars. Today, half a century later, that little boy can still go outside on a clear night and tell you, while noting their celestial positions, the story of Perseus and Andromeda, or in the late summer he can easily point to the center of the galaxy and offer some opinions of Pluto's imminent passage across that spot. His life, no matter your own disposition towards cosmic vagabonds, is no less rich for that.

acknowLedgments

In a book that seeks its purpose in the infinite potentialities of the universe and the virtually limitless manifestations of human character, there is definitely some danger of overdoing the appreciations. One comfortably begins with the Creator, of course, but it gets a little murky after that. Please accept the fact that I am entirely sincere, as well as literal, when I say I'd like to acknowledge everything and to thank everyone.

As this last presents a logistical problem, kindly indulge me the less than stellar solution of a categorical approach. At least this methodology is resonant with the presentation of the book's material. And I think it will help me to overlook fewer of the deserving, which I now realize is the great fear of any author granted the privilege of proffering testimonials.

So kindly allow me to start my thank-yous with the astrologers, those who have taught and counseled me directly, and the many more who have passed on their stimulating, and not infrequently sage, observations in books and journals. Many of these good souls are mentioned throughout the text although I would like to here again mention my first teacher, David Horbovetz, who convinced me that smart people might take this material seriously. I'd also like to mention Jody, who set me on the path; Nancy, who insisted a guided tour of the path was desirable; and the collegial community of the Arizona Society of Astrologers, who had a much larger impact on my remaining on the path than they may have ever imagined.

I must also offer the deepest of bows to all of the friends, colleagues, employers, and clients in my business sphere who have encouraged me to keep my mind open and to call it the way I see it. I know that for most of them an appreciation of astrology is marginal at best, but they most always let on that they appreciate me, and for that I am immeasurably grateful. The material and spiritual generosity of Ken Beller, Louis Patler, Michael Chase, Curt Gibson, Janna Trout, Jan Croatt, Jim Adams, Will Chizmar, Judy Shoen, Sherri Daye Scott, John Pryor, Larry Weissman, and Suzanne Miller, Mark Leibovit, Lisa Ekus, Jim Anderson, James Brewer, and Neil Cumsky, among others whom I will hate myself in the morning for having inadvertently omitted, has been nothing less than essential to the existence of this book.

As for the special souls who have worked directly on this project I have to begin with my agent, John Willig, who flawlessly cautioned and counseled, and then could have been knocked over by a ray of sunshine when AMACOM, a great name in business publishing, expressed enthusiasm for the project. On the AMACOM side I will be forever indebted to Hank Kennedy and Ellen Kadin, and their brilliant colleagues, for what can only be described as intellectual courage in bringing this book to light under the AMACOM imprimatur. I am especially beholden to the associate editor, Mike Sivilli, creative director Cathleen Ouderkirk, the promotion team under the direction of Vera Sarkanj, and to Niels Buessem, who in editing the text lived up to every bit of his Aquarius potential for genius and a deft human touch.

Ironically, it is generally the people who pay the greatest price who come in last on an acknowledgments list. To my friends and family there is nothing I can say that adequately expresses my gratitude to you for your love and support and infinite patience. And mom, I am particularly aware that I wouldn't have made it this far without your weekly long-distance declamation of the horoscope column in the *TV Guide*.

Finally, I need to thank one Ann C. Johnson for her unflagging stewardship of a matter that doubtlessly seemed almost trivial to her but was important to me. There is goodness yet in the universe. That's the important thing.

PROLOGUE
Do You Really Believe in This Stuff?

The universe is full of magical things patiently waiting for our wits to grow sharper.

—Eden Phillpotts, *A Shadow Passes*

Some years ago I was meeting with a close friend and valued client, celebrating a moment of considerable professional and personal triumph we had just shared. I said something about my role as a consultant in his business efforts and he responded that he didn't think of me as a consultant. I of course asked what he meant.

"You're not a consultant," said my friend. "You're a scout. I use you to find out stuff that I need to know about."

That distinction resonated then and has continued to resonate throughout my career. Perhaps as most business consultants, I'd like to think that my best contributions are in the substantive areas of analysis, planning, and execution. It is quite often the truth, however, that my role as a consultant has been more that of an idea prospector, bringing back intriguing and hopefully useful raw material for the mills of executive minds that are ultimately saddled with the twin headaches of making decisions and taking responsibility for them.

Over the years my own path has admittedly been more that of the journalist and researcher rather than that of the management guru. It is my nature to be excited about discovering, and to want to communicate, interesting "stuff." If I am trained by professional experience, it is to identify and report unique and (I hope) business-relevant phenomena.

Against this background it is time to confess that I've long considered the field of astrology worthy of at least a little serious attention from business executives. Personally, I've embraced its teachings and techniques in my business dealings far more than I've ever willingly acknowledged (and occasionally shared its insights with clients, some of whom would be troubled by the implications of credulousness if their names were revealed here). After nearly forty years of sincere avocational interest in the field, including the production of one book and a number of journal articles—not too mention attendance at incalculable seminars and classes—you may consider this a full coming out of the cosmic closet.

This immediately brings us to the essential interrogative that always pops up when astrology is advanced as a serious subject. Sometimes this inquiry is breathlessly posed as, "Have you lost your mind?" More politely the question is put, "Do you really believe in this stuff?"

To answer this as straightforwardly as possible, astrology is not well focused as an issue of beliefs. Astrology is an art dressed up in the scientific guise of astronomy, so the proper question may well be, "Do you believe that intuition, inspiration, and creative understanding may sometimes be based upon celestial mechanics and mathematics?" It really should suffice to people of curiosity that, whatever its status as a rational pursuit, astrology has existed since the advent of civilization and has been seriously and appreciatively remarked upon by some of history's greatest thinkers. It has also been employed to advantage, of this there is no doubt, by some of mankind's greatest leaders and achievers.

Astrology, although hardly a science in any rigorous and completely rational sense of the term, deserves a commendation for its rigorous examination of data, for the intellectual forms into which this data is organized, and for its ability to inspire some sort of "life-giving" awareness. At its core, astrology builds inspiring constructs of archetypes and understandings and values that have enormous relevance to the processes and personalities of the world, including its commerce. Terms like "psychological profiling" and "effective habits" and "team building" may be more to modern business tastes, but that seems a poor excuse for leaving unexamined a rich antecedent of psychology that exceptional minds have been pondering for the past 5,000 years.

This understanding that astrology organizes and describes data, in particular human behavioral data, on a comprehensive level at least as rich as that offered in more "scientific" personality analyses, is where much of its potential business value lies. It is this insight in its relation to the lives of business greats—that astrology elegantly traces archetypal patterns of historical success that would-be leaders and associates would do well to recognize and emulate—that forms the backbone of this book. Yet there are also other useful limbs to this particular knowledge tree.

Beyond its application regarding personality/values profiling, another great use of astrology is in identifying the cycles related to business and consumer trends. The great American social commentator Mark Twain reputedly once observed that "history doesn't repeat itself, but it rhymes." In all the years I have spent tracking trends as a journalist and marketing consultant, nothing in my experience more accurately reflects the periodicity of market enthusiasms and cold shoulders like the timing associated with astrological cycles. Cigars, denim, and gourmet hamburgers are, I have learned, just some of the consumer products on multiyear "planetary" cycles as nearly dependable as sunset and sunrise. No fooling.

Of course, there is also the real nut of this sometimes-squirrelly subject: prognostication. This matter will be dealt with in some depth a few pages from here, but every beginning in the business world—the opening of a new unit, the launch of a marketing campaign, the hiring of a key employee—would seem to embrace the intuitive every bit as much as it embraces the factual. Astrology purports to identify auspicious and inauspicious moments for getting into such things and, I know this strains credulity, *appears* to work when undertaken by a *competent* caster of horoscopes far more often than would seem possible on a random basis.

Again, none of this is meant to convey a too strenuous *rational* defense of astrology. But if I may be permitted a contemporary cultural observation, now seems like a pretty good time to consider the supra-rational gifts of the spirit and imagination.

We live at a time in which we are being devoured by the capabilities of technology applied to data collection and transmission. As my co-authors (Ken Beller and Louis Patler) and I observed in our recently published demographic study, *The Consistent Consumer* (Chicago: Dearborn Trade Press, 2005), this has a lot to do with the increasing influence of a generation whose early adolescent values were formed during the emotional chaos of the Vietnam era. Finding heroes neither among belligerent hawks nor spaced-out doves, this generation in its adulthood has reasonably come to value scientific empiricism salted with a liberal dash of cynicism as a saner approach than self-righteousness to human problem solving.

Unfortunately, this sober attitude tends to narrowly exalt empirical data and rational utilitarianism over the full variety and depth of human interests and potentials. With ever increasing speed and efficiency the "facts" are collected, the spreadsheets are filled, and the results are communicated. But something in the way of genuine experience and assimilation, not to mention passion or entirely satisfactory results, is missing. What we have in ascendance in the world is a race of engineers, when we could honestly also use a few more sociologists, cultural anthropologists, humanistic philosophers, and perhaps, astrologers.

Certainly there is irony in the fact that astrology, at least on one level, is another data-based system that is only made practicable in a broad sense by the very technology I may seem to be disparaging. Prior to the proliferation of computers, functional astrology was made remote to the general population by the considerable rigors of its arcane and precise astronomical calculations. Today in a host of formats astrology is available to virtually everyone, and its mathematics and elaborate classifications may provide just the right veneer to seduce all those of the engineering temperament.

In fact, it is worth acknowledging that any serious student of astrology will today encounter an enormous amount of data-driven research and technical instruction comprising matter so rarified and dense that a Black Hole might be put to shame. A virtual infinity of astronomical bodies, all in motion, and all in constantly changing relationships to one another may be the handiwork of the gods, but at this time and planet it is also the food of the geeks. Some very smart people are doing excellent and valuable work, but one is bound to question whether every grain of sand must be exhaustively inspected, singly and in aspect, before something may be declared a beach.

If it ultimately comes down to a matter of this author's "belief," whether the subject is business or astrology, it really boils down to accepting at least some occasional separation of measurement and meaning. The argument here is that the pendulum needs to swing back a bit from the one to the other—not from rationality to irrationality, but from obsession with minutely measurable "hard data" to an appreciation of the inspiring *real-world* conceptual possibilities within the broad context of what Einstein calls imagination. The key to negotiating our difficult times may be found, so the argument goes here, not just in some slavish devotion to what we can count and total but in the unapologetic admission to our spirits of that we can intuit and, at levels far beyond the merely logical, truly understand.

All I can add to that is that I'll do my best to be diligent and fair about presenting for your business consideration what seems to be some pretty interesting and useful stuff. Scout's honor.

 part one

the general business applications of astrology

Millionaires don't have astrologers. Billionaires do.

—J. P. Morgan

This much repeated quote derives from multiple sources. It is quoted throughout the astrological financial community and has appeared in general publications such as *Time* and the *San Francisco Chronicle*. One astrology site, bellastartalk.com, directly sources Norman Winski, a highly regarded financial astrologer, who is the library curator of Evangeline Adams, Morgan's astrologer.

CHApteR 1

INRODUCtION

A World of Opportunity

Astrology, in short, belongs not only to the past but the present. Efforts to treat it as a purely marginal phenomenon reflect not the superior rationality of scholars and scientists but their own marginal position, which prevents them from observing the culture they themselves belong to.

—Anthony Grafton, *A History of Western Astrology*

In most nations outside of the United States, the World Cup Finals is considered the planet's premier sporting event. According to international soccer's regulatory body, the Fédération Internationale de Football Association (FIFA), more than one billion people in 200 countries watched the 2006 championship match on television, the climax of a month-long media event that yielded more than $2 billion in global ad revenue. Universally popular and profitable, as well as a nest of strategic competition, the World Cup is an excellent place to begin an American business leader's appreciation of astrology.

Consider Brazil, the most successful World Cup competitor in history (five titles) and one of many countries where the sport best known to the world as football is a de facto secular religion. Despite its fabled status in the soccer world, the nation's 2002 team was struggling in the qualifying rounds to make the tournament. So the team coach, Luiz Felipe Scolari, did what any enterprising Brazilian leader might do: He hired an astrologer, who consulted on team personnel decisions and helped to scout opponent vulnerabilities on the basis of their horoscopes.

Scolari initially denied doing this, for even in places where there is greater implicit tolerance for astrology a prudent soul will guard against appearances. But when a photocopy of the cancelled check used to pay the astrologer surfaced in *O Globo*, Rio de Janeiro's second-largest-circulation newspaper, it didn't exactly make Scolari's denial more convincing. Apparently nobody in Brazil complained, though, when a freshly assembled confluence of stars with names such as Ronaldo, Rivaldo, and Ronaldinho managed a remarkable team turnaround that resulted in the Brazilian team bringing back the World Cup championship hardware from Yokohoma that year.

In 2006, the French national team, Les Bleus, was even more down and out and a likely candidate for first-round tournament elimination. Again it was revealed that the national team coach, this time one Raymond Domenech, was a devotee of astrology. Here's how the *International Herald Tribune* reported it when Domenech dismissed popular veteran Robert Pires from the team:

> The reason, depending on which version you believe, was either because Pires was a Scorpio or because he had led a revolt against Domenech. Of course if, like Domenech, you believe in astrology, the two might be related.

Led by their cosmically inclined coach, Les Bleus vastly exceeded expectations in the 2006 World Cup in Germany, making it to a penalty kick shoot-out in the championship game before succumbing to Italy. Fans of the sport will long remember the game as the one in which the French national football hero, Zinedine Zidane, playing in his last match, was booted from the game after head-butting an Italian opponent who had just insulted Zidane's mother and sister. Afterwards the world expressed bewilderment about what would make a great athlete hero overreact to such an extent in such a crucial game, but Zinedine, acting like any other self-respecting Cancer leader operating under great emotional stress, was not one, as we shall explore later on in this book, to suffer a family insult blithely.

It now seems reasonable to ask, did the *Italian* coach know this?

It is all well and good to personally believe or not believe in astrology. What the modern globally oriented business leader should first acknowledge, though, is the extent of astrology's existence and its influence in the affairs of other cultures. Simply dismissing the subject is to put oneself at a disadvantage in understanding international clients and consumers, and to perhaps surrender an important edge to the competition.

Take India, for example, a rapidly growing global economic power with increasingly important ties to the economy of the United States. India's population is over 80 percent Hindu, and the Vedic forms of astrology—and the tradition of astrological consultation—have vested in India over many millennia. While there is certainly a sober modern world tendency on the part of some prominent personages and university academicians to play down the influence of astrology in the affairs of the nation, a more accurate assessment is probably delivered by the BBC on its World Service website, when it comments, "It is estimated that over 90 percent of the Indian population, scientists included, believe in astrology."

It is worth noting here that Vedic forms of astrology, sometimes referred to as *jyotish* (the ancient forms) and *panchang* (embracing some more modern characteristics), are currently taught at a number of Indian universities and are considered to be particularly potent forms of predictive astrology. An Indian businessperson might consult an astrologer to determine auspicious dates for such activities as striking a deal, opening a store, or making an investment, as well as for determining such things as fortunate business names and locations. Western astrology, which is the primary contextual background of this book, derives a lot of its flavor from psychology and is somewhat more effectively, although certainly not exclusively, inclined toward character analysis than fortune telling.

One can point to other strong astrological traditions throughout most of Asia, which as enduring historical/cultural aesthetics are usually afforded some respect even by nonbelievers. China's sixty-year horoscope cycle of animals and elements continues to play an important part in the nation's cultural representation and, like much of Western astrology, tends to stress personality and self-awareness over specific predictions. Japanese astrology, which has an animal zodiac very similar to the Chinese, also borrows liberally from the Western system and is consulted by many modern Japanese on a daily or near-daily basis through popular media—a rapidly growing number via premium short message service (SMS) features on their cell phones.

"A lot of people subscribe to more than one horoscope service, so they have a consensus on what their day will be like," representatively explains eighteen-year-old Yumi Shimbun, a native of Tokyo, in a research piece on the Sun Microsystems website that discusses popular SMS features. "It's a weather report for your life; you just have to have it."

Similar enthusiasm, anecdotal and statistical, can be found for astrology throughout the rest of the world. One reported Helsinki-based study of 16,000 respondents, endorsed on her website by noted and admittedly controversial French astrologer Elizabeth Teissier, concludes that 52 percent of Europeans "consider astrology as a science." Although fortune telling is forbidden in Islam, the world press is rife with coverage of astrologers and psychics in Muslim nations making very public, and sometimes uncannily accurate, predictions about national and global events.

For Americans who are resistant to the charms of cosmic correlations, the greatest surprise may be Great Britain, where according to an article by James Silver in the London-based *The Independent* more than 90 percent of Britons can tell you their sun sign and two-thirds of the population consult their horoscope on a regular basis. Silver points out that the Sun sign horoscope was invented in 1930 by a British astrologer, RH Naylor, who made some dazzlingly accurate predictions about news events and was thereafter invited to become a regular contributor to the *Sunday Express*. In substantiating British interest in astrology, however, Silver might have just as readily gone back through centuries of documented cosmic dabbling of the nation's most august personages, including the revered Queen Elizabeth I, whose personal astrologer, Simon Dee, was a well-documented if historically under-reported confidante and advisor.

Beyond the embrace of popular astrology, it should also be noted that many of the West's most influential astrological societies, including the august Astrological Association of Great Britain (AA) and the Faculty of Astrological Studies (FAS), are England-based. The half-century-old AA is especially highly respected for its ambitious conferences, and for publications such as *Culture and Cosmos*, a scholarly journal dedicated to the study of "the history of astrology and cultural astronomy," whose contributors include scholars and tenured faculty from many leading educational institutions throughout the world. Similarly, over the nearly sixty years of its existence, the FAS has enrolled more than 10,000 students from ninety countries in its astrological programs, which are considered among the finest available.

Not to leave an impression that the English are overly credulous about astrology—indeed there are many, many influential and vocal detractors—but they are at least culturally comfortable and conversant with the subject. Ex-Beatle Paul McCartney, in explaining some of his own behavioral inconsistencies, found it much easier to declare he was a Gemini, according to biographer Christopher Sandford's *McCartney* (London: Carroll and Graff, 2006), than to attempt to explain schizophrenia. And former Prime Minister Margaret Thatcher, in a comment to certain MPs about her fairness of mind, once famously observed, "I was born under the sign of Libra, it follows that I am well-balanced."

Meanwhile, back in the United States, at almost the same moment that Margaret Thatcher was making her Libra observation, the American president Ronald Reagan was trying, and ultimately failing, to be much more circumspect about his own starry self-awareness.

Despite the famous, and to most Americans bewildering, 1987 revelation that Ronald and Nancy Reagan were serious astrological devotees, the *open* admission of any sort of metaphysical infatuation has long been taboo in American corridors of power. Never mind that fairly convincing evidence exists of the interest in astrological affairs by numerous American historical figures ranging from Benjamin Franklin to Walt Disney. You say your behavior is affected by Neptune? In the one nation on the planet that calls football soccer, a public statement of this nature will almost invariably draw a career red card.

Nevertheless, there is mounting statistical and anecdotal evidence that even in America there are relative degrees of taboo regarding interest in astrology. As with soccer, one is tempted to see the astrology phenomenon in terms of global creep. Once marked by disinterest and disdain, American interest in international football is now at least measurable, and perhaps that is also true of astrology.

In 2002 and 2003, a spate of studies attempting to gauge American interest in astrology was undertaken by such reputable polling agencies as Gallup and Fox News. These studies variously reported that somewhere between 29 percent and 37 percent of all Americans give at least some credence to astrology. The Fox study, Reagan evidence to the contrary, confidently asserted that Democrats are more likely to be credulous than Republicans. Sweeping demographic assessments of the astrological "crowd," however, are not easy. In a pitch to potential advertisers, MSN described the 1.3 million unique monthly visitors to its astrology website as 40 percent college degreed, 30 percent professional/managerial, and 54 percent with household incomes over $50K. Perhaps the most intriguing of the MSN figures, considering that astrology is a nearly universal inclusion in women's-interest media, is that 74.8 percent of the visitors to the MSN astrology website are male!

Certainly the Internet itself is a huge contributor to the spread of astrology and extremely useful in tracking growth of interest. In 2005, AOL announced that the number-two search term for the year at its portal was "horoscope," closely on the heels of "lottery." Entering "astrology" as a search term on Google presently yields in excess of 38 million results.

Less frivolously, there is the contribution of the venerable American Federation of Astrologers, the nation's oldest and largest certifying astrological organization. The AFA has 3,500 tested and approved astrologers among its membership, although there are certainly as many practitioners, if not more, who eschew the AFA certification route. A statistic of which the AFA seems particularly fond is their estimation that 70 million Americans start their day by reading their horoscope.

On what may be fairly described as the professional level of astrology, there are other quite active America-based astrological associations. Some of these are: the Association for Astrological Networking (AFAN); the International Society for Astrological Research (ISAR); and the National Council for Geocosmic Research (NCGR). There are philosophical differences and political dust-ups among these organizations, but all seem sincerely committed to fellowship, research, education, and commendable quality standards. In addition to these national organizations, there are several dozen serious state and city associations that hold regular meetings for professionals and serious hobbyists for educational and social purposes.

Also defining the American astrological community of today is the increasing amount of serious open-minded scholarship being brought to the historical and cultural consideration of astrology in works by Anthony Grafton, Richard Tarnas, and Benson Bobrick. Also of considerable and understandable pride to the American astrological community is Kepler College, based in Lynnwood, Washington, a state-accredited institution that in 2003 became the first accredited college in the Western Hemisphere to offer a B.A. degree, and shortly thereafter an M.A., in astrological studies.

So there is clearly some juice in astrology, foreign and domestic. Yet the key question remains. From the perspective of leadership, and in particular business leadership, is there really value here? Should you care?

Worthy of consideration is a remarkable article in the September 2005 issue of *Harper's Bazaar*. Written by Merle Ginsberg and shot by Karl Lagerfeld, the piece "It's All in the Stars" is a photo essay that exhibits and comments upon the works of famous designers according to their zodiacal signs. What makes the piece so exceptionally arresting in the current context is the absolute conviction and familiarity with which nearly all of the designers discuss their astrological natures, relating an intimate awareness of their personalities, their creative tendencies, and their leadership styles based on traditional interpretations of their astrological signs.

"Astrology has affected so many aspects of my life," says Donna Karan representatively. "As a Libra, I live in two worlds and try to find a balance—I'm creative, but I find it very difficult to make decisions."

Yet fashion designers, even those who own and run major business enterprises, are a special subset of flaky, right? Fine, but what accounts for the recent astrological infatuation of the Allstate Insurance Company, dependable personal insurer of 17 million American households? Allstate based a recent ad campaign on the knowledge derived from breaking out auto insurance claims on the basis of astrological signs, and then followed this up with "Retirement Reality Check," a very sincere analysis of American retirement attitudes similarly based on zodiacal insights. According to an Allstate spokesperson:

> We're not looking at (astrology) as a science, but there's an emotional connection that people have to money that's not being addressed in the financial arena right now. Retirement is not an optimistic topic, and we're just trying to reach people on a level that is universally engaging and yet very personal. The point is that people who have a daily connection to their horoscopes should be checking on their retirement status every day as well.

If one digs a little there seems to be no shortage of financial consultancies and institutions that *are* looking at astrology as a science, or that are at least taking it seriously. The American tradition of financiers and their astrologers most notably originates with the great turn-of-the-century capitalist J. P. Morgan, who consulted regularly with famed astrologer Evangeline Adams, a fact established in *Time* magazine among other reputable sources. Zoom forward the better part of a century and one confronts numerous financially oriented and well-subscribed astrological websites that boldface a quote attributed to Donald Regan, the former U.S. Secretary of the Treasury and White House Chief of Staff, who blew the astrological whistle on the Reagan administration: "It's common knowledge that a large percentage of Wall Street brokers use astrology."

Even the venerable business publication *Forbes* has gotten into the astrological swing of things, with an amused but in no way condescending consideration of the subject. In 2006, the magazine invited four noted astrologers to analyze the sun sign distribution of the world's billionaires, with a tip of the top hat going to Virgo at 12 percent. In January 2007, the magazine invited the talented Michael Lutin, best known as the regular astrology columnist of *Vanity Fair*, to come back and discuss the astrologically-based prospects of ten of America's best known celebrity CEOs in the coming year.

Still, with regard to business matters, any pervasive presence of astrology remains achingly anecdotal, an itch at the outskirts of awareness and acceptance. Executives who may use it in their private and professional dealings generally don't want to risk the cultural repercussions of being "found out" and, perhaps just as likely, wish to keep its effective use as a secret advantage, a competitive edge. Even astrologers who hang out a shingle in the business community and have something to gain from the publicity, are generally reluctant to talk for fear of attracting too much attention or betraying client confidences.

Although she agrees with the premise that some secrecy is attractive to those who deal with astrology and that it is essential to honor client confidences, Madeline Gerwick is a successful author and business astrologer who wishes that some of her colleagues would show a little more moxie when marketing themselves and their profession. "Astrologers are an impoverished lot," observes Gerwick, whose background includes an economics degree and considerable corporate experience. "They have to stop being so secret . . . you have to be in the phone book, get on the radio, do some advertising."

Gerwick estimates her own practice at some 900 clients over the years, and her excellent yearly *Good Timing Guide* (Fulton, Calif.: Elite Books, 2007), whose title pretty much describes its purpose, has a subscription base of 2,000. The process of reading a business chart, she explains, is one of generally "talking to businesses about strengths and weaknesses, cycles, and maximizing opportunities," and specifically consulting on matters including "finances, customers, vendors, legal issues, sales, facilities, contracts, new product launches, trade shows, and so forth" because "the chart has everything." As for why so many presumably sober-minded businesspeople seek out astrology, Gerwick, the woman who wrote *The Complete Idiot's Guide to Astrology* (New York: Alpha, 2003), is unequivocal:

> Most people get into it because a moment comes when they realize it works. Often in business you don't have the time to assemble all the data necessary to make a decision, and you have to operate on the fly. If you're open to using your intuition, astrology can prove itself to be an exceptionally helpful tool.

So, based upon a few interesting examples and relying on the testimony of the reticent, can astrology really support a claim of proof regarding its usefulness? It is helpful to look at the matter on the basis of three key business applications, which running from the most specific to the most general are: *timing, trend prediction,* and for the purpose of maintaining alliteration, *team building*—a composite organizational form of personality analysis that apparently appeals to soccer coaches. Don't close your mind just yet.

tIMINg

Auspicious Moments for Action

The only function of economic forecasting is to make astrology look respectable.

—John Kenneth Galbraith,
widely ascribed and quoted by *BBC News*

according to the conventions of astrology, every moment in time is a seed event that generates a record of all of the future potential manifestations of that moment. More ambitious authors might immediately consider the fate versus free will implications of such an assertion, but right here the goal is to simply recognize the mechanics of the proposition. Astrology may ultimately be a fortune-telling device or a psychological profiling tool but it first needs to be appreciated mechanistically as a very complex timetable or clock.

Just like the train schedule a commuter may glance at on the way to work, an astrological chart will reveal the name and nature of energetic conveyances coming down the track, when they are expected to arrive and depart, where they are heading and when they are supposed to complete their passages. What makes it especially hard to read an astrological chart—a representation of the planets and other heavenly bodies as seen from a specific point on Earth at a given moment in time—is that the astrological chart incorporates every perceivable energy "engine" in the universe simultaneously on a shifting moment by moment basis, with all the engines in constantly varying kinetic relationships to one another, and all positioned against a wavering and virtually limitless backdrop of space, history, and behavioral possibility. Certainly the complexity is compounded further by the fact that, whether one comes down on the side of fate or free will, there will always be a fair amount of subjectivity in the ascription of *meaning* to the passenger's *purpose* and *outcome* in making the trip.

It may "help" to think of a clock with nine major and, as we establish orbital data for an increasing number of celestial bodies, potentially hundreds of thousands of minor moving hands. And the hands need to be seen in constant relationship to one another. And, oh yes, the time varies with personal perspective.

What this regrettably dense abstraction boils down to in the timing of business events is two-fold:

1. The first factor is that there is absolutely nothing in the life of a business—incorporation, contract signing, real estate matters, unit openings, product launches, banking, partnerships, capital improvements, marketing initiatives, hiring, expansion, trade relations, regulatory affairs, employee relations, litigation, behind-the-scenes maneuvering, leadership acts, etc., etc., etc.—that is excluded from a temporal analysis by astrology.

2. The second factor is that the ambitious theoretical inclusion of all factors impinging upon the business at all times raises a large cautionary flag about absolute analytical precision and the limits of human perception (even when aided by computers).

Is it any wonder then that the modern scientific establishment tends to turn apoplectic over the suggestion of too specific a link between cosmos and causality, despite the precision of the astronomical observations? Way out of the ordinary is an empiricist such as Michel Gauquelin, a mid-1900s French psychologist and statistician, who started out as an astrological doubter but ultimately recorded some chart-based statistical career anomalies that seemed to give astrology a fighting chance as a credible phenomenon.

One of the more interesting current studies of the link between astronomical factors and earthly event timing is the Merlin Project, under the guidance of Paul Guercio, a noted futurist, and Dr. George Hart, a "Star Wars physicist" and winner of the prestigious Rank Prize for his work in laser optics. Guercio and Hart have harnessed the power of supercomputers to crunch an enormous amount of astronomical cycle data that is used to, mostly successfully, project times of peak energy flow in the lives of individuals, nations, corporations, and anything else that may have a birth moment. It is significant that Guercio and Hart play down the term "astrology" and that they tend to stress "the onset, intensity, and duration" of peak events rather than the prediction of specific good or bad outcomes, although they can't seem to resist occasionally going out on some gaudy interpretive/predictive limbs that don't *always* yield fruit.

Truly, though, any utility a business leader may find in employing astrology to time and interpret specific events is not best framed as the application of an exact empirical science. Perhaps ironically, as Madeline Gerwick suggests, one seems to be on more solid ground when ascribing any predictive value of astrology to its ability to aid the intuition. Perhaps as Anthony Grafton, a Princeton University professor with a deep respect for the place of astrology in the history of ideas, suggests in his essay *Starry Messengers: Recent Work in the History of Western Astrology* (*Perspectives on Science* 8 [1], Spring 2000), astrology is best considered a blend of "rigorous mathematical data" and "rich mysterious insight"; "a highly rational way of treating otherwise inaccessible and intractable problems"; an encyclopedic historical activity "connected in vital ways to the pursuit of power"; and, most tellingly, a forecasting activity in which "the arrival not the journey matters."

Some of these thoughts are echoed in an important series of essays titled *Why Economists Should Study Astrology*, written by author and financial consultant Robert Grover for the estimable StarIQ astrology website. Grover passionately and intelligently explores the premises and practices of economists and astrologers, and he reasonably concludes that it is difficult to identify which ones are the "witch doctors." He shares an enormously valuable insight when he observes that in the codified explanation of cultural phenomena, "belief trumps evidence."

So it is in this most challenging application of astrology, the prediction of very specific conditions and events, that one must proceed most cautiously. One may be comfortable that an astrologer is looking at very specific and carefully delineated factors in the examination of any business question brought by the seeker. What one may be less sure of are the additional filters, the layers of complexity and subjectivity that can cause the teller to give out a false reading.

Can an artist tell time as well as well as a scientist? Sure. Just keep in mind that either way everything's endlessly relative.

So what are we to make of the true alchemists, the men and women in financial occupations who book serious speculative transactions, sometimes enormous ones, on the basis of astrology? Almost certainly the quote ascribed to Donald Regan about a majority of stockbrokers using astrology is an overstatement, but at the same time it is hardly seems an entirely ridiculous exaggeration. The anecdotal evidence is compelling that there are many money handlers who believe that, with a certain amount of metaphysical assistance, the fabric of the universe can be woven into well-timed wealth accumulation.

You are reading this correctly, by the way, if you discern a whiff of skepticism (dearly-earned, incidentally) regarding this particular sort of voodoo economics. While this study is certainly credulous regarding the worth of astrology, its ultimate mission is an advancement of the value of applying astrological iconology and psychological archetypes to personality issues in the workplace, not as a straight-out endorsement of fortune telling. Yet insofar as this is a business book, and business is a voyage run aground without profit, it seems imperative to spend a few moments with the folks who willingly and sometimes successfully put their serious money where there mysticism is.

While economic pursuits, from identifying suitable times for crop planting to the indication of a fortuitous moment for raiding the enemy's treasury, have always been avid concerns of astrology, the serious astrological timing of financial market movements is a relatively recent historical phenomenon. Although there are instances of earlier involvements, the driving event here is the devastating worldwide depression of the 1930s, which launched the modern iteration of an historical notion that such catastrophes (and the attendant recovery periods) are written in the stars for those who can discern the appropriate cyclical patterns. A name that deserves particular mention is that of W. D. Gann, a pioneer of modern financial astrology and other mathematics-based predictive cyclical systems. It is credibly documented that Gann, in 1928, predicted with amazing precision the time, depth and trading specifics of the stock market crash in 1929. His theoretical work, to the extent it is comprehensible, is greatly valued on Wall Street to this day.

A partial list of names that carry cachet in today's cosmic money world includes David Williams, Norman Winski, Larry Pesavento, Ray Merriman, Bill Meridian, Arch Crawford, and Carol Mull. In the mid-1980s Mull, a former corporate accountant, published collections of the astrological incorporation charts of all of the companies in the Standard and Poor's 500 and of 750 OTC stocks, thereby producing arguably two of the most costly books in the history of publishing. Many more astrologically inclined financial gurus and their consultancies can be traced through professional associations, including the Copenhagen-headquartered International Society of Business Astrologers (ISBA).

Representative of the modern breed of financial astrologers is Henry Weingarten, managing director of the well-respected Astrologer's Fund, based in New York. Trained in mathematics and psychology, Weingarten takes a Goldilocks not-too-hot, not-too-cold approach toward the usefulness of astrology in following stocks, commodities, and other financial instruments. He stresses that astrology is "not a perfect tool," and that its application is "a necessary but not sufficient condition" for business and investment success. However, he also comments that its popularity is rising due to the ever-increasing internationalism of financial markets and the influence of foreign astrology-intensive cultures. According to Weingarten:

> Billions of dollars watches this stuff, but these are serious people and astrology is not their only tool. The type of individual who gets into this is the type of person who is willing to look around and have an open mind about whatever might contribute to their success. With the Baby Boomers who were exposed to this stuff in the 1960s taking over, it's more widespread than you think.

Like Weingarten, most financial astrologers who have reputations for success are cautious about not appearing overly credulous, and they will invariably stress credentials that are as vested in financial, mathematical, and psychological positions as they are in metaphysical ones. Investors who follow the work of these astrologically-inclined gurus closely will further observe that successful predictions are treated as banner headline stuff, and those that fail are treated as so much ticket litter for the trading floor. That, of course, is just common sense marketing, although one is certainly permitted to wonder why an individual who can consistently and successfully predict market movements, say, 75 percent of the time, would ever have to sell advisory services or write books on investing.

The last is actually a serious question, and the answer is more complex than a simple count of the take. In Bill Meridian's *Planetary Stock Trading* (New York: Cycles Research, 1998), which many traders consider the seminal text of modern astrological trading, the personal essence of the trader comes across as clearly as the rules for trading. Meridian's observations regarding the choice of the appropriate seed chart to use (the first trade of a stock vs. the incorporation chart of the company) and the desirability of choosing a trade chart that aspects well to the chart of the *individual* trader are clearly indicative of the subjectivity inherent in any given trading proposition. In addition, Meridian's confession that the "major reason" he pursued astrology is that "it is based upon phenomena that is known to occur at a fixed point in the future" strongly suggests that if astrological trading is a science it is one seasoned with liberal dashes from one's own psychological chemistry set.

But hey, c'mon. Who wouldn't want to predict the future and make money at it and have the whole world know about it? The allure of astrology-based financial trading is hardly that it's infallible. It's simply that to certain edgy psychological predispositions, it's irresistible.

There was this one time.

I was working on a menu consultation project with a small chain of Midwest-based restaurants that had decided to open a place in Arizona. During the course of the project it emerged that one of the brothers who owned the business had a fairly sophisticated interest in astrology. The suggestion was made, and enthusiastically accepted, that it might be fun to use astrology to build an electional chart, i.e.

to create a business chart by basing it upon a moment pre-selected as fortunate for opening the new restaurant.

Now I happen to be of like philosophical mind with the stock trader Bill Meridian, who builds his charts based on the moment of the first trade rather than business incorporation. To this way of thinking, one is only operating a theoretical business until there's a customer who actually buys something. So the idea with a restaurant is to invite someone to consume the first meal and to orchestrate the precise moment at which this meal is paid for.

As is usual in this kind of exercise, upon this occasion there was an explicitly defined window of opportunity. In other words, there was a three-day period during which the restaurant *had to* open, and we could only be time flexible within these three days. Problem.

Some pains have been taken in this section to convey just how many variables and how much subjectivity may factor into an astrological timing analysis. In fairness, in astrology all those variables hardly carry the exact same import. Some energy configurations in an astrological chart are in fact so potentially significant that they are as centuries to seconds in the measurement of time.

In the construction of the chart for this particular restaurant opening we were going to have to deal with a conjunction of Saturn and Pluto. *Conjunction* is an astronomical term for planets that are simultaneously transiting through the same degree of the zodiac. In astrology, when planets are *conjunct* it means their influences combine.

Saturn travels around the Sun in an orbital period of just under thirty years, and therefore on a mathematical average basis occupies any given degree of the zodiac for about one month (360 degrees × 1 month = 30 years). For Pluto the orbital period is just under 250 years and the average stay at a given degree is about 8.5 months. Net-net, astrologically phlegmatic Saturn and Pluto visit one another just once every 33.5 years and they were certainly going to be visiting for every second of the allotted three-day span.

Entire books have been written on the respective symbolic import of Saturn and Pluto, but it's probably fair to boil down the general sense of their combined natures to a single term: alarming. Saturn, which traditional astrology describes as a "malefic" or evil planet, even in today's more theoretically tolerant interpretive environment represents such stern qualities and attributes as prolonged effort, fixed structure, and vested tradition, and is considered a generally harsh taskmaster whose benefits are revealed only after serious dues have been paid. Pluto, its recent astronomical demotion to "minor" planethood notwithstanding, is an unconscionably aggressive and irresistible transformation force, historically associated with the advent of the nuclear age and atomic energy.

Certainly good things, even miraculously positive things, may happen when irresistible transformation at the atomic level meets fixed structure at the cultural level. To be perfectly candid, though, a sanguine outcome is not likely to be most astrologers' first guess at this pairing. Saturn meeting up with Pluto is generally heavy business—a structural crisis written in plutonium.

Anyway, there was simply no alternative but to place this potential time bomb somewhere in the electional chart of the restaurant. Depending on the "house" of the chart in which it was placed, the Pluto Saturn conjunction would have particular potential to influence a specific facet of the business. (*Note*: A western astrological chart looks like a pie cut into twelve pieces, each piece called a house. Houses, numbered one to twelve starting at the eastern horizon and running counter-clockwise, are associated with specific realms of activity. In a business chart, for example, the sixth house is usually identified with employee affairs, the third with community image and local marketing, the eighth with relationships to financial institutions, and so forth. More on this later in Part Three.)

Confident that the best engineers and inspectors available have pronounced the restaurant's physical plant fit, the client is comfortable about selecting the fourth house to host the potentially ornery pair of planets. Not to get lost in the astrological mumbo jumbo, but a night comes some three months after the successful restaurant opening when Mars (action) and the Moon (security) enter the energy picture in so-called negative aspect to the Pluto-Saturn pairing in the electional chart. It's a hot Arizona summer night and my phone rings.

It is the manager of the restaurant. I ask her how business is going and she sighs. Both of the big rooftop air conditioner units have just failed. And with a mixture of sadness, awe, and bewilderment in her voice she adds that earlier in the evening the main plumbing (an energy endeavor traditionally linked with Pluto) leading to the restrooms had become blocked (Saturn) and literally exploded.

She reminds me of my astrological read of the situation (as if I might have forgotten). We chat for a few more minutes. A few weeks later the restaurant closes for good and I never hear from anyone in the organization again.

It's a sad story as far as business goes. But it still gives me a shiver to think of the astrological foreshadowing of the event. And that, briefly, is an example of how astrological timing sometimes actually does work in a business situation.

Why it would work is anybody's guess.

CHAPTER 3

tReND foRecastING
The Rhymes of the Marketplace

 History is Philosophy teaching by examples.

　　　　　　　　　　　　　　　　　　—Thucydides

It is in the prediction of very specific events as noted in the last chapter that astrology most urgently attempts to pass itself off as a science. In the next chapter the application of astrological iconography to personality types will be introduced, and the emphasis will move strongly towards astrology as a largely intuitive values-based facilitator of human relationships. What will be briefly examined here is the use of astrology to forecast broad cultural trends, a most useful application, that is compelling as the astrological realm in which the scientific and the intuitive really do their best to create a working partnership.

Trend forecasting with astrology, while not always easy in the execution, is actually a fairly simple concept to grasp. Planets representing distinct types of energy (aggressive, compromising, acquisitive, intellectual, emotional, inspirational, transformative, etc.) move through zodiacal signs invoking thematic coloration (self-involvement, preoccupation with heritage, personal relationships, material concerns, etc.) and one makes social or economic predictions based on the dates of passage and the symbols involved. For example, one energy association of the planet Mercury is communication, and one association of the sign Aquarius is humanitarian concern, so a reasonable general trend forecast for a period when Mercury passes through Aquarius is news of altruism.

Of course there are many planets and signs, and each has many thematic associations, both positive and negative; it's no easy call to say which planetary passage or subsequent interpretation will dominate a particular period of future time. As with other predictive forms of astrology, one must also deal with the planets in their varying spatial relationships with one another, with many trend-oriented astrologers certainly as interested in the cyclic periodicity of planetary energy combinations as they are in sign placements. A "favorite" of the astrological community in this latter regard is the so-called twenty-year presidential death cycle, a phenomenon linked to the time it takes for Jupiter and Saturn to cycle around to a zodiacal meeting in the heavens, an event that since 1840 has curiously coincided with the death in office or an assassination attempt (successful except for Ronald Reagan) for every U.S. president elected in a year coinciding with the Jupiter/Saturn conjunction.

What does tend to separate the trend followers from the fortune-tellers is a reasonable awareness that the longer the time period involved and the larger the abstraction the more likely it is that at least some legitimate confirming evidence will appear. Trend followers are much more likely to emphasize the slower moving outer planets, as well as cosmic phenomena such as sunspot cycles and nodal regression cycles (please don't ask) that take at least a decade and up to centuries to fulfill a complete cycle. Pluto for example, the energy of transformation, moving through the individual signs in periods ranging from a dozen to three dozen years due to the planet's eccentric orbit, has caught the fancy of some trend observers as a generational significator. In other words, changes in the broad cultural values and collective behavioral tendencies of large age-demographics seem aptly timed by Pluto as it moves from one sign to the next.

A problem that arises when one moves out to the slowest planets, however, is that it is hard to find the sort of cyclicality that is useful in a modern business sense. It may be of interest when major wars, economic collapses, or technology revolutions take place when Pluto (248 years) or Neptune (165 years) or Uranus (84 years) comes back to a sign it has visited in the past. However, usually too much time has passed to make the use of the knowledge an especially effective forecasting tool for a short-haul business executive wondering whether jeans will be "in" this season or whether the price of crude is likely to go down the next.

Also, when one concentrates on the slowest moving planets, there is a tendency to invoke the mythological correlations over the material ones. But if one settles in the middle, with the likes of Saturn (29.5 years), Jupiter (12 years), the lunar node cycle (18.5 years), and the sunspot cycle (11 years), one gets to make surprisingly rich periodic associations with actual events that are hardly foreign to present day market concerns or, under the right intuitive circumstances, future ones. Take the following example:

It is a disturbing photo. A tall rectangular office building is on fire with smoke and flame billowing from nearly every window on several floors. The image is in an ad for an electronic record keeping service and appears in a copy of *Business Week* magazine with a cover date of August 21.

Two weeks later, in an edition dated September 11, the same magazine runs an article led by the headline, "What Would Happen If a Jet Hit a Nuclear Reactor?" The chilling lead of this article is as follows: "Airplanes falling from the sky and demolishing buildings have become an almost routine, if frightening part of nightly newscasts."

One week later, in the September 18 issue, *Business Week* runs an article entitled "Sliding Out of a Towering Inferno." Here the lead is: "Imagine being trapped by fire in a high rise building, above the reach of rescue ladders which can stretch only to the seventh floor."

These words and images all appear in the late summer of the year 1989. At the time the planet Jupiter is passing through some early degrees in the zodiacal sign of Cancer. The next time Jupiter passes through these same degrees is the late summer of 2001, when airplanes crash into the World Trade Center towers.

Kindly forgive the gruesome example, but the truth is I had no intention of finding this correspondence when I undertook the research for this section. I intended to look at the period just before 9/11, presumably forgotten in the historical maelstrom that swallowed it, to demonstrate various cultural correspondences with periods of similar astrological demarcation. Sometimes, though, astrology just makes it its own business to hit one over the head.

Jupiter, if we may move past the acknowledgment of our sorrow and move back to the business at hand, lends itself particularly well to trend tracking. In part this is because its twelve-year path around the Sun places it in the various astrological signs for almost exactly one year, making period examination and referencing fairly easy. The allure (and an endorsement) of the twelve-year cycle is also reflected in Chinese astrology, predicated on a twelve-year animal cycle that ascribes special distinction to the purported characteristics of each of the animals and the people born under their influence in their processional year-long turn.

Most students of astrology are taught that Jupiter is a planet of "good luck" and "expansion," serving as a metaphysical counterbalance to Saturn, which is said to govern "obstacles" and "restriction." But as one may surmise from the historical example just offered,

Jupiter will expand anything with little regard to its potential for good or bad. Jupiter's utility for trend trackers is that it enhances the areas upon which its influence falls, making it a symbolic demarcator of the "big things" going on at any given time.

In the symbolic language of astrology, the passage of Jupiter through the sign of Cancer would tend to make big issues out of such things as family, real estate, security, and issues of emotional intelligence. One may well argue that this preconception clouds an objective search for meaning in the identification of parallel periods, but such knowledge is only a kind of theoretical map. The location of actual treasure is another matter.

So let's say one is working on new product development or a marketing launch or a STRAP plan (Strategic Action Plan) for the summer of 2013. The shadow periods one will unveil with regard to Jupiter are August/September 1977, August/September 1989, and July/August 2001. Every bit of recorded information produced during these time periods, especially as they tend to reveal strong correspondences, will in astrological theory point to useful iterations in the 2013 period.

In the United States, for example, there are clear similarities in the *zeitgeist* of all three of the shadow periods. In each instance it is the first year of new presidential administration, so there is a bit of both a hangover and a grace period still in operation regarding politics, although the natives are just starting to get restless about policy and results. In all three cases there is a broad and palpable *perceptual* unease about the economy that is related to debt, inflationary fears, and job cuts; and there is a sense of defenselessness in international affairs related to trade imbalances, dependence on foreign commodities, and a sense of competitors and enemies growing stronger in ways that seem combative and other than "level playing field" fair.

Even a cursory review of the three eras' popular media reveals an enormous emphasis on the themes of vulnerability and protection, hardly an astrological surprise during a period represented by a creature that wears a shell. A popular theme of the period is a psychological pulling within for protection, both personally and in term of one's clan, only to be confronted with the potential for terror that lurks at great depths. It is noteworthy that the number one box-office movies of these years are respectively the first *Star Wars*, the first *Batman,* and the first *Harry Potter*, all series in which the dark characters (Darth Vader, Batman himself, Valdemort) are psychologically and even biologically intertwined with the heroes they oppose. One may of course search for correspondences in both broad and narrow areas of interest. Research in the specific summer time periods mentioned above, for example, yields consistent consumer and general business themes related to:

- *Automobiles.* The emphasis is on safety, dependability, and economy. The auto as personal fantasy is dealt with as a classic collectible.
- *Computers.* Even back as far as 1977, the theme of these periods is the computer's threat to privacy and the risks regarding data security.
- *Family.* Enormous energy is poured into the cultural consideration of traditional family roles and dynamics in an untraditional world. Think of the television series *Soap* and the movie *Parenthood.*
- *Food.* All of these are eras that emphasize native produce and regional comfort cuisine, even in fairly *haute* establishments. Seafood gets the summer salad treatment.
- *Health.* It's hard to accept until one researches it, but there is an enormous emphasis on the disease cancer itself during these periods.
- *Inflation.* Unhealthy expansion is the enemy during these time periods, whether one speaks of cancer, monetary conditions, or per-

sonal appearance. Issues range from corporate controllers in ascendance in the workplace to the threat of fatty foods that impair brain function to a fashionable counter-trend youth emphasis on tight and/or revealing clothing (hip huggers and low rise jeans, for example). A representative article in a 1989 magazine that says it all is titled "Pudgeball Nation."

▪ *Patriotism.* In many instances it comes across as much as an appeal as a given, but there are countless cultural instances in the material of these eras regarding the symbolic importance of protecting eagles and waving the flag. Net-net, these are times to circle the wagons and ward off the heathens.

▪ *Real Estate.* Homes become enormously important as places of psychological refuge and as expressions of tribal values. Existing real estate, available under stressed-out conditions, tends to be touted as an investment of choice during these periods.

▪ *Stress.* If these periods have a background chord, it's a shrill one. In no particular order, and spanning all three of the shadow periods, here are some titles of prominent articles in popular journals:

"What Makes Our Moods?"
"Your Anger Can Kill You"
"Staying Ahead in Tough Times"
"Which Emotions Raise Your Cholesterol?"
"Make Hard Times Work for Your Marriage"
"The Emotional Hazards of Work"

Other intensely resonant correspondences range from a preoccupation with the emotional challenges of little league baseball, to psychologically revealing movies about oceans with monsters in them (*The Deep, Orca, The Abyss, Atlantis*), to any number of articles in magazines ranging from *Reader's Digest* to *Psychology Today*, which dwell upon the dynamics of psychic phenomena, twilight states of consciousness, the importance of faith, and the sometimes over-looked importance of such nonlinear intellectual assets as intuition and creativity in a quantitative world.

Speaking of nonlinear (or partially linear, or cyclical) intelligence, one may readily appreciate how there is at least creative value in projecting the irrefutably real themes of the shadow periods into the future corresponding time frames. Admittedly the summer of 2013 does not sound like a blithe period, but one can be fairly assured that buying and selling will take place there. And who doesn't love an edge?

The refinement and expansion of this sort of analysis is made virtually limitless by the countless astronomical factors already alluded to in this work. But sometimes a fair amount of truth and beauty can coincide in the simplest of cyclical analyses, such as the twelve-year runabout of Jupiter. Certainly it's the potential for useful insight and application, not the complexity of the analysis itself, that makes the effort seem at least worthy of consideration.

team BUILDING
Know Thy Colleagues, Thy Competitors, Thy Customers, Thyself

I've used 360-degree feedback with our executives. They don't like it. I've set them down and delivered performance feedback. They resent it. I've scheduled coaching sessions to remedy long-standing development problems. They undermine it. Through a stroke of luck, I've discovered a more viable alternative: I now read them their horoscopes.

—Kenny Moore, *Executive Development and the Fates: A Case Study*

Whether one references a marketing department's use of customer segmentation studies or a human resource team's involvement with personality profiling, it is clear that modern business is manifestly involved with sorting human beings into categories. It is ironic, of course, that so much of this work is predicated on the notion that customers and colleagues are most fulfilled when recognized for their individual attributes, but clearly the imperatives of time and money demand that we make some useful generalizations about mass markets and employee "types." The obvious issue here is whether the analytical categories proposed by astrology deserve a place at the sorting table.

Once again the first question that is likely to occur to a reasonable person is whether there can possibly be any cause and effect correlation between the icon–based machinations of astrology and actual human behavior. But while this may be a *good* question, it may not be entirely the *right* question. A better question with regard to personality typing may well be framed around not *how* astrology works but *whether* it works (e.g., Is astrology meaningful)?

A helpful place to start searching for an answer to this question is in the work of Glenn Perry. A licensed psychotherapist and certified professional astrologer, who founded both the Association of Psychological Astrology and the Academy of Astro Psychology, Perry makes a significant historical contribution by chronicling the mid–1900s rise of humanistic psychology and the attendant appearance of a similar developmentally oriented understanding of astrology. The key factor in both, reports Perry, is a change in emphasis from a deterministic approach to human behavior (i.e., personalities and events are caused by outside forces) to one of self-actuated human potential (i.e., experience is predicated upon an individual's subjective handling of an inner world of perceptions, values, thoughts, dreams, etc.).

The figure at the center of this radical change in perspective is the eminent Swiss psychologist Carl Gustav Jung. One should consult Perry's analysis (chronicled at his www.aaperry.com website) for the full development of the argument, but it is readily clear that Jung, the father of analytical psychology, had an enormous respect for astrology, which he once appreciatively cited as "the summation of the psychological knowledge of antiquity." Perry makes a very good case that Jung viewed astrology as also more than just a little useful in a modern sense, embracing it as: 1) a useful diagnostic tool in counseling; 2) evidence of the phenomenon of *synchronicity* (the planetary positions at birth did somehow seem to Jung to correspond with a subject's psychological make-up); and perhaps most importantly, according to Perry, 3) a fully formed "language for understanding the basic psychological drives of human beings."

On the strictly astrological side of the equation, according to Perry, the name Dane Rudhyar comes into prominence. In an enlightening and exhaustive body of work dovetailing with the insights of Jung and such other humanistic psychologists as Carl Rogers, Rollo May, and Abraham Maslow, the French-born Rudhyar sets out an inspiring case for astrology as preeminently a tool for the seeker of self-realization and psychic wholeness. In 1969 he formed the International Committee for Humanistic Astrology, an organization dedicated to the notion that rather than being used as a tool for prediction, the primary use of astrology should be as a contributor to the understanding of human nature.

Although marketing segmentation will be more fully addressed in Chapter 19, here might be a good place to note the considerable enthusiasm the corporate human resources world presently has for the Myer-Briggs Type Indicator (MBTI)® personality-profiling tests, and its imitators, which also and contemporaneously with Rudhyar's efforts grew directly out of Jung's work. Cited by the Center for Applications of Psychological Type as "the most widely used personality inventory in history," the MBTI® is currently professionally administered to an estimated 2 million individuals every year. Anti-astrology supporters of the MBTI® ardently contend that it is not astrology. Yet to anyone who has given a fair look to astrology in the spirit defined by Rudhyar (whose first astrological book, *The Astrology of Personality*, appeared in 1938, four years before the MBTI®), the old saw about looking and quacking like a duck is bound to occur, especially in terms of reciprocal categories and analogous personality descriptions.

Admittedly a profound sense of the metaphysical works its way into the Rudhyar embrace of astrology that is not particularly apparent in standard personality profiling tests. With its emphasis on spiritual context, self-discovery, and individuation, the humanistic approach to astrology may actually seem to be in logical opposition to the collective and often rigidly deterministic generalizations of astrology, such as sun sign descriptions. Yet as has already been duly noted, whether one goes at it deterministically or via free will, there are always many unique interpretive factors recorded in an individual astrological chart, and humanistic astrology simply embraces the potential for subjective manifestations of chart factors that are primarily geared to an individual's current level of growth and awareness.

All of this is offered in fairness to an appreciation of astrology, because it is the nature of business to veer away from the ambiguous and the ephemeral. Okay, fine, the busy business reader is thinking, so tell me what it means when somebody's an Aquarius. Frankly, the rest of this book presents a detailed response to that kind of question, but if one doesn't first appreciate the rich contextual depth and the overarching presence of developmental free will in the "astropsychological" universe, there can never be a completely fair or adequate reply to the question.

When the language of astrology is invoked in a thoughtful psychological sense for segmentation or typing purposes, it is not just an exercise in simplistic description and deterministic babble. As much as "Aquarius" is a defined concept, it is also an artistic and spiritual one that speaks to deep-seated values on the most resonant levels of human character and awareness. Business efficiencies require acts of collectivization and simplified definitions, but that need not necessarily entail diminishment of respect for human potential.

Madeline Gerwick, a business astrologer cited in Chapter 1, captures the spirit of all this when she speaks of companies as "work tribes" and the role of an astrologer as a "shaman." Such terms may put off the buttoned down, but Gerwick makes a compelling case that companies rise and fall on their ability to motivate workers to create value, and that the key to that process is appreciating the relationship between the enterprise values and the values of the workers themselves—a purpose that astrology serves well. Corporations that believe monetary incentives and an inherent urge to compete will solve all motivational dilemmas, says Gerwick, are overlooking just how many "de-motivated" people are searching for a different "higher vibration" around which to rally their workplace existence.

That such observations have a foot on solid ground is apparent in the work of Kenny Moore, author of *The CEO and the Monk: One Company's Journey to Profit and Purpose* (Hoboken, N.J.: John Wiley and Sons, 2004), who is quoted at the outset of this chapter. Formerly a monastic priest, Moore made a mid-career shift into the world of corporate human resources. Once there, according to an article by Linda Tischler that appeared in *Fast Company* magazine ("Kenny Moore Held a Funeral and Everyone Came," February, 2004), he readily came to the conclusion that there are three major trends in corporate human resources:

1. Nobody trusts.
2. Nobody believes in top management.
3. People are too stressed to care.

Now it has to be quickly observed that Moore hardly sees astrology as the one big permanent solution to these problems, although he admits "on a bad day that is exactly where I tend to wind up." It's just that in the attempt to engage people's minds, hearts, and spirits, Moore is wise enough to note what astrology has that can't be derived from more traditional and corporately-sanctioned forms of personality and performance feedback. As he explains in an essay entitled *Executive Development and the Fates: A Case Study* that appears on the Institute for Management Excellence website (www.itstime.com), astrological feedback is not only valuable for its often uncanny accuracy; it is popularly rooted in a general perception of fatalism, fortuitous timing, and fun that allows even "star-crossed" colleagues to discuss "harsh business realities" with genuine amusement and "without placing blame on anyone or having to chart a developmental plan."

Thus, one gets down to the wry understanding that astrology may be of considerable benefit in the corporate workplace because it links an appreciation of diverse and wandering human dispositions and a sense of impenetrable mystery. Humanistic astrology, honorably vested in a studied appreciation of psychological insights, holds out the hope that an individual's role in a social network can be worked out with nonjudgmental tolerance for value differences and applied inner growth, but that any sense of ultimate resolution is mostly written in stardust. Astrology accepts both doubt and destiny, as they exist in the real "stressed-out" world, with an unduplicated combination of amusement and awe.

Moore writes of his workplace application of astrology:

> I know it's not professional. [Learning Organization guru] Peter
> Senge would surely deride me. And I don't yet have statistical data
> to document it as a Best Practice. But it seems to work.

Three potential business partners, whom we shall call Smith, Jung, and Rudhyar (disguised but not fictional), are considering the formation of a consultative agency. They think it might be enlightening, or at least amusing, to approach a business astrologer. Certainly they are interested in matters of timing and any general indications of business success, but being humanists as well as capitalists they are also interested in any insight that the astrologer might offer regarding their respective business orientations and compatibility of values.

Here, without laboriously explaining how the trick is done, is a scaled-down portion of what a reasonable astrologer might provide. S=Smith; J=Jung; R=Rudhyar.

What is the nature of business in general?

S: Business is an optimistic expression of one's creative power that leads to an increase in assets.

J: Business is an intense expression of one's personal identity through various tests of will.

R: Business is a communal expression of one's ability to profitably interact with peers.

How will you derive emotional satisfaction from business?

S: Satisfaction is derived from taking beneficial actions.

J: Satisfaction is derived from taking powerful actions.

R: Satisfaction is derived from involvement in communicating ideas to the public.

Where in a business is there the strongest need for organization?

S: One must track finances to ensure profitability.

J: One must track actions that affect public perception of the company to ensure reputation.

R: One must track finances to ensure honesty.

What is the most valuable personal resource you are likely to bring to business?

S: I bring the ability to manage financial and creative assets.

J: I bring the ability to facilitate workplace structure and group interaction.

R: I bring the ability to innovate with regards to financial and creative assets.

What is the area of a business that is most likely to draw your spontaneous energy?

S: Management of assets.

J: Communication of corporate philosophy to prospects and clients.

R: Communication of inspiration to peers.

Where is the true mission of a company best expressed?

S: The mission is in the company's ability to motivate and inspire individual achievement.

J: The mission is in the ability to allow individuals to participate in a successful group dynamic.

R: The mission is in the successful accumulation of assets.

Where do you have the talent to lead?

S: Peer communication and internal directives.

J: Marketing activities conducted with the public on an interpersonal basis.

R: Marketing activities expressed to the public on the detail level.

Where do you have the potential to be a brilliant innovator?

S: Management processes.

J: Allocation of employee resources and partnership assets.

R: One-on-one relationships.

Where are you most likely to experience either real spiritual insight or crippling self-deception?

S: Precipitate actions that are an expression of will.

J: Beliefs regarding the nature and responsibilities of partnership.

R: The role and motivations of leadership within a partnership.

The business destiny of this individual is to make a mark in:
  S: Leadership by systems management.
  J: Leadership by force of personality.
  R: The broad dissemination of ideas.

The competent astrologer who has discerned the preceding from the individual reading of the principles' three horoscopes would next doubtlessly compare the horoscopes for direct positive and negative (+/−) energy dynamics. For example:

Smith/Jung
  + great harmonious energy for accomplishing tasks of any sort
  + ability through sympathetic genius to express real wisdom
  − desire to transform the other into something they are not
  − some incompatible ideas may lead to loss of self-confidence

Smith/Rudhyar
  + an unusual similarity of thinking coupled with intellectual detachment
  + friendly interest in seeking out new experiences and opportunities
  − strong urge to competitiveness
  − enormous drive can cause more problems than it solves

Jung/Rudhyar
  + likely an extremely beneficial growth relationship
  + many warm and positive feelings—a relaxed feeling of affection
  − incessant mental stimulation—goading to see what happens
  − friction caused by lack of synchronization—working at cross purposes

The beauty of astrology is that at this point there is no scoring system, and only an educated guess regarding how the relationship dynamics of the business might play out (although in this case it's hard not to see the problem at mission control). All that is really provided, since another competent astrologer might find a wholly different way to articulate the energy indications, is a set of insights that could conceivably resonate with the principles. At the least, they might have some direction toward a productive conversation regarding roles and expectations, with or without moderation by a shaman-referee, prior to hooking up. On an ongoing basis such an analysis is also likely to prove of benefit during a dust-up or an impasse, providing a nonjudgmental, nonlinear route around loggerheads or a washed-out business bridge.

What if it all goes to heck in a handbasket anyway? Well, then astrological analysis always makes a great I-told-you-so.

A CEO of a national merchandising display company serving the bricks-and-mortar retail industry contacted me after reading *The Consistent Consumer*, a book I co-authored with Ken Beller and Louis Patler (Chicago: Dearborn Trade Publishing, 2005). That book presents a values-based segmentation analysis of America's major age demographics. The book advances the sociological premise that generations are culturally imprinted by the values of their natal times, yet move beyond those values by developing their own set of generational values that serve as survival and growth mechanisms in direct response to the vested values dominance of the preceding adult generations.

The CEO in question, whose company employs several-hundred field reps who visit the stores to work on the merchandise displays, found compelling the characterization of a demographic we call the

Believers, born between 1972 and 1983; more than half of the CEO's field staff belong to that group. The CEO felt frustrated about what she perceived as the group's inconsistent work ethic, and was eager for any insight regarding training, motivation and retention.

We looked over the Believers material together. Broadly, the Believer description is of a group that often has an underdeveloped sense of urgency and commitment regarding work processes, a distrust of any sort of autocratic leadership or hierarchical organizational models, and a desire for peer connection and social consensus over externally imposed standards and operational efficiencies. Dealing with this group requires such executive tactics as openness to democratic discussion, stepping off the pedestal, and granting a fair amount of behavioral latitude regarding personal styles and interests.

Somewhere during this discussion I suggested half-jokingly (A note to would-be astrological business consultants: This must almost always be done half-jokingly.) that a useful dimension to this analysis might be obtained if we included an astrological overlay. Intrigued, the CEO provided a list of birth dates for the entire field staff, which was then run through an astrological sun sign grid. Factoring in both the number of individuals involved and attendant length of service it was determined that the Believer workforce at this business has a very strong Scorpio component, with serious secondary accents of Leo and Cancer.

Whereas the business iconology of sun signs will be explored in depth in Chapter 5, what we learned from this is that, in this particular instance, the socially bonded and egalitarian Believer generation was perhaps fiercely competitive and ambitious below the surface. The fact that the CEO herself had a strong Scorpio theme in her own astrological chart further indicated that the culture of the organization, which Believers tend to embrace or reject en masse, was likely to be modeled on close observation of the CEO's values. This suggested a caution to the CEO that she might be uncomfortably looking in many mirrors if her own edgy persona became too accessible to the rank and file.

Regarding secondary characteristics, it was worth noting that Leo wants to be a creative star and Cancer needs to be secure. The composite indicates an organization that thrives on a limelight image of leadership yet needs to have a committed parent figure. Everything in this analysis suggested the centrality of the CEO and a strategic need for her to create a delegator/head coach presence amidst her own workforce. She most likely was best off as the powerful "outside" rainmaker persona of her company who could avoid undesirable imitation, preserve the illusion of glamour, and serve as the keeper of the sacred tribal culture by guardedly selecting opportune times to make well-designed and emotionally satisfying connections, on both individual and group bases, with her troops.

What also became interesting in the analysis was how little presence in the workforce there was of the astrological signs that are most commonly associated with structure, systems, communications and, in general, a rational/intellectual outlook on life. Far more disposed toward intuitiveness and emotion, this was likely the sort of workforce that doesn't adapt particularly well to the strict requirements of standardized formats (the CEO admitted that one of her great concerns was getting this group to fill out even simple reports). From a training perspective, this appeared to be a crowd that would do better with group-centric behavior modeling and real human beings to present policy rationalizations than with the self-administered instruction materials or merchandising display models simply sent over the Internet.

There is more to this, and the company in question is still working out specific policies and procedures as this book heads to press. Yet it should be apparent from this sample that an astrological analysis of one's workforce is at the very least a useful generator of perspective. I can vouch for at least one happy "display" client in this regard.

 part two

tHe SUN SIGNS

 *We are born at a given moment, in a given place, and we have like celebrated vintages the same qualities of the year and of the season which saw our birth.*

—Carl Jung, *Modern Man in Search of a Soul*

CHAPTER 5

Leadership and Sun Sign astrology

*When you come right down to it all you have is yourself.
The sun is a thousand rays in your belly. All the rest is
nothing.*

—Pablo Picasso, quoted on *Humanities Web*

The single grain of stardust that tipped the scales with regard to creation of this book was an article that appeared in *Fast Company* magazine (Issue 98, September 2005). The piece, written by Bill Breen, was an accolade for a new book on business leadership authored by Harvard Business School professors Anthony J. Mayo and Nitin Nohria. Their book is titled *In Their Time: The Greatest Business Leaders of the Twentieth Century* (Harvard Business School Press: Cambridge, Mass., 2005), but what really hit home was the title of Breen's accolade, "The Three Ways of Great Leaders."

Now keeping in mind that there may be only three ways of great leaders, it is noteworthy that a search for books on "leadership" at Amazon.com yields in excess of 200,000 hits, and a Google search for "leadership books" returns an astounding 71 million–plus entries. Doubtless every one of the authors behind this biblical flood of leadership divination, present company included, believes their work to indispensably describe the rules and regulations of leadership. But for professors Mayo and Nohria, who contend that three ways of great leadership are all you get, there is a particularly potent leadership mojo that centers on a concept they identify as "contextual intelligence."

While Mayo and Nohria certainly deserve to be read in their own words (really, *In Their Time* is a very engaging work), what they seem to be getting at is a thesis that the opportunity for leadership is greatly defined by an individual's specific moment in history. Great business leaders, the argument is made, have a gift for appreciating the cultural essence of their times and capitalizing on the conflux of demographic, technological, regulatory, geopolitical, labor, and social trends of the moment. "Understanding how to make sense of one's time and to seize the opportunities it presents is at the heart of this book," they write.

You sure won't hear any astrologers objecting to the premise. In fact, after applauding the thesis most astrologers would simply be prone to pointing out that there is a big old cosmic clock hanging on the wall. And this clock can be quite an aid, not only to matters of timing but also to an understanding of the significant archetypal rhythms and patterns of the moment with all those nascent trends in it.

It's just that if you have four years to write, and the help of dozens of brilliant graduate students and paid researchers, and the faculties for polling 7,000 current business leaders about what they think, and you come up with 1,000 candidates for great business leaders of the twentieth century that you eventually whittle down to the top 100, it's hard to believe that you will come up with only three types of leaders. Three! These are, by the way, identified as the *entrepreneur,* the *manager,* and the *charismatic leader,* although professors Mayo and Nohria don't exactly make their historical-context case a whole lot clearer by stating that "all three types coexist and are pervasive through every decade."

Now all of this is not to imply that the professors haven't in fact hit pay dirt and come up with the exact right number of "ways of great leaders." It's simply that astrology is so often characterized as trivial, even by its own practitioners, for dealing in *only* a dozen macro-personality types. Yet even a Harvard Business School professor would have to grant that's four times as many as Mayo and Nohria stipulate . . . and that's without the help of any graduate students.

Disbelievers and professional astrologers alike understandably denigrate sun sign astrology, piteously trivialized in horoscope columns that appear on the newspaper comic pages for a good reason. Not that they find it false, but professional astrologers tend to view sun sign astrology as the cheeseburger on the astrology menu, an item whose mass appeal is only matched by its lack of imagination. Without it, however, the study of astrology is like climbing a ladder that is missing its first rung.

It is clearly not the object of this book to teach the techniques of astrology, for which there are likely as many resources as there are leadership books. It is worth mentioning, however, that a technical appreciation of astrology often emerges when one "gets" the fact that, from the perspective of earth, we see the sun in a regularly recurring year-long passage against the background of twelve major constellations that we call the zodiac. That the earth actually wobbles and produces a phenomenon called precession of the equinoxes should be taken up at a later date, but the gist of what we're looking at here is that the sun observes an apparent year-long regularity that allows us the atypical astrological/astronomical luxury of knowing someone's zodiacal sun sign on the basis of their month and day of birth, whatever the year may be.

Symbolically speaking, and in reference to the sort of astropsychological analysis discussed in Chapter 4, the sun has come to represent the ego. While torn on the horns of a free-will-versus-fate dilemma, it is helpful to appreciate that sun sign astrology embraces the consideration of an individual's unique expression of imprinted values. In other words, sun sign astrology posits that personal expression is a free will offering, but that the values that underlie personal expressions are more or less lifelong and "fated."

So it is that we come to the study of leaders as avatars of value patterns that have been observed in the human record since the beginning of records. Even when, as some of these avatars unfortunately do, they express the negative aspects of the values they represent and fall from grace, they are at least for a while stars that light up not just our history but also our understanding of human nature—which for the sake of this argument comes in the variety 12-pack rather than the budget *threefer*.

Speaking of variety and budget packs, in the Mayo/Nohria book, one of their subjects is C. W. Post, an itinerant salesman who went on to found Post Cereals, the company that became General Foods. According to the Mayo/Nohria analysis, Post's genius was variously manifest in his early adaptation of product sampling, in his eventual recognition that an increasingly industrialized America would embrace convenience products, and in his shrewd perception that nationally distributed women's-interest media could be instrumental in base-building a national brand. Post is presented in the Mayo/Nohria work as an example of the *entrepreneur*.

In the analysis you will encounter in the next twelve chapters of this book, this same C. W. Post will again make an appearance. Here, however, he will be dealt with as an individual who stole many of his best ideas from the Kellogg brothers, who once fired dynamite into the sky in an attempt to make rain over an arid piece of Texas land he hoped to develop, and who once wrote a book on the psychosomatic root of all illnesses some years before committing suicide. Post is presented as an example of the *Scorpio*.

Certainly it is a reader's decision as to which set of facts is of potentially greater use in a business encounter. Imagine you are walking into Mr. Post's office tomorrow morning. Will your greater concern really be that he is an entrepreneur?

CHAPTER 6

aries

The Value of Force

Do you want to know who you are? Don't ask. Act!
Action will delineate and define you.

—Thomas Jefferson, broadly ascribed, and quoted
on *The Democratic Party* website

✦ MARCH 21 TO APRIL 19 ✦

Thomas Jefferson	April 13, 1743	U.S. president
J. P. Morgan	April 17, 1837	J. P. Morgan and Co.
Andrew Mellon	March 24, 1855	U.S. financier
Will K. Kellogg	April 7, 1860	Kellogg's
Walter Chrysler	April 2, 1875	Chrysler
Robert W. Johnson, Jr.	April 4, 1883	Johnson and Johnson
James Casey	March 29, 1888	United Parcel Service
Donald Douglas	April 6, 1892	Douglas Aircraft
Henry R. Luce	April 3, 1898	Time, Inc.
Joseph F. Cullman	April 9, 1912	Philip Morris
Sam Walton	March 29, 1918	Wal-Mart
Hugh Hefner	April 9, 1926	Playboy Enterprises
Cesar Chavez	March 31, 1927	United Farm Workers
Elisabeth Claiborne	March 31, 1929	Liz Claiborne
Clive Davis	April 4, 1932	Arista Records
Gloria Steinem	March 25, 1934	*Ms.* magazine
Tom Monaghan	March 25, 1937	Domino's Pizza
Ken Lay	April 15, 1942	Enron
Rosie O'Donnell	March 21, 1962	*Rosie* magazine
Larry Page	March 26, 1973	Google

Style: Direct

Objective: Primacy

Strength: Energy

Weakness: Impatience

Communication: Forceful

Tactic: Confrontation

Belief: Action

Reward: Spoils

With an Aries leader you must allow for personal compulsion. Here is character defined by a raw fiery drive towards self-realization that must have, in all things great and small, immediate manifestation and gratification. If you work for an Aries get ready to move fast, to hide your personal stash, and to put any needs you may have for coddling and reflection way back in the wimp closet.

Dynamic as a rocket launch, when they are firing on all cylinders their achievements are beyond awesome. J. P. Morgan, who at one time ran both the American railroad and steel industries while simultaneously functioning as the nation's de facto central banker, fitly bore the nicknames Jupiter and Zeus. *Time* founder Henry Luce defined the corporate capitalism of the American Century, invented the omniscient voice of modern journalism, and became the most pervasive voice in the formulation of American foreign policy in the twentieth century.

Whatever the field of endeavor, speed, indomitability, and tireless effort are key concepts here. The stories of Aries leaders are filled with early starts and inexhaustible rising to meet hopeless conditions and challenges. These qualities reflect a passion for personal accomplishment that, even when the life purpose suddenly careens down a new road (Aries leaders love new roads, anything new actually), rarely burns out in a lifetime.

There is irony in the fact that Aries leaders tend to talk a lot about developing the self-esteem of others. In his autobiography, *Made in America* (New York: Bantam, 1993), Wal-Mart's Sam Walton observes, "Outstanding leaders boost the self-esteem of personnel." Similarly, Domino's Tom Monaghan has upon numerous occasions commented that creating a feeling of self-worth in individuals is the purpose of leadership. Also, legendary feminist Gloria Steinem, in an essay created for National Public Radio's *This I Believe* feature, extols the "unique core self born into every human being."

All of this is well and good, of course, as long as you never quite forget whose self-esteem takes precedence in your relationship with an Aries leader. These ambitious souls are not generally disposed towards sharing power or credit, will not brook anything hinting of insubordination, and are not likely to ever let you get in the last word. One's overriding purpose in an Aries-led organization is to contribute energy, surrender personal will to the leader's ideology, and to do whatever it takes to get a win.

It may not be exactly what you have in mind when you consider your own self-actualization. But what a ride!

aries Leaders: value statements

The Food of the Gods Is Action

Perhaps Will Kellogg would describe the state of the Aries soul as "snap, crackle, pop." If so, the champion of corn flakes and crisped rice would be right on the mark, because while leaders of any as-trological persuasion tend not to be lazy, Aries is preeminent in the capacity for what seems like the mother of all sugar rushes. It is so befitting that an Aries first popularized pre-sweetened, ready-to-eat breakfast cereal.

The many tales of Aries' energetic efforts honestly seem like ex-aggerations, something that schoolyard toughs might try out on each other to gain status. One learns of a 100-hour/7-day workweek (Tom Monaghan); an 18-hour workday and three short vacations in twenty years (Gloria Steinem); the incomparable effectiveness of working hard "23 or 24 hours a day" (Cesar Chavez); and the capac-ity for personally directing a virtually unprecedented 24-hour service company (Jim Casey in the early days of UPS). And there will always be that much-circulated image of Hugh Hefner perennially in paja-mas on a document-covered bed, working, always working.

Indeed, an Aries leader is the sort that tends to have a huge problem with delegation, preferring by nature to be directly in-volved with all aspects of an enterprise. Music impresario Clive Davis, a lawyer with no formal musical training, is legendary as one of the few major recording company executives who discovers artists, picks their material, and shows up at recording sessions to make comments about the volume of the bass player. With Aries micro-management is almost as much about limitless energy as it is about control.

David Glass, a key associate of Sam Walton, summarizes this Aries quality when he talks about a management style that Walton himself characterized in his autobiography as "management by walking and flying around." Notorious for being constantly on the go and involved in every aspect of his business, Walton demanded work on weekends and found it impossible to stay retired when per-suaded by family to do so. According to Glass, Walton's management style was actually best characterized as "management by wearing you out."

Do It First; Do It Fast

Robert W. Johnson, Jr., according to a 2003 *Fortune* magazine profile, started attending Johnson and Johnson business meetings at the age of 5 and became general superintendent of the family trust at the age of 25. James Casey began working at the age of 11 and started the company that was to become UPS at the age of 19. At the age of 14, starting quarterback-honor student-class president-steady jobholder Sam Walton became the youngest person ever in the state of Oklahoma to attain the rank of Eagle Scout.

While such information may be interesting to most people, it is the stuff of thrills to an Aries leader. No other sign is so devoted to being or doing something before anyone else. J. P. Morgan creating America's first billion-dollar company (U.S. Steel), Elisabeth Claiborne becoming the first woman CEO of a Fortune 500 company (Liz Claiborne), and Clive Davis creating the first major recording label exclusively dedicated to album-length rock and roll (Arista Records) are just some of the examples of this quite intentional rush to glory. Even when an idea is occasionally derivative, as in the case of Larry Page's Google not being the very first search engine, you can be sure that the issue is going to become one of top speed; the rapidity of search execution and the early introduction of service extensions have always been a prime Google concern.

It is in this light one can best appreciate Hugh Hefner's wry declaration of his own feminist trailblazing while simultaneously appreciating fellow Aries Gloria Steinem's rise to prominence as the first person to do an inside expose on the life of a Playboy bunny. One may also bemusedly reflect upon the fact that Aries leaders are responsible for the national emergence of rapid delivery (UPS/Domino's) and the introduction of Band-Aids (Johnson and Johnson). And there is also Henry Luce's instructive comment to a *Time* magazine bureau chief that, "the function of enlightened journalism is to lead, to put in what ought to be."

It is sometimes said, not entirely unfairly, that an Aries leader will lose interest in a specific project over the long term simply because it no longer seems fresh or innovative. Certainly, the truth of this assertion will be astrologically qualified by factors in the horoscope other than the sun sign. Few Aries leaders would, however, find fault with Hugh Hefner's observation in an *Esquire* magazine article that "the best part of any relationship is the beginning."

It Is Better to Be an Ideologue Than an Intellectual

Henry Luce endorsed a way of approaching information that he called "directed synthesis." The essence of this outlook is that life's inescapable complexity begs for an over-arching, simplified, and somewhat omniscient summarization. This theory received expression via the all-knowing journalistic style invented by Luce's *Time* magazine and was even more apparent via the photo-journalism orientation of his *Life* magazine. And if you think about it, "directed synthesis" is not all that different from what is being addressed by the rankings of the Google search engine.

In all manner of communication, it is the Aries leader's fervent intent to get to the point as quickly as possible. The Aries-led meeting is summarized as one of marshaled facts, instant answers, and snapping ridicule of those who wander into the weeds of resistance, delay, or obfuscation. Along with Zeus and Jupiter, the powerful J. P. Morgan also proudly bore the nickname "yes or no Morgan." As Morgan once observed:

No problem can be solved until it is reduced to some simple form. The changing of a vague difficulty into a specific, concrete form is a very essential element in thinking.

Unsurprisingly, in the lives of great Aries leaders one comes across a great deal of reliance on belief systems or creeds. These creeds range from religious fundamentalism to militant patriotism to sexual role definition to personal health habits to the rightness of big league capitalism, all of which exist to establish in the eyes of their adherents the underlying and, most importantly, the inarguable values and acceptable limits of human behavior. All considerations of the "rightness" or sincerity of such creeds aside, the Aries leader appreciates better than anyone that while contemplative introspection breeds caution, ideology is hot-wired to action.

The Rules Are Meant to Be Broken, but Only by Me

Thomas Jefferson wrote the American Declaration of Independence, one of the greatest expressions of man's inalienable right to liberty that has ever been recorded. The debt owed by all Americans to this great and courageous visionary can hardly be calculated even to this day. And yet it is a simple fact that Jefferson himself owned human slaves.

It's certainly not the intent here to pick on Thomas Jefferson, but it is essential to recognize in an honest discussion of Aries leadership a propensity to sometimes be a little less than personally rigorous about strongly espoused ethical beliefs. The deeply religious Sam Walton was an admitted talent stealer and spy; the ardently feminist Gloria Steinem had romantic trysts with notorious woman haters; the venerable J. P. Morgan was a leader of the Society of Suppression of Vice but was a well-known adulterer; the ardently anti-handgun

Rosie O'Donnell was discovered to have an armed body guard escorting her son to kindergarten; and Enron's Ken Lay once simply announced, "We don't break the law."

Let it quickly (Aries-style) be stated that no one astrological sign has a monopoly on roguishness or regrettable actions. But Aries, as has already been mentioned, does like to quote a scriptural party line and then to start firing away. Just keep in mind the subtlety of the observation by Henry Luce that "a useful lie is better than a harmful truth," and J. P. Morgan's observation that "a man always has two reasons for the things he does . . . a good one and the real one."

In short, for an Aries leader business is business. Don't say you haven't been warned.

It's a Man's World

With apologies to popular relationship author John Gray, both men and women Aries leaders tend to hail from Mars. This is no slap at the femininity of Aries, but it is a caution to those who would simply see all women, including leaders, as fundamentally subordinate and reactive. Befitting the war god and zodiacal ram, who lend their mythic personae to the natives of this sign, an Aries damsel can initiate a hack and a head butt with the best of them.

Speaking of hacking and butts, there was a time when the surest way to spot an Aries was through the haze of cigarette or cigar smoke that surrounded them. Aries leaders of an earlier era, as most memorably exemplified by the cigar wielding J. P. Morgan, were famous smokers. Joseph Cullman, former CEO of Phillip Morris, is an Aries best remembered for a tenure that includes the creation of the uber guy, the Marlboro Man.

An even more prevalent icon for an Aries is the vehicle built for speed, be it car, boat, train, or airplane. Unlike Henry Ford, who championed the bland Model T, Aries-born Walter Chrysler saw his opportunity in adapting the far larger and more powerful cars he originally built for racing to a general consumer market. Along with amazing cars, Aries history includes a near-legendary fascination with boats and airplanes; J. P. Morgan owned a famous series of sleek yachts (his company also built the Titanic), and it was Aries-born Donald Douglas who changed aviation history when his company introduced the swift and luxurious DC-3.

Hugh Hefner has to be mentioned here again, of course, as the testosterone-fueled icon of icons. Ironically, some critics have said that what Hefner actually accomplished was to turn the male of the species into a peacock. But in the natural world that doesn't equate to any less "action."

As for the women leaders born under this sign there is obvious recognition that the male of the species has traditionally held the power and now it is time to share. With all the overtly aggressive feminist pronouncements of someone like Gloria Steinem, there is just as much revealed by a women's fashion mogul like Liz Claiborne. "We didn't want to be women dressed as men," she once explained to the Montana Academy of Distinguished Entrepreneurs regarding her breakthrough line of women-in-the-workplace clothing created in the late 1970s.

Only after her business was established did she deem it of consequence to add a line called Claiborne for Men.

★ tips for dealing with aries

- The Aries coin of the realm is action. Do not dwell on what you have done or prattle on about what you are going to do. Do it.

- But first make sure it is something your Aries boss wants to have done. It is their army. No matter your salary or your title, never forget you are basically a grunt.
- An Aries tells it like it is. The overly sensitive need not apply.
- *Hint*: If entertaining an Aries, there is often appeal in trying out the newest, high-visibility, high-energy hot spot. Aries hates to come late to a hot trend, and gifts should emphasize innovation along with quality. Also, most Aries are morning people, and you will generally have their best attention at a pre-lunch meeting . . . just don't waste their time.

taurus ♉

The Value of Fixedness

I want you to become the highest paid women in America.

—Mary Kay Ash, quoted in the *Toronto Star* and
frequently expressed during motivational speeches

✦ APRIL 20 TO MAY 21 ✦

William Randolph Hearst	April 29, 1863	Hearst Corporation
Henry J. Kaiser	May 9, 1882	Kaiser Industries
Daniel F. Gerber, Jr.	May 6, 1898	Gerber Products
Alfred N. Steele	April 24, 1901	Pepsico
David O. Selznick	May 10, 1902	Selznick International Pictures
Edwin H. Land	May 7, 1909	Polaroid
Edward J. DeBartolo	May 17, 1909	Edward J. DeBartolo Corporation
Jack Eckerd	May 16, 1913	Eckerd Corporation
William R. Hewlett	May 20, 1913	Hewlett-Packard
I.M. Pei	April 26, 1917	I.M. Pei and Associates
Mary Kay Ash	May 12, 1918	Mary Kay, Inc.
Queen Elizabeth II	April 21, 1926	United Kingdom
Cathleen Black	April 26, 1944	Hearst Magazines
George Lucas	May 14, 1944	Lucasfilm
Stacey Snider	April 29, 1961	Universal Pictures
Marc Andreessen	April 26, 1971	Netscape

taurus signatures

Style:	Persistent
Objective:	Wealth
Strength:	Patience
Weakness:	Self-indulgence
Communication:	Sincere
Tactic:	Endurance
Belief:	Abundant Nature
Reward:	Valuables

It's not so much that time slows down in the Taurus leader's universe. Rather, it expands to take in a deeper sense of domain. Taurus is inclined to plow the field rather than race across it.

What dynamic drive accomplishes in the Aries universe, Taurus replaces with perspective, stable strength of purpose, and self-possession. Collected, calm, and competent, Taurus is generally the quiet sort of commander who doesn't speak much because there is no requirement to do so. A steady demeanor suffices, with just the glint of an iron fist.

The magic in Taurus leadership stems from a bullish tenacity towards principled behavior, a belief in the limitless power of focused talent coupled with hard work, a faith in the natural order of things, and a conviction that most people would rather be productive and prosperous than lazy and estranged from life's material and social rewards. Taurus leaders have a gift for trusting and encouraging both the dreams and the practical efforts of their colleagues, even graciously allowing for the inevitability of a certain amount of crooked furrows. Perhaps more frequently than those of any other astrological sign, and albeit with important exceptions (we'll get into William Randolph Hearst in a bit), historically significant Taurus leaders are uniquely described as both "authoritative" and "beloved."

A recent museum retrospective of the life of famed Taurus industrialist Henry Kaiser is instructive in this regard. The 2004 Oakland, California exhibition was organized according to various mottos by which Kaiser ran his business, including: "Find a need and fill it," "Together we build," and "Dare to dream." Doubtless it is easy to respect the levelheaded authority of a leader who not only makes such mottos but who also actually lives them.

The Taurus leader's appeal is suggested in a true story about William Hewlett, the cofounder of Hewlett-Packard. In 1959, Hewlett placed a dollar bill on his desk, observing that his employees were so trustworthy and dependable and filled with *esprit de corps* that "I could leave it there and it will be there forever." Today in Hewlett's "enshrined" office in Hewlett-Packard's headquarters, that dollar remains, along with a significant pile of money that other people have left over the years.

Certainly, Taurus leaders are not always perfect. They can be stubborn about procedure, slow to react to a changing consumer market, and naïve about the motivations of others. When their carefully checked tempers do occasionally blow, the fall-out can be legendary.

For the most part, though, these authoritative yet approachable, stolid but generally warm-hearted human beings inspire much confidence and loyalty in those who serve with them. Taurus leaders rarely define the success of an enterprise in personal terms, believing rather that success lies in the development of talent, the accomplishment of enduring works, and in the participation in material rewards by all who have contributed to the prosperity generated by accomplishment.

Sounds pretty close to perfect at that.

taurus Leaders: value statements

The Human Story Is an Enduring One

Taurus movie impresario George Lucas insists that his *Star Wars* movies are not about space gizmos. In an article written by entertainment editor Rob Lowman, which appeared in the *Los Angeles Daily News* (May 15, 2005), Lucas comments, "I have been saying this ever since day one, when people were saying [*Star Wars*] was all about spaceships. You could do it with chariots and tell the same story."

Right or wrong, the idea that human existence is the perennial reliving of a single archetypal drama underlies the Taurus leader's approach to life. In the Taurus worldview there are big enduring Shakespearian (who most literary historians believe was born a Taurus) themes that inevitably dominate our energy and our consciousness. In addition to *Star Wars*, Taurus-produced movies such as *Gone With the Wind* (David Selznick), *Citizen Kane* (Taurus Orson Welles portraying Taurus William Randolph Hearst) and *King Kong* (originally produced by David Selznick; big budget remake created on the watch of United Artist's Stacey Snider), reveal the compelling Taurus fascination with big-picture themes, such as power, ambition, greed, hate, beauty, love, and heroism.

It is within this conceptual context that the Taurus leader always seems to be dealing with the issue of long-term success—and two strategic beliefs tend to present themselves. The first of these is that meaningful human existence is predicated upon our ability to manifest such timeless virtues as bravery, sacrifice, patience, loyalty, faith, kindness, and generosity in our daily lives. The second of these is the recognition that life is indeed hard and that occasionally stopping to do a little rose smelling—having a nice supper, taking a bubble bath, catching a fish, telling a joke, flirting with the deliveryman, giving peace a chance—is the only way to remain balanced and sane.

Plain old-fashioned hard work, though, takes a particularly compelling place in such an earnest and traditional worldview. Edward De-Bartolo is said to have commented that one should always work harder than one plays. And Jack Eckerd grew to be so fed up with what he perceived as a declining American work ethic that he co-authored a book about it, *Why America Doesn't Work* (Dallas: Word Publishing, 1991), in which he comments, "Meaningful work is a fundamental dimension of human existence, an expression of our very nature."

This is a good thing to know if you happen to work for a Taurus.

Success Is Built from the Ground Up—Literally

If you are a typical Taurus leader you likely believe that God is an architect. This is not a sign of disrespect. On the contrary, it is hard for a Taurus to imagine that anyone would prefer to think of God as some sort of nebulous abstraction dealing primarily with ephemeral things, such as an afterlife.

In a discussion of great Taurus business leaders, it's hard not to notice how many of them have made their fortunes from moving dirt and building something. Edwin DeBartolo and Jack Eckerd mined the gold of suburban shopping centers; Henry Kaiser built massive roads and dams before turning his attention to the urban development of Oahu. The great architect I.M. Pei designed or refurbished some of the world's greatest buildings, including museums ranging from the Louvre to the National Art Gallery to the Rock and Roll Hall of Fame. Even William Randolph Hearst, whose original wealth came from his father's mines (and if a little metaphorical license may be allowed), mined the nation's "dirt" and published it into a business empire.

Even those Taurus leaders whose enterprises are not directly connected with building or land development tend to have serious outdoor interests, including farming, ranching, riding, fishing, hiking, gardening and, yes, even conservation. Particularly well-regarded in naturalist circles is William Hewlett, who once sued the developers of the Squaw Valley ski resort for cutting down a hidden copse of trees and who donated a sizable tract of Lake Tahoe beachfront to the U.S. Forest Service to protect it from condo development. And there's just something quintessentially Taurean in the fact that Netscape founder Marc Andreessen was born to an agricultural seed salesman and an employee at outdoor outfitter Lands' End.

If one takes the classical sense of history vested in most Taurus leaders along with their appreciation of the land, it is not surprising to discover an affinity for significant historical edifices, particularly those with a sense of natural setting and housing important creative works. I.M. Pei's work has already been mentioned, and the lives of Taurus leaders are filled with projects such as Henry Kaiser's Hawaiian Village and the American Academy of Arts and Sciences founded by Edwin Land. Ultimately, though, the essential Taurus architectural icon is likely the castle,

It's easy to see where Queen Elizabeth fits into such an observation, but the most compelling example of the castle phenomenon is reflected in the life of William Randolph Hearst. His 165-room, 127-acre San Simeon estate, now a designated historical landmark best known as Hearst Castle, was every bit, as one observer has described it, the kingdom of a feudal lord. In its day the most prestigious site for Hollywood hobnobbing, the estate at one time boasted the world's largest private zoo and what was estimated to be the world's priciest private collection of art.

As famed playwright George Bernard Shaw once commented,

no doubt to Hearst's inestimable delight, the estate was "the place God would have built if he had the money."

God Wants You to Have a Pink Cadillac

If God is the universal developer, as many Taurus leaders believe, then his favor is revealed in a bounteous harvest of high quality stuff.

Materialism is a primary and unapologetic fact of most Taurus lives. It is without the slightest trace of irony or self-consciousness that Mary Kay Ash, named by Lifetime Television as the Most Outstanding Woman in Business in the twentieth century, dangled diamond brooches and pink colored luxury goods as the carrot before the aspirants in her tribe of cosmetics salespersons. Mary Kay talked most sincerely and convincingly about the importance of faith and family in a successful life, but she always seemed to be implicitly adding, "Wouldn't you also like a mink coat?"

For Taurus leaders, the issue is not whether having stuff is good—that's a given of human existence—it's whether the stuff is used to good purposes. What makes a figure like William Randolph Hearst so interesting in an astrological study is his truly atypical, for a Taurus leader, position that his resources fundamentally existed to please himself. Ruthlessly pushing his political and economic agendas against enemies real and imagined, all the while indulging his appetite for more of everything, Hearst became, according to one PBS observer, "a Depression-era symbol of all that is hateful about the rich." (*Astrological Note:* Hearst was born with the Sun in direct conjunction with the planet Pluto, the ruling planet of Scorpio. This would add a powerful sense of competitive compulsion to the more socially-empathic, Venus-influenced Taurean nature. More on this later in the Scorpio section of the book, Chapter 13.)

Fortunately, the great Taurus leaders are more disposed towards being the stewards of value rather than mere consumers (although, in truth, one rarely encounters a Taurus ascetic). Most Taurus leaders innately grasp two things about wealth: 1) it is rarely amassed without serious time and toil; and 2) the best one can do with it is to dispense it meaningfully for the benefit of others. Serious development and beneficent distribution—it's the godlike thing to do.

Invest for the Long-Term

It is somewhat ironic that the man who invented instant photography, Edwin Land, as quoted in a biographical essay written by Victor McElheney for the website of the National Academy of Arts and Sciences, had the following to say about introducing a new product into the marketplace:

> Neither the intuition of the sales manager nor even the first reaction of the public is a reliable measure of the value of a product to the consumer. Very often the best way to find out whether something is worth making is to make it, distribute it, and then to see, after the product has been around a few years, whether it was worth the trouble.

Although this attitude may seem cavalier to some, if not downright heretical in today's world of the quarterly report, it offers an awfully valuable insight into the Taurus leader's soul. Taurus leaders simply do not see the world in short-term increments. Their sense of tomorrow's payoff is predicated on steady asset growth over an extended period of time.

Although Taurus pays much attention to the growth and preservation of all sorts of asset classes, great Taurus leaders have nearly universally recognized that the most significant investment one can make is in the development and recognition of human talent. The history of Taurus leadership reaches a high point in William Hewlett's enlightened policies towards his workforce, immortalized in business history as "The H-P Way." This set of practices, which is reflective of the honest esteem of the worker found in many Taurus-led businesses, combines trust, respect for the creative process, and a package of benefits and participatory rewards that reflect a true material and spiritual honoring of loyal, dedicated effort over the years. (*Note:* A lot of the credit for the design of the "H-P Way" belongs to Hewlett's partner David Packard, a Virgo, who appreciated the efficiencies and ethics inherent in a system based upon motivated, fairly rewarded, and loyal employees. With Virgo one tends to get an appreciation for sensible and decent systems; with Taurus there is more emphasis on the long-term fellowship of the "herd.")

This appreciation of the compounding power of history rightly served is evident in the best moments of Taurus leaders in all their affairs. One notes Queen Elizabeth's sincere thanks to a throng of 80th-birthday well-wishers for appreciating that the British monarchy is "more than a meaningless survival." And there is Cathleen Black of Hearst Magazines, who when asked by a representative from her college alumni magazine what she planned to do with the rest of her business career as she approached her 60th birthday simply responded:

> I'm thinking of leaving this place in great shape for the next generation.

Let Your Creed Be Social Responsibility

To a Taurus leader philanthropy is rarely an afterthought. While they are certainly not alone among business leaders in donating to good causes, there is a passion and purity to the good works of Taurus that is unique among astrological signs. Theirs is an innate appreciation that serious material resources and long-term commitment, not just good intentions or splashy publicity, are required to help remove some of the of the hardship from humanity's shoulders.

One finds ample evidence of this in the Herculean efforts of The Gerber Foundation, The Kaiser Foundation, the William and Flora Hewlett Foundation, the Mary Kay Ash Charitable Foundation, and the George Lucas Educational Foundation. William Kaiser's Kaiser Permanente pioneered the inestimably important field of nonprofit HMOs. Jack Eckerd's Eckerd Youth Alternatives has touched the lives of 60,000 at-risk children and is reported to be the nation's biggest nonprofit organization for troubled kids.

Beyond the quantification, however, one takes the sense that Taurus has a builder's sense regarding what material is really important, and a true benefactor's soul regarding what must be addressed for society to benefit in the long-term. How indicative of the Taurus character that Netscape founder Marc Andreesen made the Mosaic program, on which Netscape is based, free to all comers, and that his current project, a Web-based social networking project called Ning, is also free to all. And there is Polaroid's Edwin Land, who in funding the new home of the American Academy of Arts and Sciences saw the value of a welcoming space where scientists and humanists could freely communicate, calling it "a house of beautiful ideas."

The final words in this chapter shall also be given to Edwin Land. A long-term advocate of public television, Land once explained in Congressional testimony why the medium had such promise. It encapsulates the best of the Taurus leader's worldview:

> We need to search for ways to tell young people what we come to know as we grow older . . . the permanent and wonderful things about life.

✦ tips for dealing with taurus

- Old-fashioned virtues, from loyalty to discretion to manners to good grooming, are essential if reporting to a Taurus boss. Especially loyalty.
- Taurus is a follower of fashion, but the classics will never be entirely knocked from their perch. Avoid trendy flashiness, which Taurus does not trust.
- Do not discount Taurus stubbornness. These generally peaceful souls are capable of detonation if you don't learn when to desist.
- *Hint:* Taurus is a sign that inherently knows both the price and value of everything. Business gifts should be predicated on high quality. Indulgent Taurus loves traditional fine foods, and the elegant box of candy or the bottle of fine wine will find an appreciative audience here.

CHAPTER 8

Gemini

The Value of Flexibility

There's a reason that executives lie. The alternative is worse!
—Scott Adams, *Seven Years of Highly Defective People*

MAY 22 TO JUNE 21		
Cornelius Vanderbilt	May 27, 1794	Shipping/Railroad magnate
Francis and Freelan Stanley	June 1, 1849	Stanley Motor Carriage Co.
Cyrus Curtis	June 18, 1850	Curtis Publishing
Alfred P. Sloan, Jr.	May 23, 1875	General Motors
John Maynard Keynes	June 5, 1883	Economist, financier
Igor Sikorsky	May 25, 1889	Sikorsky Aircraft Corporation
Armand Hammer	May 21, 1898*	Occidental Petroleum
Bob Hope	May 29, 1903	Entertainer, investor
John F. Kennedy	May 29, 1917	U.S. president
Katherine Graham	June 16, 1917	*The Washington Post*
Robert Maxwell	June 10, 1923	Maxwell Communication Corp.
George H. W. Bush	June 12, 1924	U.S. president
Paul McCartney	June 18, 1942	Musician, investor
Donald Trump	June 14, 1946	The Trump Organization
Tim Berners-Lee	June 8, 1955	Creator, World Wide Web
Scott Adams	June 8, 1957	Dilbert

*In 1898, the Sun entered the sign of Gemini early on May 21st. Also, as Armand Hammer was born with four additional planets transiting the sign of Gemini, he is appropriately included on the Gemini list.

gemini signatures

Style:	Alert
Objective:	Expression
Strength:	Agility
Weakness:	Fickleness
Communication:	Impulsive
Tactic:	Dexterity
Belief:	Perception
Reward:	Respect

the mind plays tricks. Rock hard certainties are illusory. Tomorrow never knows.

With Gemini one enters into the experience of life as actually lived on a daily basis, particularly as processed through the maze of the human mind. The prominent personages of this sign, and there are many, thrive on an awareness that mental adroitness and situational flexibility often have an advantage over an appreciation of the way things are "supposed" to be. Their instrument of success is lightning-quick perception, engaging and insightful, and right on the mark.

The downfall of Gemini in a traditional corporate leadership role, and the reason why so few of them actually wear the crown, is that they find long-term consistency constraining and predictability way too prosaic for their nimble intellects. Long-range corporate goals and immediate personal gratification can be too closely balanced in their accounts. Their looking glass allows them to see squiggly things in astonishing clarity, and then a sudden shift of light or mood makes them capriciously adjust the focus to fuzzy.

The Gemini's natural métier in business is in consulting, research and development, or any of the marketing functions (PR, advertising, and especially, sales) in which idea dissemination and persuasion take precedence over organizational structure and standard operating procedure. At their best Gemini manages to convey some brilliant moments of insight and expression, things so in total synchronization with their time and place that they may attain icon status. Consider Kennedy's "Ask not what your country can do for you," or Katherine Graham's bold decision to pursue the Watergate scandal in the pages of her Washington-insider newspaper, or Tim Berners-Lee creation of the World Wide Web, or even Donald Trump's original inspired blurting of "You're fired!" (And it would be regrettable to not mention Gemini Clint Eastwood's "Make my day," or Gemini Marilyn Monroe's "Happy Birthday, Mr. President," or Gemini Bob Dylan's, "Blowin' in the Wind.") Sometimes, of course, the Gemini is reading from someone else's script, but the power of the association of the specific phrase with the Gemini is undeniable. You get the idea.

Even these blazing moments of contemporary cultural connection cannot hide the fundamental truth that Gemini tends to experience the world in terms of its inconsistencies and contradictions and manipulations and short-lived resolves. Workplace-skewering cartoonist Scott Adams has amassed quite a nice fortune from the principle he has espoused on *The Dilbert Blog*, "I'm suspicious of anyone who has a firm belief about anything." Paul McCartney, arguably the world's richest rock musician and an acknowledged astrological devotee, has unapologetically summarized his Gemini birthright to his biographer Christopher Sandford as "we're sort of schizo."

Even when one gets to a leader as revered in corporate management circles as GM's Alfred Sloan, it is essential to understand that his greatest contribution is an understanding of the fleeting quality of commitment and the shortsightedness of rigid centralized control. A pioneer of consumer research and the first advocate of model redesigns in every auto year, Sloan was the first major CEO to really understand consumer diversity ("A Car for Every Purse and Purpose" was his slogan) and the role of aggressive salesmanship in stimulating desire and cooperation both within and outside of the corporation. It is also enormously befitting in a Gemini sense that the major research and awards thrust of the foundation that bears his name is toward workplace flexibility.

Not always prized in the corporate throne room, flexibility *is* at the heart of the Gemini matter.

gemini Leaders: value statements

Life's Greatest Trial Is Boredom

Gemini gifts include a rich and playful curiosity, exceptional vigor (famously pronounced "vigah" by John Kennedy), a way with words, and considerable charm. Their shortcomings run towards bouts of impatience with the "ignorant" input of others, petulance when they don't get what they want, and a rather apparent lack of enthusiasm for mundane tasks and responsibilities. In so many words, there is something about them that stays, to paraphrase Bob Dylan, "forever adolescent," and not just a little reminiscent of Peter Pan.

Apparent in the lives of many Gemini "greats" is a constant need for amusement and stimulation. This can be seen in both the personal and professional aspects of their lives, and in ways not always condoned by polite society (more on this in a bit). Finger-wagging aside, however, one really gets the business sense of this in the life of the great American shipping and railroad magnate Cornelius Vanderbilt, who in his day was the largest employer of labor in the United States but purportedly hated the daily routines of work.

Certainly the life and career of Donald Trump is instructive in this regard. Is there any doubt that his various roles as a television personality *and* a McDonald's pitchman *and* a presidential candidate *and* an author *and* a self-styled ladies man are every bit as dear to him as his real estate career? Is there a chance that "the Donald" would trade in his tabloid life for a greater level of respect on the financial exchanges?

In a leadership context it should simply be kept in mind that the "inner child" will often surface with Gemini. A Gemini appreciates George H. W. Bush's strikingly firm assertion that as the President of the United States he no longer, whatever his mother's instructions, had to eat his broccoli. A Gemini "gets" whatever it is in Scott Adams character that caused him to wear a disguise and give a consulting presentation to a major technology firm in which he boasted of having previously helped P&G to develop better *tasting* soap.

"I don't think Dilbert will age unless I do," Adams once responded to an online inquiry, "and I've stayed twelve-years-old for quite some time now."

One Is an Insufficient Number

Gemini sees the world in terms of ambiguous choice, believing most matters to be grayish rather than black and white. So much about their lives suggests two souls warring in one body, and the classic image of an angel on one shoulder and a devil on the other resonates strongly here. Gemini is very aptly symbolized in astrological iconography as the sign of twins.

In a business analysis, the first thing that becomes readily apparent in this regard is that even a very successful Gemini tends to pursue a dual career. Many, for example, whatever their careers are also very successful authors. But while such an observation can be made of the leaders of other astrological signs, the duality with Gemini runs towards particularly striking dichotomies. For example:

- Donald Trump, as already noted, is as famous as a television personality and political candidate as he is as a real estate developer.
- Robert Maxwell, famous as a media baron, was also an international money launderer and a spy for both the Soviet Union's KGB and Israel's Mossad.
- Ditto for "philanthropist" Armand Hammer, chairman of Occidental Petroleum, who was also a money launderer and a spy, and was once described by *New Republic* magazine as "the greatest confidence man of the twentieth century."
- Igor Sikorsky, Russian-born father of the modern helicopter, was a highly regarded religious visionary and philosopher.
- Bob Hope made serious stabs at boxing and butchery before embarking on his entertainment career.
- Scott Adams, famed as the creator of the Dilbert cartoon empire, is a vegetarian food manufacturer and restaurateur.

In a particularly neat trick of astrological fate there are the actual Gemini twins, Francis and Freelan Stanley, who at the turn of the twentieth century invented the highly esteemed Stanley Steamer automobile. By all accounts a remarkable vehicle, one that in 1906 set the land-speed record of 127 miles per hour, it was this steam-propelled car that might have well become the prototype of automobiles in service to this day. While historians advance various reasons why this did not happen (basically, it took a long time to heat the steam), some say the Stanleys' relative lack of interest in industrial mass production was key, as they were just as avid about pursuing studio photography and building concert-quality violins.

Although not entirely germane to a business study, it is worth mentioning that the other area where duality (or triplicity, or quadruplicity, etc.) quite frequently rears its head in the lives of Gemini leaders is that of intimate personal relationships. Driven by a requirement for diversity, stimulation, and approval, the lives of the Gemini "greats" are often quite speckled with philandering and/or multiple matings. This becomes culturally important when, as a National Public Radio survey revealed just a few years ago, more teenagers knew about of John Kennedy's hanky panky with Marilyn Monroe (both Geminis) than were aware of JFK's political party affiliation (Democrat).

Some Geminis, of course, remain devoted to a single career focus and to happy, committed partnerships. For others, personal consistency just doesn't always count for much. In a personal or professional relationship it's well worth noting with which Gemini you are dealing.

Thanks for the Memory

If you have never actually listened to the lyrics of *Thanks for the Memory*, Bob Hope's familiar theme song, you might understandably take it as a sweet and melancholy farewell. Yet if you really listen to the words it becomes quite clear that the song is a classic kiss-off. Gemini is rarely a paragon of long-term sentimentality.

Perhaps both the best and worst that can be said of Gemini is that they tend to be dominated by thinking, and their minds tend to be enormously focused in the moment. For good, this allows remarkably cool and cogent analysis of a current state of affairs. For bad, this allows the memory to become short and the heart to appear ungenerous.

It is discomforting to come across key moments in the lives of so many Gemini leaders in which appreciation of the past and responsibility to the future is given short shrift. Character revealing anecdotes abound in which Gemini bosses rather pragmatically, if not cruelly, sever ties with long-term associates without so much as a handshake. Consider Robert Maxwell's massive embezzlements from his employee pension funds, Bob Hope's unceremonious dumping of partners in each move up the ladder of success, the other Beatles throwing bricks through Paul McCartney's window when the latter sued for self-interested business dissolution of the band, and, of course again, there is Trump's cold-hearted trademark phrase, "You're fired!"

Ironically, Gemini leaders do have a pretty good memory when the issue is a perceived slight against their own interests. Donald Trump, who by all accounts lost a lot of other people's money and went through some bleak financial times himself, is reported to have written "f—— you," on the requests of disgruntled past lenders when his affairs started to improve. Paul McCartney acknowledges having carried an active 25-year grudge against record producer Phil Spector, whom he blamed for ruining the album *Let It Be* with changes not run by Paul.

So the best one may expect from a Gemini is a burst of in-the-moment brilliance, such as occurred during the Cuban Missile Crisis, when John F. Kennedy very astutely calculated that his adversary Khrushchev, with greater military vulnerability and politically more to lose, would pull back from ultimate confrontation. As for sentiment, though, the best one may do with Gemini may be Kennedy's subsequent comment, "Forgive your enemies, but never forget their names."

Truth Is Negotiable

When most people hear the word "truth," they have a tendency to think of ethical principles carved in granite or scientific verities as constant as the law of gravity. A Gemini, on the other hand, tends to think of truth as a sharpshooter hitting a bull's-eye or an Olympic gymnast sticking the perfect dismount. The difference is that while truth will remain constant in the first example, in the Gemini world, tomorrow's truth may be a jammed gun or a fractured ankle.

Eschewing big principles as far more conditional and ambiguous than others will admit, Gemini leaders prize the brilliant considera-tion and expression of what is going on right here and right now. The wonderful things that can emerge from such an outlook are great daily newspapers such as Katherine Graham's *Washington Post*, great monthly magazines such as Cyrus Curtis' *Saturday Evening Post* and *Ladies' Home Journal*, and great yearly car redesigns such as those produced by Alfred Sloan's General Motors. It is similarly worth not-ing that a tight and conditional Gemini focus is usually essential to successful advertising strategy. It was Alfred Sloan who made General Motors the country's largest advertiser, and Cyrus Curtis who on a large scale developed the now widely accepted practice of placing advertising near relevant editorial.

The trouble some people have with the Gemini outlook is sim-ply that opportunism is no dirty word in the Gemini businessperson's lexicon. Yet many of these same detractors would agree that there is no better state of mind for performing a marketing or sales function than guiltless opportunism. That there may even be something ap-proaching a kind of business nobility in such an outlook is evident in a brilliant project undertaken by Cyrus Curtis and the Curtis Pub-lishing Company that derived, in true Gemini fashion, from an un-derstanding of adolescent boys.

Recalling his own start as a newsboy, Cyrus Curtis put together what was likely the greatest sales training program for boys in our nation's history. The League of Curtis Salesmen was an early twentieth-century network that touched the lives of 250,000 youths, who sold the three major Curtis magazines—*Saturday Evening Post, Ladies Home Journal,* and *Country Gentleman*—door-to-door for commissions and prizes. Provided with training materials, given stationery and business cards, and afforded opportunities for advancement on the basis of their sales performance, many of the boys in that program embraced their skills and successes and went on to outstanding sales careers as adults.

Keep this in mind when you hear such Gemini statements as Armand Hammer's observation that "those who insist on telling the truth never have a future," and Bob Dylan's pronouncement that "all the truth in the world adds up to one big lie." These are just the other side of Alfred Sloan's reflection that "Bedside manners are no substitute for the right diagnosis" and Clint Eastwood's insistence that "If you want a guarantee, buy a toaster." A Gemini, blessed with a quick mind and unburdened by constrictions of philosophy or tradition, will sell that toaster better than most.

Talk Is Anything but Cheap

It is the passion of Gemini to make life more interesting for themselves and for others. They accomplish this primarily through the written word, although the spoken word, sung word, and acted word are also very much in their arsenal. Self-involved as they may sometimes be, an evolved Gemini describes the existing culture with great clarity and truly inspires that culture to come up with ideas for the betterment of the human situation.

Pulitzer Prizes, Academy Awards, and Emmys, more so than business honors, do tend to pile up for these charming and fascinat-

ing individuals who are so quick with a turn of phrase or a lively observation. Indeed, in business circles and elsewhere their candor can
make vested traditionalists somewhat nervous. It is undeniable that
they demand more than a fair share of attention and that they sometimes play fast and loose with responsibility and the rules.

Sometimes though they channel the exact thing that needs to be
said at the exact right moment, and for this there should be some
genuine appreciation.

✦ tips for dealing with gemini

- While they are capable of throwing themselves into their
  careers, do not expect long-term consistency in action or
  thought or commitment from the Gemini individual. It's just
  not in their nature to endure too much sameness or drudgery.
- Because Gemini is most often an original and impulsive
  thinker, it is difficult for them to experience deep empathy
  with others. They have not forgotten their debt of gratitude
  out of malice. Their minds have simply and totally moved on
  to something else. (No, you don't have to like it.)
- Gemini is a communicator and needs to *hear* praise. Quiet
  appreciation, and even a little something extra in the pay enve-
  lope, are nothing compared to approbation paid out loud.
- *Hint*: The best thing one can do for a Gemini is to create
  situations where they can present their ideas in a spontaneous,
  reasonably unedited format. Keep in mind that when you
  invite them out for a social occasion, what they hear is that
  they are being invited out for mental gymnastics. Choose
  venues where the ambient noise is not a conversation killer.

CHapter 9

canceR

The Value of Foundation

Winning is the most important thing in my life, after breathing. Breathing first, winning next.

—George Steinbrenner, quoted on
the *Baseball Almanac* website

JUNE 22 TO JULY 21

P. T. Barnum	July 5, 1810	Barnum and Bailey Circus
John D. Rockefeller	July 8, 1839	Standard Oil
George Eastman	July 12, 1854	Kodak
Juan Trippe	June 27, 1899	Pan Am
William Lear	June 26, 1902	Learjet Corporation
Estee Lauder	July 1, 1908	The Estee Lauder Companies
Robert E. Rich	July 7, 1913	Rich Products
Leona Helmsley	July 4, 1920	Helmsley Real Estate Holdings
Merv Griffin	July 6, 1925	Merv Griffin Enterprises
H. Ross Perot	June 27, 1930	Electronic Data Systems
George Steinbrenner	July 4, 1930	New York Yankees
Donald Rumsfeld	July 9, 1932	G. D. Searle and Company
Bill Cosby	July 12, 1937	Bill Cosby Productions
Michael Milken	July 4, 1946	Drexel Burnham Lambert
George W. Bush	July 6, 1946	U.S. president
Vera Wang	June 27, 1949	Vera Wang Fashion
Richard Branson	July 18, 1950	Virgin Enterprises
Howard Schultz	July 19,1953	Starbucks
Judy McGrath	July 2, 1954	MTV
Donna Dubinsky	July 4, 1955	Palm Computing

cancer signatures

Style: Moody

Objective: Security

Strength: Loyalty

Weakness: Stubbornness

Communication: Emotive

Tactic: Defense

Belief: Clan

Reward: Protection

Leaders born under the sign of Cancer experience a central paradox of business life with unparalleled emotional intensity. On the one hand Cancer leaders fully accept that business is a matter of black and red numerals, that it is a fiercely competitive blood sport where you are either a winner or a loser and nothing in between. On the other hand most Cancers are sensitive custodians of culture, genuinely concerned about the welfare of those whose lives they touch.

More than the leaders of any other sign, Cancers see themselves as part of an historical chain of values, with both financial and emotional components. They are stewards of the link between past and future, and their job is to preserve and enhance the literal and figurative assets of the cultural system in which they place their trust. Their passion, ambition, and focus in this regard are unparalleled.

For people who see their essential task as the victorious oversight of a strong culture, life tends to be dominated by rules and convictions, rights and wrongs, and intense beliefs about the appropriate forms of government, religion, and other key organizational units of society. The opportunity created here is for rich and successful nurturing of a long-lived tribe. The danger is the destructive side of zealotry, a self-righteous knowingness that belligerently challenges suspected disloyalties and alternative interpretations of rightness.

Thus with Cancer one encounters the lives of business builders and nurturers, such as Kodak's George Eastman and Starbucks' Howard Schultz, whose exemplary success and social consciousness have brought the world long-term multidimensional satisfactions on people, policy, and product levels, as well as on the bottom line. And then there are those Cancer leaders who, whatever their contributions, will be remembered for nothing so much as their cranky self-righteous confrontations with competitors, colleagues, and employees. Even in these latter cases, though, the strong sense of caring that is the foundation of all Cancer success shines through.

With Cancer leaders, it is the attribute frequently characterized as "heart" (reflecting earnest determination as much as loving consideration) that makes them such formidable figures, even when mired in controversy. Michael Milken, whose mammoth financial market manipulations earned him a jail sentence and the wholesale ostracism of the investment community, is suddenly recast as a not-so-bad hero of the free market system, sponsoring an influential capitalist think tank and backing enormous philanthropic commitments. Ditto for America's first billionaire, John D. Rockefeller, who—although described as a man possessed by greed during his active business years—retired in his mid-fifties and devoted the rest of his long life and most of his fortune to philanthropic causes.

One gets a good feel for the Cancer leader's soul and the public's reaction to it in the person of Richard Branson, the self-made British billionaire, who created Virgin Enterprises. Criticized for everything from a lack of formal education and a "hippie" back-ground to an almost pathological addiction to daredevil risk, the relentless Sir Richard is one of Britain's most culturally vested and even beloved figures. A poll in a British newspaper a few years ago said that after Mother Teresa, the Pope, and the Archbishop of Canterbury, Branson would be the most appropriate person to "rewrite the Ten Commandments."

"I believe in benevolent dictatorship," Branson once remarked resolving all paradoxes, "provided I am the dictator."

cancer Leaders: value statements

May Your Tribe Increase!

In the February 2001 issue of *Town and Country*, author Janet Freed Carlson writes of fashion designer Vera Wang's husband, financier Arthur Becker, who likes to tell the story of the couple's first date. According to Becker, Wang expressed a preference for choosing the restaurant. When the couple arrived, every member of Wang's im-mediate family was seated at a table awaiting them.

The preceding may be an example of an Asian custom, but its astrological spirit is also pure Cancer. To Cancer the primary foun-dation and focus of one's life is the essential values-affirming, support-providing cultural unit, the family. Generally, Cancers will consider nothing more important and nowhere will they place greater alle-giance than this heritage-bound repository of personal source and communal destiny.

Thus it is hardly surprising that the lives of Cancer business lead-ers are often literally predicated on close family relationships. Whether one addresses business inspiration, early instruction, start-up financing, entrepreneurial legacy, or chief purpose, Cancers are inclined to cite family as the chief source of involvement and consideration. With an inflexible sense of rectitude Cancer leaders will take care of their own and expect that you will do likewise for yours.

For good and/or bad, there is something quintessentially parental about Cancer leadership. On the upside there is an understanding of the need for instruction, nurturing, and patience. As Howard Schultz, who claims his own father's work tribulations inspired the labor-friendly policies at Starbucks, writes in his book, *Pour Your Heart Into It* (New York: Hyperion, 1999):

> There are a lot of similarities between rearing a family, where the parents imprint values on their children, and starting a new business, where the founder sets the ground rules very early.

Less fortunate implications arise, as they often do in families, when the dad or mom is inclined to emotional imperialism. Working for H. Ross Perot meant observing total loyalty to a creed that was articulated on the fly by a very stubborn and ethically inconsistent man. Even that ultimate father figure, Bill Cosby, put his foot into it when he began to publicly bash black families for the problems of the black community, and when it was subsequently discovered that his own morality had a touch of green around the gills.

Ultimately though, the trick to "getting" Cancer is to accept that their chief ambition is to take care of and go home to the ones they love. Thus it was true of John D. Rockefeller, who basically spent the last four decades of his life entertaining grandchildren, attending church, and playing golf on his own estate courses. Thus it is true of Palm Computing's Donna Dubinsky, who has commented that her chief goal is to retire and spend more time with her family and to maybe teach a bit.

It may not be sexy, but it is a whole lot thicker than water.

The Best Offense Is a Good Defense; the Best Defense Is a Pile of Cash

When one sees the world in terms of "us" and "them," there is inevitable worry about vulnerability, be it from actual threat or the result of good old-fashioned paranoia. Either way there often seems to be some palpable sense of fear in the lives of Cancer individuals regarding openness to attack. Often this fear simultaneously becomes both "the enemy" and a weapon in the Cancer's own arsenal.

Sometimes this manipulation by and of fear is just not pretty. One encounters Leona Helmsley illegally shoving the prospect of imminent home loss (the greatest of Cancer catastrophes) at apartment renters with the temerity to resist going condo. On a much larger stage there is the role that fear of homeland destruction has played in the evolution and conduct of Cancer George W. Bush administration's War on Terror, notably coordinated by Cancer Secretary of Defense Donald Rumsfeld.

Lest this last seem too much a political comment in what is essentially a business text, let it be noted that many Cancer-led organizations tend to run on a military paradigm, with tight behavioral codes and strict conformance expectations. George Steinbrenner says he learned all about leadership from his military experience. Annapolis graduate H. Ross Perot demanded his employees adhere to rigid standards in everything ranging from dress to marital fidelity, and specifically sought out military veterans to staff his various enterprises. He even engaged some of them in paramilitary operations—most famously in southeast Asia in a hunt for missing Vietnam-era prisoners of war and in Iran when some of his EDS executives were kidnapped during a business deal.

Maybe just a bit more obvious in business than in the military, though, is the awareness that the chief weapon of defense is money.

The Cancer's simple rule regarding competition and allies is that you crush the resources of the one and purchase the allegiance of the other. That morality doesn't always figure into it can be surmised from the write-your-own-rules/take-no-prisoners styles of Rockefeller (monopolistic practices), Milken (insider trading), and Perot (heavy-handed political contributions).

Of course, the very notion of "morality" is a bit weak-kneed in the context of what Cancer leaders might see as a business-based "holy war." In such a worldview greed may not be good, but it is necessary. As Vera Wang coolly observed to *Town and Country* (February 1, 2002):

> It's grow or die, as they say on Wall Street. It's about the bottom line. Anybody who says it isn't, isn't really in business.

As a Cancer always seems to appreciate, a healthy bank account calms many fears.

Empathy Trumps Intellect

A common theme among Cancer leaders is how relatively few have taken an institutional education especially seriously. John D. Rockefeller, George Eastman, Richard Branson, Estee Lauder, and Leona Helmsley are just some of the phenomenally successful Cancer leaders who never attended college. Others who did, like Juan Trippe and George W. Bush, were pretty much there to have a good time, gain credentials, and make contacts. Even famed Cancer inventor William Lear, who gave the world products such as the car radio (on the back of which Motorola was built) and the Lear jet, did not matriculate past the eighth grade.

Of far more visceral and educational importance to most Cancers is their first salaried job, generally taken at an extremely early age. Cancers tend to make an early connection between hard work and money, as well as early discovery about the miracle of dividends and compound interest. Institutions of higher education sometimes just muddy these fundamental points besides serving as hotbeds of dogma, a portion of which will generally not conform to the Cancer's tightly maintained definition of desirable cultural values.

Just as relevant here, however, is the fact that the Cancer genius rarely resides in the formal intellect. Rather, Cancers are the masters and mistresses of deep feelings. They may not know what you are thinking, but they do know what you want.

Thus, the Cancer genius traditionally manifests in the product and service arena as both an anticipation of and an improvement upon deeply held consumer desires. For example:

- Photography was enormously popular before Kodak, but it took George Eastman to figure out how to make it a portable everyman process, "as easy as using a pencil."
- Cosmetics existed before Estee Lauder, but it was this great entrepreneur who appreciated that "touching the customer" through expert demo counter application, sampling, and free gifts needed to be part of the beauty package experience.
- Overseas air travel was once the sole province of the elite, but it was Pan Am's Juan Trippe who saw it as an experience that should not just be reserved for the ultra-rich.
- People were drinking coffee in coffee shops and diners long before Starbucks, but Howard Schultz saw the upside of offering premium product and a creating a truly inviting "third place" for socialization.
- Bridal gowns certainly pre-existed Vera Wang's work, but she made her fortune on an understanding that to a bride true fashion on a wedding day is more important, not less, than on any other day.

Similar insights abound regarding Robert Rich and Rich topping (in a world of wartime shortages, how great to have an appealing substitute for whipped cream!); Merv Griffin and shows like *Jeopardy!* and *Wheel of Fortune* (people wanted TV quiz shows that were more honest and easier to play than the tainted *21*); Judy McGrath and the growth of MTV (style-conscious young people wanted to *see* their music); and Donna Dubinsky and Palm Computing (computer users required a constant electronic companion).

Or maybe the Cancer genius is best summed up by P. T. Barnum, a promoter of outrageous attractions that eventually morphed into the modern circus, who appreciated that nineteenth-century America was eager to push past its Puritanism. Interestingly, one thing history now knows is that Barnum, who invented such customer friendly policies as the rain check and the outrageous publicity stunt, never uttered his alleged observation that "there's a sucker born every minute." Cancers are way too smart to ever let on in public that they feel that way.

Howling at the Moon Is Optional

The discrete way to get at this touchy point may simply be to point out the astrological symbolism. The heavenly body most closely associated with Cancer is the moon, constantly phase-changing by reflected light so that its countenance is never quite the same from night to night. The stellar constellation/animal icon of Cancer is the crab, a creature who lives through alternative seasons of thick shell and shedding, and who by nature would rather lose a claw then let go of the prize.

The less discrete way to put this is that inside every Cancer, even the best of them, there seems to live a creature who is part crabby lunatic. It's Leona Helmsley screaming at busboys, George Steinbrenner changing Yankee managers twenty times in twenty-three seasons, H. Ross Perot independently hiring a bigoted mercenary named Bo

Grits to travel to Laos and look for POWs. It's the fine line that exists between tenacity as evidence of one's patience and courage of convictions, and tenacity as evidence of hysteria—and it is a line with which most Cancers have some familiarity.

The smart ones recognize this quality in themselves and make a keen effort to remain as private as possible. Capable of great emotional chemistry with a crowd, Cancer leaders will rarely choose to place themselves in unscripted public circumstances. It's Rockefeller being deadly serious about avoiding chance meetings, Branson refusing to maintain a personal corporate office, and Eastman declining to have photographs taken of himself.

To put it bluntly, these are not the folks to whom you want to recommend thriving on uncertainty.

Charity Starts at Home

It would be unfair not to mention all of the impressive philanthropic work undertaken by Cancer leaders. As hard as they compete in the business arena, they bring an equal measure of commitment to aiding the downtrodden. And while there is often little sympathy for passive charity, the contributions to causes that encourage others to help themselves in realms such as education are frequently profound.

Where one may encounter the best of Cancer leaders, however, is in their loyalty to and support of their own workforces, which the best of them see as extended families (and which sometimes are). It is almost hard to comprehend the goodness and generosity of a George Eastman, who set awesome precedents with respect to salaries, retirement annuities, life insurance, and disability coverage, and who in 1919 simply gave one-third of his stock to his employees as a thank you.

Today, similarly, much deserved praise is heaped upon Howard Schultz, with Starbucks being one of the first big restaurant companies to ever offer stock options to hourly employees, health benefits to part-time employees, and fair trade prices to its Third World coffee suppliers. Schultz is also of the belief that his company generally benefits much more through local cause marketing that supports a community rather than major media marketing that supports an ad agency. He proselytizes about "relationships"—with staffs, suppliers, stockholders, and customers—and there's real meaning in the word. Schultz once observed:

> There is a direct link between how I grew up and how we tried to build Starbucks.

That is something any Cancer understands.

✦ tips for dealing with a cancer

- No matter how much logic you bring to bear on a situation, a Cancer will almost always make a gut-level decision. Don't over-explain or fake your feelings.
- Cancer holds grudges and feels empowered when the competition suffers. Don't let your heart bleed for the enemy.
- More than any other boss, a Cancer will let you know that success is measured in terms of profit, with nothing in second place. You will rarely get something for nothing here.
- *Hint*: Although the Cancer boss is capable of being a moody SOB at times, the truth is that this is a very sentimental individual with an old-fashioned set of loyalties and a powerful sense of tradition. Birthdays, anniversaries, and most importantly, the major holidays, are loaded with powerful personal associations for Cancer, and you would be wise to circle them on your calendar and honor them.

CHAPTER 10

Leo

The Value of Flamboyance

All the things I love is what my business is all about.

—Martha Stewart, *The World According to Martha*

JULY 22 TO AUGUST 21		
Henry Ford	July 30, 1863	Ford Motor Company
S. S. Kresge	July 31, 1867	K-Mart
Clarence Saunders	August 9, 1881	Piggly Wiggly
Jack L. Warner	August 2, 1882	Warner Brothers
Lucille Ball	August 6, 1911	Desilu Productions
Malcolm Forbes	August 19, 1919	Forbes
Anne Klein	August 3, 1923	Anne Klein and Company
George Soros	August 12, 1930	Quantum Fund
Charlotte Beers	July 26, 1935	Ogilvy and Mather
Martha Ingram	August 20, 1935	Ingram Industries
Yves St. Laurent	August 1, 1936	Yves St. Laurent
Martha Stewart	August 3, 1941	Martha Stewart Living Omnicom
Frederick W. Smith	August 11, 1944	FedEx
Lawrence Ellison	August 17, 1944	Oracle Corporation
William J. Clinton	August 19, 1946	U.S. president
Steve Wozniak	August 11, 1950	Apple
Meg Whitman	August 1, 1956	eBay
Mark Cuban	July 31, 1958	Broadcast.com (Dallas Mavericks)
Earvin "Magic" Johnson	August 14, 1959	Magic Johnson Enterprises
Stephen Case	August 21, 1958	AOL

Leo signatures

Style:	Radiant
Objective:	Glory
Strength:	Charisma
Weakness:	Details
Communication:	Assured
Tactic:	Theatrics
Belief:	Self-expression
Reward:	Praise

The sign of Cancer, which we have just visited in Chapter 9, is astrologically linked to the Moon. Signified by reflected light, night shadows and constant phase changes, Cancer individuals manifest a tidal emotional life that ebbs and flows across a moonlit beach of tribal rituals and relationships. Leo on the other hand, represented by the brilliant Sun, has little business with hoary dogma or dark dancing nuance and simply needs to get its shine on.

In many ways Leo is simultaneously the least complex and most effective of all the leadership signs. Impatient with the rule of history, Leo leaders believe that it is the will of a solitary individual, the charismatic tribal chief, that gets everyone productively and happily through to tomorrow. Not to be overly simplistic about it but the Leo's lot in life is to be a contact high and a radiant inspiration, right here right now.

While Leo leaders may not have invented the personal pronoun they get a heck of a lot of mileage out of it. We sometimes condemn ego in society as selfishness, especially if we are void of talent and/or spirit ourselves. But Leos see their birthright as the bright burning of a spirit that exists in all people, but is usually only recognized by a fortunate few born in the middle of the Northern Hemisphere's hot season.

Now it should be noted here that the last three paragraphs all basically say the same thing. This, too, is what Leo is about. Leo delivers a profound yet very simple message about the power of an illuminated personality. And while they personally realize this insight to the core of their being, with a purity and passion no less than that of Apollo delivering fire to mankind, they will repeat this message over and over . . . until YOU get it.

Of course, when one is the human incarnation of the sun there is a tendency to suck up all the oxygen in the room. Leaders of the Leo persuasion don't always get the highest grades when it comes to "works well with others." An Achilles heel is a tendency to prize an audience over an ally (although the most successful Leos tend to prize talented specialists who will support and execute the Leo vision without stepping into the limelight).

When one looks at some of the names listed here—Henry Ford, Lucille Ball, Martha Stewart, Magic Johnson, Malcolm Forbes, etc— it is virtually impossible to separate enterprise identity from individual identity. Creative entrepreneurship is the stamp of the true Leo leader, frequently taken to the point of personality cult as well as to fortune and fame. In addition to the Leo leaders already mentioned here, just try to imagine a one-for-one fill-in for Mick Jagger or Julia Child or Arnold Schwarzenegger, all with long-lasting larger than life personalities that are simultaneously subject to caricature and adoration.

Ask a Leo about the secret of leadership or a successful life and they will invariably list enthusiasm, tenacity, and a predisposition towards joy as the proper tools for the job. "A man can succeed at almost anything for which he has unlimited enthusiasm," says Charles Schwab. "Find something you're passionate about and keep tremendously interested in it," says Julia Child. "It's a helluva start," Lucille Ball once commented, "being able to recognize what makes you happy."

Perhaps above all else, Leo brilliance stems from being as powerfully vested in the present as the noonday sun. Even with his Hall of Fame basketball career behind him and an HIV-positive medical condition, Magic Johnson enthusiastically told Seth Rubinroit, a young reporter from the *L.A. Youth* newspaper: "I am a businessman. This is what I do each and every day. I love it. I love coming to work. I never have a bad day."

Leo Leaders: value statements

I Am What I Am

Leo-born Clarence Saunders revolutionized the retail grocery industry when he introduced the self-serve Piggly Wiggly supermarket chain. In time Saunders lost control of the business due to some unfortunate stock market risk-taking. Prohibited by the remaining Piggly Wiggly enterprise from ever using the Piggly Wiggly name again, Saunders launched a new chain of stores actually called, "Clarence Saunders, Sole Owner of My Own Name."

The original Henry Ford Motor Company eventually went on to produce not the Ford Model T, but the Cadillac. More passionate about engineering than street sales in the early days, Henry Ford had a run-in with his board and resigned from the company. "I resigned," Ford said, "determined never again to put myself under orders."

Lucille Ball was willing to take a significant pay cut for creative control of the landmark *I Love Lucy* series. Her insistence that the show be shot on quality film stock rather than kinescope recording tape, and in California rather than New York, led to the rise of Desilu Productions and the subsequent installation of Lucy as the first woman to run a major television production company. "You really have to love yourself to get anything done in this world," the Queen of Comedy once observed.

Again it is urgent to understand that for a Leo the power of one's inner light is primary, and the right to live by that light is a birthright. "I've got to be me," is the lyric playing in their brain. There is definitely some ego involved, but the rapt attention paid by the world to Leo greats is more like a photosynthetic phenomenon than an act of free will.

As Apple cofounder Steve Wozniak once told a writer for the *San Jose Mercury News*: "I wonder why, when I just did kind of normal things—some good engineering and just what I wanted to do in life—why everywhere I go, some people think that I'm some kind of hero or a special person."

Were Henry Ford around to counsel "the Woz," he might remark as he once did upon an earlier occasion: "Asking who ought to be the boss is like asking who ought to be the tenor in the quartet? Obviously, the man who can sing tenor."

The Devil Is in the Details

Leos fully intuit their connection to the divine. They walk (or in Mick Jagger's case, strut) with nearly Olympian self-possession through a cosmos of brilliant conceptual flashes, incandescent human interactions, and profound acts of creativity, celebration, and indulgence. Possessed of monarchial tendencies, Leo leaders' chief shortcoming is sometimes finding it a compromise of their "station" to admit fallibility or clean up their own mess.

It is quite true that leaders of every astrological sign occasionally

get beaten up a bit by setbacks. Even so, there's a special set of circumstances magnifying the downside for Leo. First of all they are gamblers
by nature, and they can be caught far out on limb when events move
against them (George Soros, for all his great investing success, badly
misplayed the collapse in tech stocks and was infamously featured on
the cover of *Fortune* with a thumb's up equities message just prior to
the 1987 stock crash). Second, they are so often eager to take center
stage that there is little opportunity for hiding in the wings during a
crisis (Bill Clinton invited universal scorn by going on television to
deal with "what the definition of *is* is"). And third, they are often
capricious about details, overlooking some and getting heavily side-
tracked by others. ("The real story is," said Magic Johnson, "I had un-
protected sex.")

Perhaps the most apparent instance of all this coming home to
roost can be found in the professional life of Martha Stewart, the
eponymous founder of Martha Stewart Living Omnicom. Martha's infamous insider stock-trading transgression, although obviously felonious, was relatively minor in the financial scheme of things. Clearly
her cocksure style and media celebrity exacerbated her punishment.

What may be puzzling in this context, though, is Stewart's obvious professional predilection towards living one of the most detail-
intensive lives on the planet (it should be mentioned that her Venus
is in the sign Virgo, which would make her both an artisan and a
lover of detail, but more of that later). It should be apparent to anyone, though, that the lifestyle she pitches is more entertainment than
education, being more or less an exaggerated parody of what Super-
man might accomplish if he were a homemaker (Hand-tied bundles
of twigs for buttering corn? Fresh-cut virgin grasses for lining a roast
pan in which to cook a holiday ham? Marabou stork feathers for a
hand-crafted tree angel with an underskirt?). Without a very large,
conscientious, and talented staff actually doing the work, there's just

no way anyone is going to "do" the Martha fantasy—and despite the credit she takes for being the über-domestic goddess, she obviously knows this very well herself.

And yet Martha deserves credit for the big concept that drives the engine, as do so many other Leo leaders, regardless of who is actually shoveling the coal. FedEx founder Fred Smith doesn't maintain the airplanes or deliver the packages, but his notion of delivering all those packages through a hub and spoke system was pure genius. "It's not efficient for one connection," Smith once wrote about his decision to have every FedEx package travel through Memphis, "but it is efficient for an enormous number of connections."

Smith's system is in fact a perfect metaphor for how a Leo generally conceives of any satisfactory organizational matrix. Call it hub and spokes, or perhaps even more accurately, sun and planets. It may not look like the center is moving with the same effort as the outer points, but surely light and gravity should count for something.

You Are the Wind Beneath My Wings

Henry Ford is often given credit for inventing both the automobile and the industrial assembly line that produces it. He personally did neither of these things, but it is unlike Leo to let a little thing like a fact get in the way of taking credit. He was the right man in the right place to allow history to make a judgment in his favor, and he didn't deem it necessary to waste a lot of time on sharing credit or engaging in modesty.

One thing Henry Ford *is* responsible for is suddenly doubling the salaries of his assembly line workers while simultaneously reducing their hours of labor. Of course he had self-interested motives for these actions, among them the desire for increased productivity and for laborers to be able to afford the cars they were building. Yet for all the caveats, how must his employees have felt about Ford on the day they learned of the new policies!

This, in a nutshell, is what one gets with a Leo leader. At one end of the spectrum you have the self-lionizing imperial tendencies of a Napoleon (a Leo), and at the other, the generous collaborative orientation of a Charles Schwab or a Meg Whitman. In both cases the affect is personal loyalty, although in the former the motivation is generalized fear, and in the latter it's a rewarded appreciation of specific talents.

Sometimes you do get both, of course. Mark Cuban, owner of the Dallas Mavericks, is famous for both his generosity to his players and his attention-grabbing, ref-baiting interference with the game as it is being played. Oracle's Larry Ellison describes the dichotomy between expressing pleasure and displeasure as a personal growth continuum, in which one must learn to cultivate empathy for human fallibility and learn to encourage and advise rather than challenge or scold.

Basically, it comes down to whether the specific Leo leader is inclined to think of people as inherently worthy or unworthy of trust, and the specific Leo will leave little doubt of that. As FedEx founder Frederick W. Smith, functioning at his Leo best, observed:

> A manager is not a person who can do the work better than his men. He is a person who can get his men to do the work better than he can.

Yet it is always worth remembering that the Leo perspective is inherently self-referential. A useful insight is unearthed in a quote by actress Simone Signoret about the often-difficult, Leo-born studio head Jack Warner, to wit, "He bore no grudge against those he had wronged."

That Simone knew her Leos.

Celebrate

Leo leaders tend to be hard workers, quite capable of burning the midnight oil. But they will not disguise the fact that they also expect life to yield some fun. In fact, they expect it to yield a lot of fun . . . a hedonistic payoff for all the work as it were.

There are many icon events ranging from sponsorship of rock concerts, to patronage of the fine arts, to opulent personal celebrations, to ownership of sports teams, to development of resorts, to assorted thrill seeking pastimes, to a taste for fine living, to all sorts of infamous romantic dalliances that can be specifically linked to the Leonine taste for sensory stimulation and celebration. Steve Wozniak's rock concerts, Larry Ellison's yacht racing, Jack Warner's building of the Hollywood Park racetrack, and Malcolm Forbes' seventieth birthday party are the stuff of business legend. Particularly high on the list of Leo pleasures is playing host at a splendid entertainment or party, as it gives the Leo the opportunity to again establish a central magnanimous position in relationship to the rest of the Leo's chosen society.

Here again the example of Martha Stewart is useful. Perhaps today's version of the hardest working woman in show business, Stewart's rise to prominence was accomplished on the back of her landmark book *Entertaining* (New York: Clarkson Potter, 1982), which she wrote while a caterer. It was the largest-selling cookbook since Julia Child's *Mastering the Art of French Cooking* (New York: Knopf, 1961). While replication of most anything in Stewart's book is as arduous as anything one might come across in the field of neurosurgery, the real insight into Stewart and Child and their Leo tribe is an appreciation of just how much fun it would be to not necessarily do the work, but to stand triumphant over the end result and accept congratulations.

In other words, the highest attainment of the working Leo's life is to make the enterprise itself praiseworthy, and thereby fun to be identified with as its leader. As has already been alluded to, this primarily entails selecting a field for which one has a passion and vesting one's spirit in the opportunity for creative evolution. Bill Clinton, for example, was speaking from the depths of his Leo soul and on many personal levels when he observed upon leaving office that "I may not have been the greatest president, but I've had the most fun for eight years."

And if that sounds a little like self-congratulations, you're beginning to understand.

All the World's a Stage

Her late husband groomed Martha Ingram, head of one of the nation's largest distribution companies, for her job as chairman and CEO of Nashville-based Ingram Industries. Much of her time prior to her full-time immersion in the distribution business was devoted to the development of Nashville's fine arts community. She wrote a book about that aspect of her life entitled *Apollo's Struggle* (Nashville: Hillsboro Press, 2004), a title that would do justice to the autobiography of most any successful Leo.

Leos, as many astrologers have remarked, live their lives as if they were starring in heroic dramas about themselves. In almost every important endeavor of their lives the connection sought is between actor and audience. Leo's self-appointed challenge is to keep coming up with a performance so bright and wonderful and captivating and full of joy that nobody would dare look away.

Rage, envy, dejection, and even occasional strategic withdrawal are all tools in their dramatic bag. Yet at the not-so-secret heart of most Leo leaders is a desire for heroism, an expression of the universal triumph of the human spirit. One of the most fascinating qualities that links Leo leaders is that they are most often truly globally oriented and concerned, and the contributions of Ford, Smith, Soros, Whitman, Clinton, Wozniak, and others are truly most impressive in this international regard for the interconnectivity of all mankind.

"The real differences around the world today are not between Jews and Arabs; Protestants and Catholics; Muslims, Croats, and Serbs," Bill Clinton publicly commented on the occasion of an IRA 1996 London terrorist bombing. "The real differences are between those who embrace peace and those who would destroy it; between those who look to the future and those who cling to the past; between those who open their arms and those who are determined to clench their fists."

It may not be that simple, and the devil is certainly in the details, but it's that very sort of Leo thing that makes Apollo smile.

✦ tips for dealing with Leo

- If it is important to you to take public credit for your work it is perhaps best to deal with someone other than a Leo. They will always believe that your accomplishment derives from their inspiration and are entitled to the lion's share of the glory.
- Leo is quite partial to the sudden brainstorm, although they will rarely flesh out the details. That, make no mistake about it, is *your* job.
- Leos are directors at heart and will have no problem with telling you how to conduct both your professional and private affairs. Unlike some other control-oriented signs, however, the Leo is sincerely interested in giving advice that will make you happier . . . something to keep in mind when you feel like strangling them.
- *Hint*: Leo loves to celebrate life and is genuinely pleased with any sincere invitation that has as its goal a good time. Keep in

mind, though, that Leo tends to like the host role better than that of guest, because it provides Leo with the much-coveted director's chair. No individual will take more offense if you turn down his or her invitation.

CHAPTER 11

VIRGO

The Value of Fastidiousness

Good enough never is.

—Debbi Fields, personal motto

AUGUST 22 TO SEPTEMBER 21

Martha Matilda Harper	September 10, 1857	Harper Method Shops
Milton S. Hershey	September 13, 1857	The Hershey Company
William Cooper Procter	August 25, 1862	Procter and Gamble
Harland Sanders	September 9, 1890	Kentucky Fried Chicken
Arthur C. Nielsen	September 5, 1897	AC Nielsen Company
Margaret Rudkin	September 14, 1897	Pepperidge Farm
William M. Allen	September 1, 1900	Boeing
J. Willard Marriott	September 17, 1900	Marriott International
David Packard	September 7, 1912	Hewlett-Packard
Henry Ford II	September 4, 1917	Ford Motor Company
F. Kenneth Iverson	September 18, 1925	Nucor Steel
Warren Buffett	August 30, 1930	Berkshire Hathaway
Muriel Siebert	September 12, 1932	Muriel Siebert and Company
Andrew S. Grove	September 2, 1936	Intel
Bernard Ebbers	August 27, 1941	WorldCom
Shelly Lazarus	September 1, 1947	Ogilvy and Mather
John T. Chambers	August 23, 1949	Cisco Systems
Carly Fiorina	September 6, 1954	Hewlett Packard
Debbi Fields	September 18, 1956	Mrs. Fields

VIRGO SIGNATURES

Style:	Diligent
Objective:	Precision
Strength:	Skill
Weakness:	Perfectionism
Communication:	Logical
Tactic:	Rationality
Belief:	Purity
Reward:	Approval

At first glance Virgos might not seem particularly well-suited for the role of chief executive. They tend to be endlessly fussy about small details, transparently mistrustful of broad motivational generalizations, cautious to a fault, uncomfortable in front of a crowd, and generally lacking in the sort of warmth or charisma that inspires colleagues to eagerly go above and beyond. So why then is the list of Virgo business leaders so genuinely impressive?

One likely answer is that Virgo skills are genuine, as are their personal convictions, and little will distract them from a task once undertaken. Rather than the old saw about seeing what you get, a Virgo tends to deliver far more than you might believe possible from a glimpse at the surface. Their real power comes from the fact that, whatever the goal and whoever sets it, nobody holds a candle to them when it comes to meticulous and conscientious delivery.

In business one generally finds Virgos in engineering and accounting, technical research and development, line/service positions, and anywhere the title of "executive assistant" might honorably apply. Virgos are most often the diligent team members devoted to task execution, preferring the concrete realities and rewards of a well-designed mechanistic solution to what they see as the ephemeral philosophizing of the "concept" departments like marketing, strategic development, and human resources. The list of exceptional Virgo leaders includes many engineers—Henry Ford II, A.C. Nielsen, Ken Iverson, David Packard, Andy Grove, among them. Many of the others, such as Warren Buffett, Margaret Rudkin, and Muriel Siebert, cut their teeth in the hard data disciplines of accounting and/or finance.

It should be readily apparent that the basic working premises of the "information age" are very congenial to this sort of leader. Data-based solutions built upon rigorous measurements facilitated by technology are the only ones that most Virgos will abide in. Add in a natural propensity for efficiency plus a willingness to work "as long as it takes," and it is easy to understand why Virgo is the face of the database/metrics generation.

Although there is decidedly an emphasis on the rational here and a love of methodical process, there is a humanistic side to Virgo leadership. Rather than through the broad dramatic style of a Leo, however, Virgo "sensitivity" gets more quietly expressed in enlightened labor policies, sincere personal friendships, a respect for nature, and significant acts of philanthropy. As Warren Buffett confesses, it's simply that Virgo usually takes more satisfaction from the work than the rewards, and for many other signs this is outside the pale of credible human experience.

Two of the names on the list featured here might be most instructive for their counter-type failures. Carly Fiorina, the deposed head of Hewlett-Packard, erred in placing what seemed to be her own career agenda and perk priorities above the conservative employee-centric cultural agenda instituted by her Virgo predecessor, David Packard.

Even more interesting is Bernie Ebbers, the convicted head of telecom giant WorldCom, who offered the following in his own defense at his accounting fraud trial: "I don't know technology and engineering. I don't know accounting. I was not technically competent to lead WorldCom for the indefinite future."

The presiding judge sentenced Ebbers to 25 years in prison for his felonious improprieties, but it may have well been the mammoth offense to the Virgo ethos that truly sealed his fate.

VIRGO Leaders: value statements

It's the Little Things That Count, So Count Everything

Virgos are motivated to drive data as the bee is driven to process pollen. As with pollen, much of this data will be lost or corrupted or proven below utility grade. But if handled expertly by the workers in the hive, with just the right amount of critical acumen, one might just end up with an accurate accounting and a sweet sense of accomplishment.

The awesome microchips of Andrew Grove's Intel, the staggeringly precise electronic measuring devices of David Packard's Hewlett-Packard, and the powerful networking connections of John Chamber's Cisco Systems are fitting enough emblems of the passion for copious detail work that underlies the Virgo spirit of enterprise. Relentless data flow and precise measurement are business mantras so vested with Virgo that they sometimes operate independently of a defined goal. Virgo leaders might argue that exhaustive measurement is at the heart of both cost control and practical invention, but Andrew Grove's observation that "a fundamental rule in technology says that whatever can be done will be done" indicates that in the Virgo universe one sometimes computes because one can. (Although, to be fair, Grove has also observed: "Not all problems have a technological answer, but when they do, that is the more lasting solution.")

The Virgo measurement mindset is not just reflected in the field of technology. Consider that back as far as 1923, long before the advent of personal computing or television, A.C. Nielsen created a company that postulated promotional investment was a crippled concept without some hard measurement of its effectiveness. Nielsen created the famed Nielsen Code that introduced the concepts of monitored test sampling and market-share tracking to business, and also exhorted his colleagues to "watch every detail that affects the accuracy of your work" and to "accept business only at a price permitting thoroughness."

Also in the marketing field, Shelly Lazarus, as quoted in the Thomas Neff and James Citrin book *Lessons from the Top* (New York: Currency, 2001), identifies the strength of the Ogilvy and Mather culture as one that eschews "a cult of personality" in favor of "institutionalized principles" and "a willingness to seek measurements." Automotive kingpin Henry Ford II is most often associated with the recruiting of the so-called Whiz Kids, a group of young engineers and accountants who brought increased automation and scrupulous auditing into Ford at a time when a leadership crisis and corporate chaos had led to rapidly declining profitability. Even such facts as Margaret Rudkin's ten-year search for the perfect cookie to complement her Pepperidge Farm bread line and Col. Sanders' nine years of fried chicken recipe development speak to the exhaustive detail orientation of the Virgo leader.

Certainly an issue here is that perfection may always be one jump ahead of any possible reality. Nevertheless, it is the honorable quest of the Virgo leader to gather as much data as possible and to drill the details down to their most constructive, reliable, and manageable essences. As Warren Buffett once summarized: "Risk comes from not knowing what you are doing."

Stick to Your Knitting

The necessary corollary to being data obsessed, although it is a factor missed by many whose lives are predicated upon quantification, is to limit the complexity of the enterprise. Again it is Warren Buffett who lends some practical wisdom in this regard, once commenting:

> You only have to do a very few things right in your life, so long as you don't do too many things wrong.

The tales of successful Virgo business leaders are rife with decisions to eschew unnecessary organizational complications, line extensions, and partnership entanglements. Pepperidge Farm's Margaret Rudkin understood that the secret to success was not rapid product diversification but a passion for vertical integration of her bread business—from farm to factory to distribution. Nucor's Ken Iverson cut entire product divisions when he became CEO, appreciating that the success of his company was predicated on an unambiguous focus on efficient steel production. Andrew Grove proudly states that Intel has succeeded so remarkably in the microprocessor market because the company has "put all its eggs in one basket."

For a Virgo leader an ultimate goal is the creation of an efficient, smooth running, controllable, replicable, and profitable system. Unsurprisingly, franchise system developers such as Harland Sanders, J. Willard Marriott, and Debbi Fields are prominent among the ranks of great Virgo leaders. Worth a special mention is Martha Matilda Harper, a Canadian domestic servant who in the late nineteenth century launched the Harper Method Shops, a network of ultimately 350 independently owned beauty salons, reputed to be the first franchised store-based service business in North America.

The greatest example of Virgo focus and single-mindedness may be discovered in an examination of the life Milton Hershey, founder not only of The Hershey Company but the entire town of Hershey, Pennsylvania. In the compelling tale chronicled by biographer Michael D'Antonio in his book *Hershey: Milton S. Hershey's Extraordinary Life of Wealth, Empire, and Utopian Dreams* (New York: Simon and Schuster, 2006), Hershey takes a single confection and executes an entire community plan around it, from factories to homes to schools to public transportation to hospitals to parks to a sports arena to a theme park/resort. Upon his death his entire personal fortune is placed in a charitable trust, most of it earmarked for the support of a remarkable Hershey-based boarding school for disadvantaged youths.

Early in his career, after several candy enterprise failures, Hershey developed and then sold a successful caramel business so that he could concentrate on chocolate production. Asked why he divested a business that finally showed a profit, Hershey had no trouble sharing an insight that any great Virgo leader might appreciate. "Caramels are only a fad," proclaimed Hershey. "Chocolate is a permanent thing."

Anticipate a Profitable Day's Work for a Profitable Day's Wages

When Ken Iverson moved Nucor's headquarters from Arizona to North Carolina he outfitted his new office simply with a folding table and a few chairs. When David Packard moved Hewlett-Packard headquarters out of his garage, he had the contractor lay out the new building in the footprint of a supermarket so the building would be easier to sell if the business failed. Andrew Grove ran Intel from a rather ordinary second floor office cubicle. Warren Buffett, whose Berkshire Hathaway offices are in a very modest Nebraska-based business plaza, managed his first investment partnership out of his bedroom and still lives in the same relatively unspectacular Omaha house he purchased in 1958.

So, one may fairly ask, are Virgos cheap?

One honest way to answer this is, "Yes, they are." They are cheap when it comes to what they would characterize as capital inefficiency. Throwing money around for the sake of ego satisfaction or personal comfort or the potential thrill of a risky speculative payoff or even to purchase loyalty is, to most Virgo leaders, the economic equivalent of fingernails on the chalkboard. One doesn't spend a business life devoted to financial metrics and then capriciously throw resources at personal indulgences, one's own or anyone else's.

Yet, at the same time, Virgo leaders have a reverence for work and an endless amount of respect and appreciation for those in the workforce who work skillfully, diligently and uncomplainingly. Perhaps more than the leaders of any other sign, Virgo has a feel for the financial, temporal and organizational burdens of a working life. In all of them there is a little bit of J.W. Marriott, who could raise all kinds of heck when a manager violated standard operating procedure but who would visit a busboy in the hospital if he was injured in the conscientious discharge of his job.

The resolution of these conflicting values of frugality and fondness is a theme worked out again and again in Virgo-led businesses. And whether one speaks of Buffett or Iverson or Grove, the resolution remains much the same. Management levels must be kept to a minimum, ego-perks are to be discouraged and, above all else, workers should be rewarded primarily on the basis of their tangible contributions to profit.

David Packard, whose enlightened "H-P Way" employment policy was discussed earlier in Chapter 7 (in the context of partner Bill Hewlett's contributions), will always be a beacon shining on the virtue of these practices. Fiercely devoted to the principle of lifetime employment, Packard toured every H-P facility when business turned soft during a recession to preach the Virgo gospel of inventory control, cash monitoring, and spending cuts including salaries across the board. Jobs were saved—and not long after H-P returned to profitability.

Shelly Lazarus, thinking like a Virgo leader, once commented, "If you are superb at what you do, then you define the terms of employment." Yet ultimately it is Warren Buffet who again best explains the Virgo mindset: "The first rule is not to lose money," says the Oracle of Omaha. "The second rule is not to forget the first rule."

Health Is Wealth

Rarely does a life go by without a significant health challenge to either people we love or ourselves. Virgo leaders may not be any more or less statistically representative of this phenomenon. Yet so many stories of Virgo leaders do seem to turn on health crises.

For Henry Ford II it was the early death of his father Edsel (of a cancer that Ford II bitterly maintained was precipitated by the stress of working for his grandfather, Henry Ford), causing him to be suddenly installed at Ford Motors while just in his twenties, head of the company that he would lead for the next thirty-five years. For a youthful J.W. Marriott it was the discovery of lymphatic cancer and the pronouncement of a death sentence, after which Marriott took his mission even more seriously and, miraculously, thrived for another fifty years. For Milton Hershey the issue was the unanticipated disappointment of a sterile marriage, which caused him to dedicate his life and fortune to taking care of disadvantaged kids.

In their book, *In Their Time: The Greatest Business Leaders of the Twentieth Century* (Cambridge, Mass.: Harvard Business School Press, 2005), Anthony Mayo and Nitin Nohria tell the remarkable story of Pepperidge Farms' Margaret Rudkin. Saddled with the sudden incapacity of her husband due to a polo accident and fearful that her son's intense asthma was exacerbated by chemical additives in processed food, Rudkin began baking additive-free bread in her Connecticut kitchen and offering it as a specialty item to upscale grocers in New York. Some of the product's earliest and best customers were doctors.

Product purity and environmental sensitivity feature in many Virgo efforts. John Procter's Procter and Gamble rode Ivory Soap, famously marketed as "99 $^{44}/_{100}$ percent pure," to national prominence. Matilda Harper's Harper Method Shops were partially conceived as distribution points for her amazingly ahead-of-the-curve all-natural shampoos. Milton Hershey settled in rural Pennsylvania because he discovered that chocolate quality was directly related to milk freshness. And whatever today's nutritionists might write about fried chicken or chocolate chip cookies, both Harland Sanders and Debbi Fields were quality-ingredient champions of the highest rank.

Assuredly it is not just the Virgo leader who understands that good health and the minimization of environmental toxicity is life affirming. But the compulsion to purify both personally and in the greater planetary sense is especially great here, perhaps another example of an inherent engineer's bias towards optimal systems performance. Purification has long been associated with the astrological sign of the Virgin, and it does seem to be the earnest Virgo executive who most naturally champions the ongoing figurative virtues of a bottle of water, a salad, and a strenuous bike ride around the block—sometimes with enough conviction to cure cancer.

Tell It Like It Is

In 1971, the U.S. Congress asked Boeing's William Allen to come up with a cost estimate for the continuation of the development of the shelved supersonic transport airplane. Allen's realistic estimate effectively killed the project. It was business that Boeing certainly could have used, but it was an honest estimate.

Retiring once and for all the notion that Hewlett-Packard could continue to support lifetime employment for all workers, Carly Fiorina told Congress: "There is no job that is America's God-given right anymore." An honest answer perhaps, but one that left a bitter taste with labor.

In one of the nation's most famous job terminations, Henry Ford II dismissed the enormously popular and successful Lee Iacocca from Ford. Many commentators said that Iacocca had established too strong a cult of personality in the job and was maneuvering too hard for the reigns of the company. Ford's own comment was, "Sometimes you just don't like somebody."

After selling Kentucky Fried Chicken to an investor group, Harland Sanders was retained as a figurehead and spokesperson. How did the new gravy taste, a reporter wanted to know. Like "sludge," was the Colonel's answer, like "wallpaper paste."

For better or for worse, a Virgo leader has a hard time with a lie. Lies may be convenient but they are not rational. They muck up the integrity of the data.

So with Virgo leaders one gets people like Nucor's Ken Iverson, whose much praised management book is entitled *Plain Talk* (Hoboken, N.J.: Wiley, 1997). It's a notion that reeks of integrity while at the same time it causes headaches for those who would rather have their CEO's a bit more slick and adaptable. But so what, really, if Intel's Andrew Grove is willing to comment that "the future belongs to the paranoid?"

He *is* laughing all the way to the bank.

✦ tips for dealing with virgo

- Virgo has an engineer's soul and is totally devoted to developing products and processes that will optimize business accuracy and efficiency. They have very little interest in, and less time for, building personal relationships in the business sphere—and that goes for customers as well as colleagues.

- It is the Virgo nature to tell it like it is, sometimes pretty harshly. They are not worried about your feelings. They are worried about the work.
- Conscientious work habits, good grooming, and intelligence are the three factors that will impress a Virgo boss. What will get you fired is a lie.
- *Hint*: Virgo usually has outdoor interests, regarding nature as the one system for which it would be rather pretentious to seek improvements (although, frankly, the Virgo would probably not be above a few well-meaning suggestions if Mother Nature was ever encountered in person). The key knowledge here is that there are Virgo hunters and Virgo vegetarians, and each is pretty likely to manifest certainty about the rightness of their philosophical position. Forewarned is forearmed when firing up the camp stove.

CHAPTER 12

LIBRA

The Value of Fairness

First they ignore you, then they laugh at you, then they
attack you, then you win.

—Mohandas Gandhi, speech to India's citizens
during their struggle for independence

 SEPTEMBER 22 TO OCTOBER 22

Henry J. Heinz	October 11, 1844	H.J. Heinz
George Westinghouse	October 6, 1846	Westinghouse Electric
Elmer Sperry	October 12, 1860	Sperry Gyroscope Company
William Wrigley, Jr.	September 30, 1861	Wm. Wrigley Jr. Company
Mohandas Gandhi	October 2, 1869	Mahatma, Father of India
William Edward Boeing	October 1, 1881	The Boeing Company
Morehead Patterson	October 9, 1897	AMF
William S. Paley	September 28, 1901	CBS
Ray Kroc	October 5, 1902	McDonald's
Charles Revson	October 11, 1906	Revlon
Jean Nidetch	October 12, 1923	Weight Watchers
Jimmy Carter	October 1, 1924	U.S. president
Lee Iacocca	October 15, 1924	Ford/Chrysler
Ralph Lauren	October 13, 1939	Polo Ralph Lauren
John Lennon	October 9, 1940	The Beatles
Jesse Jackson	October 8, 1941	The Rainbow Coalition
Mary Sammons	October 12, 1946	Rite-Aid
Donna Karan	October 2, 1948	Donna Karan/DKNY
Anne Mulcahy	October 21, 1952	Xerox
Russell Simmons	October 4, 1957	Rush Communications
Michelle Peluso	October 2, 1971	Travelocity

Style: Diplomatic

Objective: Balance

Strength: Charm

Weakness: Indecisiveness

Communication: Receptive

Tactic: Diplomacy

Belief: Harmony

Reward: Peace

Libra represents an important juncture in the zodiacal progression. The first six signs, Aries through Virgo, are similar in that they describe personality types that are primarily self-referential and concerned with the expression of individually defined traits and passions. Beginning with Libra, and continuing on through Pisces, the emphasis shifts to the primacy of the external world and the ways in which individuals derive their *primary* roles from their dynamic interaction with the social, natural, and spiritual collectives.

As the antithesis of hard-charging Aries, Libra introduces the notions of reflection and balance into the leadership equation. Immediately let me point out that this does not imply an absence of energy or aggression, passive or otherwise. It's just that Librans tends to derive motivation and inspiration from external forces applied to their consciousness by others, manifesting a natural and often gifted capacity for resolving duality and imbalance and for identifying the desires of the masses.

Thus, on the highest plane of Libra achievement one comes across the names of great political leaders like Mohandas Gandhi, Desmond Tutu, Lech Walesa, Jesse Jackson, and Jimmy Carter—individuals whose lives were consecrated to the balancing principles of peace, justice, and human equality in the face of bigotry, aggression, and oppression. In our relentlessly hostile world, giving peace a chance, to paraphrase Libra John Lennon, does indeed often become part of the Libra mission. Even so, the trickiness of the Libra dynamic is captured by a famous John Lennon observation about his song "I'm a Loser," that "part of me suspects that I'm a loser, and the other part of me suspects I'm God Almighty."

The lives of great Libra leaders are filled with epic struggles regarding the achievement of grace and balance, both in the professional and private realms. Here are the considerate consensus-gathering leaders who may detonate over imagined disloyalty. Here are the perpetual-motion, street-smart hustlers who often swear by meditative retreat. Here are the perfect romantics engaged in the most inspiring of marriages and then, sometimes, the most ethically compromising of extra-marital affairs.

Perhaps more than any other astrological leadership group, Libras collectively take on the characteristics of those psychological inkblot tests. Accurately reflecting the complex reality of others, including fears and aspirations, these generally empathic souls have a capacity for inciting consternation and affection in equal measure. Perception of them is a constantly meandering fine line between challenge and complement.

Likely their greatest business strength is that somewhere these receptive folks do develop a magnificent feel for public trends. Uniquely and truly tuned in to what the masses want they have little trouble in building their business missions around the fulfillment of collective desires. Most often possessing great personal intelligence and style themselves, Librans are often the laissez-faire culture leaders who unapologetically build fortunes upon the likes of ketchup, chewing gum, fast food hamburgers, lipstick, electric toasters, rap music, and sitcoms.

"What we are doing is satisfying the public," once commented CBS founder William Paley with regard to his network's programming. "That's our job. I always say we have to give most of the people what they want most of the time."

So say what you will about *The Beverly Hillbillies,* Juicy Fruit and the Big Mac. When that many people will support a thing, however slight, it is often the Libra who feels and fulfills the collective desire. Sadly, the peace thing may just take a bit longer.

Libra Leaders: value statements

Life Hangs in the Balance

A brilliant real-world example of the Libra approach to leadership is revealed in the life of Jean Nidetch, founder of Weight Watchers. Incapable of motivating herself to lose weight on her own, this Brooklyn housewife hit upon the idea of a social solution. Her notion was to gather together individuals in similar heavy straits to her own in order to communally share the tribulations of pursuing dietary moderation, developing a process famously highlighted by the ritual of public confession and a weigh-in.

Certainly there is in this instance the happy astrological coincidence that the Libra icon is a balance scale. But the purest Libra essence of this tale is to be found in the linkage of a personal self-improvement enterprise to the earnest feedback of the communally troubled. It is the greatest drive of the Libra leadership personality to serve as the facilitator of counter-balance to all the things that bring down our collective faith in ourselves, to serve as a patient accommodator and a sympathetic facilitator in the midst of all of the things that are out of whack in this wacky world.

Libra leaders labor to clear a compromise through the clash of egos and conflicting experiences that make up so much of our lives. In their public pronouncements one frequently comes across the depth of their understanding in statements such as Lee Iacocca's, "You need sorrow to experience happiness" or Donna Karan's, "There is no pleasure without pain." Similar in tone is President Jimmy Carter's observation that "unless both sides win, no agreement can be permanent," or Gandhi's thought that "my imperfections and failures are as much a blessing from God as my successes and my talents, and I lay them both at his feet."

In their daily business lives no phrase is more likely to appear on a Libra leader's lips than "balancing act." This is true in the case of a Ray Kroc, who contrary to popular belief always understood the need to balance the cookie cutter imperialism of McDonald's with the retention of local neighborhood identity. Similarly one hears the phrase in the public remarks of Rite-Aid's Mary Sammons, who understands her greatest executive challenge as management of the opposing fiduciary demands of debt reduction and business development.

On a personal level, the drive toward balance can seem perplexing but nevertheless appears to spring from a most sincere source. It's not necessarily easy to assimilate that Henry J. Heinz, father of the industrially produced table condiment, was also a major presence in the World Sunday School Association, or that Russell Simmons, one of the pioneers of the rap music phenomenon, is a vegan and a yoga practitioner. Yet it is just this willing immersion in the experience of opposites that, as Simmons once described it, facilitates "a better relationship with the higher self."

And with Libra in charge, the betterment of self is a topic on which everyone gets to weigh in.

Consensus Building Is a Process, Not a Destination

There is perhaps irony in the fact that Libran leaders, for all their studied equanimity, can be outright despots. Despite the considerable energy a Libra boss will put into garnering feedback and opinion, a moment inevitably comes when an important threshold of perception is reached. At that point the Libran will decide his vision is as refined and focused as it's likely to get, and will have little patience with associates who subsequently waver from or compromise that vision, even if its full dimensions are comprehensible only to the Libran.

One encounters this phenomenon frequently among the numerous famed designers born under the sign of Libra. Here the vision can be almost as particular as that of Virgo, although with Libra the emphasis tends to be on detail execution rather than data compilation. Legendary in the beauty and fashion industries are the stories of Charles Revson and Ralph Lauren bawling out associates over barely perceivable aesthetic imperfections.

In a more comprehensive sense, the decisive Libra leader is actually defending his or her sense of the culture that enables the enterprise. McDonald's Ray Kroc, who once proclaimed, "You're only as good as the people you hire," is equally famous for his insistence that "the organization cannot trust the individual; the individual must trust the organization." Lee Iacocca identifies the ability to share burdens, delegate responsibilities, and work well with others as career killers in their absence, but he has no hesitation about the CEO's obligation to act unilaterally when the appropriate moment has come.

Indeed, this insistence upon making forceful decisions, whether the Libra in question is a delegator or a micromanager by nature, seems to be something of a learned trait that flies in the face of the Libra's feedback gathering temperament. Lee Iacocca takes great pains in his autobiography, *Iacocca* (Bantam Books: New York, 1984), to address this issue, assuring his readers that "in most cases there is no such thing as certainty," and he advises that when one is 75 percent sure of something it's time to act. Intriguingly, Travelocity's Michelle Peluso describes the "comfort range" for fact-gathering as 60 to 80 percent, after which "it's time to move on."

"I've always really admired people who have exceptionally talented people around them," Peluso once told a National Public Radio commentator. "It's incumbent on me to understand deeply what's going on in all aspects of our business and to question things when I think we're off the mark."

Shortly afterwards, though, Peluso adds the insight that truly separates the Libra leaders from the rest of the balance-seeking herd: Says Peluso:

> You need to debate pros and cons but, you know, in some cases the last piece of analysis, the last piece of data, isn't always necessary.

Time Is on My Side

To know Libra is to experience an ongoing series of coin flips in which the coin hardly ever lands on the same side twice in a row. Although Libra leaders, as just described, most often come to an understanding regarding the necessity for decisiveness, they are hardly of the "always take action" persuasion. Aggression may have its place, most Libra leaders would grudgingly agree, but it is hardly always superior to patient opportunism or the restorative power of recreation and retreat.

One of the most truly remarkable and revealing facts about Libra leaders is how late so many of them come to their true calling. Many people are aware that Ray Kroc was in his mid-fifties when he first came across the McDonald brothers and their California hamburger restaurant. But consider these additional Libra leader age anomalies:

- William Paley was being groomed for the family cigar business when, in his late twenties, he engineered the purchase of a small group of radio stations to promote the tobacco product. What grew into CBS, much further down the road, was at the time an afterthought.
- William Wrigley, Jr., was working for the family baking-powder business when he realized the chewing gum that the company gave away as a premium was more popular than the baking powder. He was thirty-one years old when he got into the gum distribution business and actually didn't become a manufacturer until he was 50.
- Jean Nidetch was already thirty-eight years old when her cookie habit prompted her to form Weight Watchers.
- George Westinghouse made his original fortune through the development of railroad air brakes. Westinghouse Electric didn't come into existence until he was 40.
- Although he was an automobile man throughout his career, Lee Iacocca had a relatively slow rise through the executive ranks at Ford. It was his firing from Ford at the age of 54 that led him to the world-renowned turnaround he facilitated at Chrysler.

In general, one needs to recognize in the Libra leader a periodic bias towards inaction and an overarching belief that the best things often happen in their own sweet time. Even their "full speed ahead" mode is comparatively temperate, and there is definitely a tendency to esteem quality over speed in deliverables. Representative of the attitude is Donna Karan's comment regarding the change brought about by the sale of her company (which she didn't create until age 37) to Louis Vuitton-Moet Hennessy, i.e. "The pace has gotten parallel to inhuman." Similarly, one may consider William Paley's famous injunction to his news commentators banning the instant analysis of presidential addresses.

The unmodulated urgency of other astrological signs is simply a necessary evil at worst and a curiosity at best to Libra. It's noteworthy that Henry Heinz, who was one of the first corporate advocates of the five-day workweek, was a famous collector of timepieces and was actually named an honorary curator of timepieces for Pittsburgh's Carnegie museum. He doubtlessly would have understood John Lennon's observation "time you enjoy wasting is not wasted."

Style Is the Handmaiden of Grace

It might seem odd that a group of leaders that has collectively made its mark in consumables, such as ketchup and chewing gum, is to be signified by its contributions to style. As has already been noted, however, Henry Heinz was such an admired collector of fine antiquities that he was made an honorary curator of an important museum. And William Wrigley, whose style contributions range from the preservation of the Chicago Cubs' Wrigley Field to a landmark collection of mansions, will be forever honored for his devotion to the protection and beautification of Catalina Island, still wholly owned by the Wrigley family. Examples abound of Libras owning world-class car collections, breathtaking yachts, fine art contributions and splendid edifices.

Certainly the style-setting names Revlon, DKNY, and Polo Ralph Lauren resonate in this regard. And while Russell Simmons might be best known for creating the Def Jam record label, he eventually sold his popular clothing business, Phat Farm, for a greater sum than Def Jam. Style is also very much in evidence in the lives of people like Lee Iacocca, who will always be associated with the trend setting styles of the Ford Mustang, the Chrysler LeBaron convertible, and the Chrysler Minivan; and William Paley, who built CBS into what was widely known as the "Tiffany Network."

A real key to understanding Libra, though, is the recognition that style is not just some superficial thing that makes something look good on the outside. Whether it's Revlon's Charles Revson tweaking the color of lipstick in an ad weeks past the production date, or Xerox's Anne Mulcahy predicating the future possibilities of her business on universal digitalized color printing, or Ralph Lauren demanding that china patterns match what he is wearing to a meeting, or Jesse Jackson telling the Democratic National Convention that he "sees the face of America: Red, Yellow, Brown, Black, and White . . . We are all precious in God's sight," there is something closer to vision than to mere style appreciation taking place here. Whether one speaks of colors or sounds or the successful coordination of an outfit, Libra apprehends a stylish result as no less than a harmonious blending of the communal zeitgeist with the manifestation of the divine that is present in everything—if only one can just get inwardly quiet and clear enough to tune into it.

Numerous earnest examples of the Libra relationship with style can be offered, but likely the most compelling is that to be found in the life of Ralph Lauren. Surely no less a word than passion can be utilized to describe how a lower-middle-class Jewish kid from the Bronx, born Ralph Lifschitz, was able to transform himself into a style maker for a legion of upwardly mobile WASP wannabes. The very strength of the style aspiration here, on the part of creator and customer alike to reflect a balanced perch on a secure and distinctive social plateau, is a real look into the secret heart of Libra leadership.

"Ralph Lauren sells more than fashion, " once commented Oprah

Winfrey in an introduction to a conversation with Lauren she recorded in O magazine. "He sells the life you'd like to lead."

Such a life is beautiful and balanced, partaking of a whiff of status and a drop of divinity. How could anyone possibly not buy a shirt that promises all that?

Give the Customer What She Wants

A story is told about Charles Revson, who founded Revlon. Supposedly he would rarely take a telephone call from a supplier, or anyone else for that matter, who did not have a scheduled appointment. However, if you were some secretary who had just purchased a tube of lipstick and called with any sort of complaint, you would be put right through to Revson's office.

In *Iacocca,* Lee Iacocca writes of the doubts he had prior to the release of the Chrysler LeBaron convertible. General advancements in air conditioning and car audio had made the American convertible sort of a dinosaur, and no American car manufacturer had released one for several years. What convinced Iacocca he had a winner was when he drove a prototype to the mall and people flocked around the car asking him where he had bought it.

In a similar fashion, Ray Kroc knew that any business that could support the simultaneous running of eight malted-milk mixers had to have something special going for it. Henry Heinz arbitrarily picked the number "57" for his labels because he liked the sound of it and thought the number seven had "an alluring significance" to most people. In the words of Ralph Lauren, "I don't have to do a focus group to know what people want . . . I feel it."

Libra business leaders never have to be told to listen to their customers. They are them.

✦ tips for dealing with Libra

- Libra leaders would really rather avoid making enemies. Diplomacy, consensus building, and compromise are almost invariably preferred to direct confrontation.
- Don't try to rush a Libra into making a decision. The inner balancing process they are performing rarely benefits from a shove, no matter how well intentioned.
- Refrain from actions that disturb the peace. Libra loses respect quickly for anyone who willingly tries to upset the apple cart or cannot keep cool under stress.
- *Hint*: Libra likes to be out with the crowd, but in one-on-one situations they tend to prefer loveliness to liveliness. Aesthetics and style count for a lot with Libra, and you are far more likely to seal the deal in the midst of harmony than mayhem.

CHAPTER 13

SCORPIO

The Value of Fortitude

The secret of our success is that we never, never give up.

—Wilma Mankiller, *Mankiller: A Chief and Her People*

OCTOBER 23 TO NOVEMBER 22

Isaac Singer	October 27, 1811	Singer Manufacturing
Charles William Post	October 26, 1854	CW Post (General Foods)
John T. Dorrance	November 11, 1873	Campbell's Soup
Peter Drucker	November 19, 1909	Management guru
Malcolm P. McLean	November 14, 1913	SeaLand
Ruth Handler	November 4, 1916	Mattel
Stephen R. Covey	October 24, 1932	Management guru
Jack Welch	November 19, 1935	General Electric
Ted Turner	November 19, 1938	Turner Communications
Tom Peters	November 7, 1942	Management guru
Anita Roddick	October 23, 1942	The Body Shop
Calvin Klein	November 19, 1942	Calvin Klein
Wilma Mankiller	November 18, 1945	Cherokee Nation
Christie Hefner	November 8, 1952	Playboy Enterprises
Scott McNealy	November 12, 1954	Sun Microsystems
Bill Gates	October 28, 1955	Microsoft
Indra Nooyi	October 28, 1955	Pepsico
Anne Sweeney	November 4, 1957	Disney-ABC
Jerry Yang	November 6, 1968	Yahoo!
Sean "Diddy" Combs	November 4, 1969	Bad Boy Records

SCORPIO SIGNATURES

Style:	Controlled
Objective:	Conquest
Strength:	Will
Weakness:	Suspicion
Communication:	Targeted
Tactic:	Stealth
Belief:	Intensity
Reward:	Power

Scorpio continues the theme of individual values best understood in the context of collective enterprises. Unlike Libra, though,
whose responsive nature tends to be directed toward a balancing of
energies, Scorpio handles life in far more aggressive and competitive
terms. Acutely aware of the jagged edges and relentless strife that
make up much of human nature and social existence, the Scorpio
leader surmises that confrontation, not complacency, is necessary
when dealing with life's harshest spiritual, natural, and man-made
challenges.

To put it plainly, Scorpio leaders experience life as a very serious
contest that incessantly puts survival on the line. Life's most obvious
characteristic, in the Scorpio worldview, is that it produces losers and
winners. Fearless, focused, and driven, the Scorpio leader is a seeker
not so much of peace or personal popularity as of masterfully managed success, even when it comes at the expense of others.

Indeed, in the field of business leadership one finds no sign more compelled to establish a set of sound (and tough!) management principles than Scorpio. One gets a taste of this in the person of General Electric's Jack Welch, whether one looks to his early tenure termination of 100,000 jobs or his landmark devotion to the Six Sigma quality program or to the fact that his autobiography is simply called *Winning* (New York: HarperBusiness, 2005). Conceptually, this passion for righteous, hard-edged, take-no-prisoners policy is also apparent in the ardently didactic writings of the many eminent management gurus who claim Scorpio as their sun sign. Thinkers such as Peter Drucker, Stephen Covey, and Tom Peters have been pushing management theory through levels of practical dogma to the domain of ethical imperative with discussions of "basic social purpose," "good and evil," and "taking responsibility" dominating much of their work.

A wonderfully unguarded glimpse into the sheer intensity of the Scorpio mindset is yielded in a 1989 television-news special, actually a post-purchase addendum to the PBS *Cosmos* series, which featured two eminent Scorpios, scientist Carl Sagan and media mogul Ted Turner, simply sitting at a desk (no fancy graphics or filmed reports) chatting about the state of the world. In the course of an hour the two men unflinchingly consider: the destruction of the biosphere; bloated weapons arsenals; the implications of nuclear winter; global poverty; the failure of the American educational system; the possibility of time travel; and the decline of cultural standards as revealed in the fact that the majority of American newspapers carry astrology columns! There is a grudging acknowledgment of the possibility of a God who cares about all this, but Sagan says that as a scientist he naturally has empirical reservations, while Turner adds that Jesus and Mohammed really make no direct mention of overpopulation or nuclear weapons. Both men strenuously agree that it is our job, not God's, to work out of this mess anyway.

If this sounds just a little cold, well, Scorpios really don't care too much about that. Empathy past a point is vulnerability, according to the Scorpio worldview, and sticky sentimentality is a flat-out disease. Numerous astrological authors have commented that if Scorpio has an Achilles heel it is a genuine bewilderment as to why there are so many weak temperaments and idle preoccupations on the planet that aren't in sync with the tough and directed and right (Scorpio) way of seeing things.

All in all, with Scorpio one is presented with the highest human iteration of the contest that takes place between the will and the world. The prize in this contest is not peace or popularity. It is power.

SCORPIO Leaders: value statements

I Will

A Scorpio leader rarely relies on charisma, although they often have enough personal magnetism to power a hydroelectric dam. Whereas some other leaders are content with the high-wattage projection of self, however, the Scorpio emphasis is on the inner glow of self-mastery. As Scorpio Stephen R. Covey might tell you, "highly effective people" have structured habits and well-planned ambitions, not personal gratifications and random desires.

Perhaps the best expression of the Scorpio purpose as it relates to business leadership is found in the work of Peter Drucker, who is given much of the credit for creating the field of modern management theory. More than any observer before his time, and most since, Drucker recognized that management is primarily a job of identifying, developing, and focusing inherent human talents rather than the dispassionate monitoring of systems and the training of tasks. While Drucker's landmark work can never be summarized in a few sentences, it is fair to say that he continuously advocated such virtues as cultivating personal strengths; finding legitimate social purpose; clearly predetermining the intent of one's efforts; working tirelessly; and, ultimately, predicting the future by having the will to create it.

The signature of Scorpio leaders is a tendency to be at their most fierce when the challenge is toughest, often equating obstacles and opposition with an opportunity to display more mettle than lesser beings. Jack Welch, named by *Fortune* magazine as the Manager of the [Twentieth] Century, once commented that the "best executive" is the one who is "overburdened and overstretched." Famed designer Calvin Klein, acknowledging what appears on the outside as an easy-going demeanor, contends that if challenged he is "like nails . . . I will kill." Microsoft's Bill Gates, the world's richest man, has observed simply that "life is not fair; get used to it."

Especially iconic in this regard are the many Scorpio women who have achieved success by transcending embedded sexual and cultural roles to achieve leadership status in a so-called man's world. Christie Hefner may be Hugh's daughter, but it is nevertheless wholly remarkable that a woman now directs Playboy Enterprises. Indra Nooyi, vulnerable to all the prejudices that might conceivably thwart a traditional Indian-born woman in corporate America, now runs Pepsico and may well be believed when she maintains, "There are no limits to what you can do." Perhaps even more remarkable is Wilma Mankiller, a woman who fought past sexual bias, poverty, geographical displacement, and vast historical tradition to become the chief of the Cherokee Nation, the first woman to ever head a major Native American tribe.

Of course, there may be some downside to a personality in which there is no quit and little tolerance for failure or second fiddle. C. W. Post, for example, the founder of the company that eventually became General Foods, is noteworthy for writing a monograph declaring that all illnesses are psychosomatic (although, sadly, Post's own mental imbalances led to several breakdowns and his eventual suicide).

Perhaps an even more lucid image is that of Post, in an attempt to produce rain in a dry portion of rural Texas, firing dynamite into the sky.

By all measures. though, one is well advised towards caution in going up against Scorpio leaders in a contest of wills, or in any other sort of contest if it comes to that. Because for every sad ending of a C. W. Post there are a dozen Scorpios who really do have it *all* under control—or who are willing to put out whatever concentrated effort it takes to get there. Their devil is more than willing to stand up to your devil if it comes to that.

"It's possible, you can never know," wryly observed Bill Gates, "that the universe exists only for me. If so, it's sure going well for me, I must admit."

You Are with Me or Against Me

Despite Bill Gates's tongue-in-cheek statement, Scorpios are deeply aware they are not universes unto themselves. Many will in fact identify their chief managerial role as the identification and development of communally integrated talent. "The task of management," writes Peter Drucker, "is to make people capable of joint performance, to make their strengths effective and their weaknesses irrelevant."

Towards this end the Scorpio leader sets the bar of expectation high, but rewards are ample for those who can clear it. Tom Peters' admonition to leaders is "give a lot, expect a lot, and if you don't get it, prune." Jack Welch, notoriously fierce about removing the deadwood, says that if you pick the right people, give them a chance to spread their wings, and provide attractive compensation, "you almost don't have to manage them."

Thus, the emphasis for Scorpio is truly on team building and the understanding that *colleagues* tend to be a lot more valuable than *subordinates*. Sun Microsystems founder Scott McNealy has always been passionate in his technical assertion that "the network is the computer." Such an understanding is also at the foundation of the approach of most Scorpio leaders to personnel.

Of course, the very notion of "team" may itself be too mild a metaphor for Scorpio's intense nature, with something closer to a military squadron or a posse perhaps a more appropriate image. Scorpios can rarely manufacture polite patience for the incompetent in their own midst, and they tend to shoot first and ask questions later when challenged by the competition. Alas, this last can even extend beyond the metaphorical, as is evidenced in the multiple violent and even lethal confrontations between hiphop artists represented by Sean "Diddy" Combs and those signed to other management.

Even in politer realms, however, the Scorpio manager generally relishes the assessment of being "kick-ass" tough. A *Time* magazine profile of Bill Gates quotes Microsoft CEO Steve Ballmer admiringly reflecting on Gates's management style: "Bill brings to the company the idea that conflict can be a good thing. . . . [He] knows it's important to avoid the gentle civility that keeps you from getting to the heart of the issue quickly." Other sources report that one of Gates's most frequent comments to associates is "that's the stupidest thing I've ever heard," although it's considered quite the badge of honor to arouse this assessment.

The mental state of the Scorpio leader regarding enmities and alliances is amply revealed in a now-infamous statement made by Pepsico's Indra Nooyi. Keynote speaker at a business school commencement, Nooyi discussed the cultural tolerance imperatives of an interlaced global economy, employing a metaphor of the hand as the globe and the individual fingers as the five major continents. Identifying the middle finger as North America, she admonished the future generation of American business leaders to make sure the hand was clearly extended in respect "so that the other continents see you extending the hand . . . not the finger."

Okay, so they don't sugarcoat it. At least with a Scorpio you do know where you stand.

Originality Is No Substitute for Success

Many people are now aware that Bill Gates got the idea for Windows during a collegial visit to Steve Jobs and his team at Apple. Gates later maintained that Jobs himself actually got the graphical user interface (GUI) idea from Motorola and that "intellectual property has the shelf life of a banana," but that still doesn't mean he didn't rip off the competition. Certainly, Gates has never felt like he's owed anyone an apology.

It's a trait that has fierce detractors, but Scorpios have a tendency to believe that anything that exists is to be considered in the public domain if you can get your hands on it. It's hardly a Scorpio leadership notion that originates with Gates. Consider these examples:

- Isaac Singer's name is synonymous with the sewing machine, but he was successfully sued by Elias Howe for patent infringement. Fortunately for Singer, time and revisions to law eventually proved to be on his side.
- C. W. Post had no exposure to ready-to-eat breakfast cereal or the sanitarium business until he became a patient at the Battle Creek, Michigan sanitarium run by the Kellogg brothers. He established competing businesses in both fields in Battle Creek.
- Ruth Handler is credited with introducing the Barbie doll to the world, thereby effectively creating Mattel. However, the original doll, with its landmark anatomical attributes, was actually a toy named Lilli that was sold as a gag gift to bachelors in Germany.

- Malcom McLean, founder of SeaLand, often gets the credit for creating containerized shipping. In truth, he successfully modified a concept that had been tested by others.
- Sean "Diddy" Combs may well be the world's greatest beneficiary of musical "sampling," the practice of recording extensive sections of other artists' hit musical creations into one's own "original" songs.

Along these lines one may also consider all of the Scorpio management theorists who basically got their starts and many of their ideas from observing the business practices of others. What seems to be business philosophy is in many cases glorified reporting. As Stephen Covey has observed, "actually, I didn't invent the seven habits . . . they are universal principles and most of what I wrote about is just common sense."

For all of the ethical questions that may arise over this issue, however, one can hardly argue with the success of the Scorpio adaptations. Ted Turner did not invent the communications satellite, but his inspired use of an available piece of hardware changed television-viewing habits forever. Jack Welch may have bought more ideas than he developed, but he single-handedly changed the notion of what it means to be a corporate manager.

And pirate or not, has anyone had more of an impact on our present day society than Bill Gates?

Money May Be the Root of All Evil, But It Certainly Helps Pay the Bills

Scorpio is too much of a competitor to ever be cavalier about money. In business, success and failure are stories written in dollar amounts. Fail to maintain profitability and you are out of the game—and that's simply not an option for Scorpio.

As passionately as Scorpio feels about the importance of financial achievement, however, there is a noteworthy complexity that enters the picture here. With some exceptions Scorpio does not seek to accrue a fortune simply so that it may be counted or applied toward the purchase of nice things. (Scorpio is hardly against nice stuff, but it is rarely an end in itself.) The notion of money as business lifeblood has a real resonance with Scorpios, and there is always an acute interest on the part of a Scorpio leader as to how financial resources may best be applied in the interest of the collective enterprise rather than just for the benefit of any particular individual.

Peter Drucker nails the sense of this when he describes the function of profit as job creation and preservation. "Otherwise," writes Drucker in *The Essential Drucker* (New York: Collins, 2001), "profit is simply a bribe to capitalists to keep the economy going." Drucker, in addition to tweaking investors, lost a lot of cache as a guru in executive circles when he suggested that no executive compensation should be more than twenty times greater than the lowest paid employee.

Although other Scorpio leaders might have a different take on compensation, the role of capital formation, and the appropriate levels of risk-reward, most would agree with Drucker that the economic sphere is *one* sphere rather than *the* sphere. Many Scorpio leaders eventually come to an understanding that the social sphere—the connected activities of all human beings on the planet—is where resources must inevitably flow. Ted Turner, the founder of CNN, commenting on his then unprecedented $1 billion gift to the United Nations and his support of many other global goodwill initiatives, said, "War has been good to me from a financial standpoint but I don't want to make money that way . . . I don't want blood money."

While much has been made of Bill Gates's decision to turn over almost his entire fortune to charitable endeavors, an equally thrilling gesture was made by Anita Roddick, British-born founder of The Body Shop, who has given her entire $100 million fortune over to global causes and then began blogging on environmental and women's rights issues at the www.takeitpersonally.org website. A lifelong advocate of the global citizenship responsibilities of corporations, Roddick captures both the scope and the tenor of the Scorpio leadership personality with regard to resources, when she comments, "If I can't do something for the public good, what the hell am I doing?"

Information Is Power

Many classic astrology texts describe Scorpio as the sign of the detective. It is simply unbearable to Scorpio to be confronted with a mystery and have it go unsolved. Worse yet is being denied information that may be known to others and being placed at a competitive disadvantage.

Thus, in the ranks of business priorities one finds the Scorpio leader nearly obsessed with unobstructed paths to information. Even big media people among the Scorpio ranks, most notably Ted Turner, decry the danger of conglomerate control of information sources. Playboy's Christie Hefner adds that when it comes to determining what material is appropriate for publication, "you're better off trusting the marketplace" than the agenda of any single person or interest group.

Many of the social causes supported by Scorpio leaders directly relate to improving access to information and education quality. Scott McNealy, retired CEO of Sun Microsystems, now has as his chief ambition the stewardship and growth of the Global Education and Learning Community (GELC), a nonprofit open source Internet community for educators dedicated to providing unfettered global access to knowledge. The Bill and Melinda Gates Foundation lists universal access to great education and the support of technology in libraries among its most important causes.

As with everything Scorpio undertakes, one should be attuned to the passion underlying the principle and the practice. Knowledge—book-learned, street-smart, derived from all manner of inquiry and experience—allows you to, in the words of Jack Welch, "change before you have to." And Scorpios hate being made to do anything, especially change on the terms of others.

✦ tips for dealing with scorpio

- The Scorpio leader demands a cool and calm work environment that reveals nothing of its true intensity to prying eyes. If you need to emote, think twice and take it outside.
- Never betray, never embarrass, never try to top the Scorpio leader. Scorpio is every bit a competitor and is hardly uncomfortable with revenge.
- Scorpio plays secrecy of intent as an advantage, so accept that you will rarely be granted a full confidence. But also know that loyalty and competence will be handsomely rewarded.
- *Hint:* In almost any situation Scorpio prefers to be master rather than student. An exception, however, is a situation in which one freely gives of one's own subject matter mastery to create an additional advantage for Scorpio. This works best, by the way, in a noncompetitive format. On the golf course or around the poker table, it's simply a good idea to have Scorpio win (although expect to catch hell if Scorpio surmises you are giving less than your best).

CHAPTER 14

sagittarius

The Value of Farsightedness

I always thought of Jaws *as a comedy.*

—Steven Spielberg, quoted in *Cosmopolitan* magazine

NOVEMBER 23 TO DECEMBER 21

Andrew Carnegie	November 25 1835	Carnegie Steel
Henry Clay Frick	December 19, 1849	H.C. Frick and Company
Richard W. Sears	December 7, 1863	Sears Roebuck and Company
Gerard Swope	December 1, 1872	General Electric
Frank Phillips	November 28, 1873	Phillips Petroleum
Willis Carrier	November 26, 1876	Carrier Corporation
Martin Clement	December 5, 1881	Pennsylvania Railroad
Branch Rickey	December 20, 1881	Baseball executive
Robert Woodruff	December 6, 1889	Coca Cola
J. Paul Getty	December 15, 1892	Getty Oil Company
Walt Disney	December 5, 1901	The Walt Disney Company
Henry Singleton	November 27, 1916	Teledyne
Helen Copley	November 28, 1922	Copley Newspapers
Charles Keating	December 4, 1923	American Continental Corporation
Gary Comer	December 10, 1927	Lands' End
Robert Noyce	December 12, 1927	Intel
Berry Gordy	November 28, 1929	Motown Records
Paul O'Neill	December 4, 1935	Alcoa
Fritz Maytag	December 9, 1937	Anchor Brewing
Reginald Lewis	December 7, 1942	TLC Beatrice International
Steven Spielberg	December 18, 1946	Amblin Entertainment, DreamWorks

saGittaRius siGNatuRes

Style: Upbeat

Objective: Wisdom

Strength: Discernment

Weakness: Insensitivity

Communication: Oracular

Tactic: Candor

Belief: Knowledge

Reward: Adventure

To a **Sagittarius,** neither Libra's balancing act nor Scorpio's confrontational posture entirely suffices. A student and a practitioner of the great breadth of human possibilities, Sagittarius tends to be enormously open-minded and philosophical of nature, recognizing that cultural predilection and human behavior most often wobble between moral extremes. Passionately interested in discovering what works conditionally in the course of human entanglements, Sagittarius is even more driven toward the hunt for the holy grail of lasting values.

This inherently brave and optimistic "seeker" quality is truly the Sagittarius signature, and it tends to set up an existence that runs an experiential and intellectual gamut far broader than what most other human beings will allow themselves. Sagittarians are the individuals who explore heaven and hell and a good portion of the world's geography if for no other reason than they are so damn curious about the what and the why of human potential. Capable of the most astounding and far-reaching insights and achievements, they often tend to cut an impossibly broad swath across the angelic and devilish in their personal conduct and commentary, leaving a sometimes-perverse mixture of glory and emotional gore in their wakes.

In order to get where an alpha Sagittarius is coming from, it is perhaps helpful to consider the value "essence" that can produce the combined creative output of a Walt Disney and a Steven Spielberg. And while you're contemplating the culture transforming impact of that historical pair, you might as well toss in the likes of filmmakers Woody Allen, Jean-Luc Goddard, and Otto Preminger. Sagittarians see life in its broadest unadulterated terms: the good and the bad, the mythical and the mundane—and the bigger the screen for rendering an observation, the better.

Acknowledging how far a Sagittarian will go to trap an insight allows for an appreciation of their greatest business advantage. For it is in the sheer tireless breadth of the Sagittarian leader's search that an "aha!" moment nearly always eventually comes a-calling. Astrologers often label Sagittarius as a visionary sign, and the most memorable among them do have an enormous facility for recognizing when they have at last come across the mother lode (or to be more metaphorically apt for the sign symbolized by the Archer, for appreciating when their arrow has finally hit the bull's-eye).

Thus, to appreciate the Sagittarian notables listed in this chapter is to recognize that nearly each one perceived and capitalized upon a moment of precise cultural opportunity. Andrew Carnegie saw the industrial promise of America and knew the very moment when the iron age was dead and one of steel had begun; Frank Phillips saw the first few passenger automobiles on the road and knew he needed to be in the oil business; Richard Sears and Gerald Swope, of Sears Roebuck and General Electric respectively, understood the product implications of a burgeoning consumer economy far earlier than most; Coca Cola may just be flavored and colored sugar water, but

Robert Woodruff knew that if it was positioned as a powerful "back home" tonic for American boys at war it would be part of the fabric of American life forever; Berry Gordy knew the instant when bringing black pop music artists into the American mainstream had become possible, just as Branch Rickey recognized the moment for black and Hispanic baseball players to enter the national pastime; and so on.

"All our dreams can come true if we have the courage to pursue them," Walt Disney once commented. But to truly appreciate the gift of Sagittarius is to recognize the clarity, the optimism, the fearlessness, the grounded humanity, the intellectual edginess, the luck, the incontestable wisdom, the self-effacing humor, and the ultimate certainty behind another Disney summary observation: "I love Mickey Mouse more than any woman I have ever known."

saGittaRius LeaDeRs: vaLue statements

Ask and It Shall Be Given

Sometimes when one employs the term "optimistic" in a character description, there almost seems to be an implicit charge of feeble-mindedness. Why would anyone with a rational world perception expect things to inevitably work out on their behalf? Well, the greatest strength of the generally brilliant Sagittarian is that success is exactly what they expect.

While some Sagittarian leaders are the beneficiaries of inherited wealth—J. Paul Getty and Fritz Maytag are examples—many more come from modest or even quite humble beginnings. Andrew Carnegie, at one time the world's richest man, knew real poverty in his early upbringing, and the stories of most of the other Sagittarian leaders rarely begin from a perch any higher than the most middle of the middle class. Even so, success from these levels is not a phenomenon that excludes the success stories of non-Sagittarian leaders.

What makes Sagittarians different is that they have their expectations focused so far down the road that they almost aren't in touch with the limitations of their present circumstances. For example, one of the remarkable things about a number of the leaders listed below is that they made some of their greatest business strides during the 1930s Depression era. This is true not just of Coca Cola's Robert Woodruff and Walt Disney, who understood the public's yearning for escape and better times, but of industrialists such as the Pennsylvania Railroad's Martin Clement, Phillips Petroleum's Frank Phillips, and the Carrier Corporation's Willis Carrier, all of whom were astute enough to see better days ahead and used the economic distress of hard times to increase their business investments rather than scale back.

Indeed, whatever the era, the stories of Sagittarian business leaders are rife with all-or-nothing gambles that most people would not take, and with strokes of luck that just don't seem to befall most people. Walt Disney, who once claimed Mickey Mouse popped out of his head during a financial bad stretch, risked every penny Mickey had made him on *Snow White*, the world's first feature length cartoon, which was broadly characterized in Hollywood as "Disney's Folly." Richard Sears, working in a train depot, launched his business from a misdirected shipment of pocket watches, which he convinced their manufacturer to let him sell on consignment. Steven Spielberg's career didn't blossom until he snuck onto the Universal Studios movie lot, appropriated an empty office and brazenly submitted his name to the corporate directory.

This is certainly not to imply that Sagittarians always win their gambles. It's just that they operate from the principle that there is meaning in the universe and its order can sometimes be glimpsed. Under such circumstances it is far more constructive to live in a world where you stipulate an agreeable providential Source than an angry Deity who is out to get you.

Beyond insight, the great business talent that resides in this optimistic attitude is an enormously charismatic gift for sales and promotion. When one is dealing with the landmark leadership of companies like Disney, Coke, Sears, GE, Motown Records, etc., the examples of promotional genius and verve are myriad. Sagittarians are the leaders who all have a bit of what Frank Phillips had in him, prior to his days as an oil wildcatter, when as a balding barber he cheerfully sold a hair restoration remedy to his customers.

This *Annie*-like "The sun will come out tomorrow" quality (a lyric written by Martin Charnin, a Sagittarian) is amply illustrated by Charles Keating, publicly humiliated and sent to jail for his part in orchestrating the Lincoln Savings and Loan scandal. Keating is now back at work (his convictions were overturned) and fond of pointing out that if the government regulators had just kept their cool, the land investments he made would have eventually paid off handsomely for everyone instead of causing the general ruin that resulted from asset seizure and liquidation at ten cents on the dollar. But is this Sagittarian bitter?

"I really haven't had it so bad," Keating says. Pass the sunshine.

The Best Things Come in Big Packages

It's the mother ship in Steven Spielberg's *Close Encounters* or the dinosaurs in his *Jurassic Park*. It's the 500-page "wish book" catalogue assembled by Richard Sears or the more than 100 companies absorbed by Richard Singleton's Teledyne. It's a truth about Sagittarius as obvious as the giant planet Jupiter that is said to rule the affairs of this astrological sign. Simply put, in the Sagittarian world, size matters.

This sense of breadth is true of Sagittarius whether one speaks of vision or enterprise or the mundane geography of personal history.

Collectively, more than the champions of any other astrological sign, Sagittarians are marked by big dreams, enormously peripatetic lives and far-flung enterprises. If you happen to work for one, don't be surprised if they are rarely in town, much less in the office.

For Sagittarius, to be moving in wide-open spaces is to be alive. Rare it is to find one who is not an outdoorsman or sportsman of some stripe. They will make as good use of today's electronic communication devices as anyone (they have to, of course, as they are always away somewhere), but they simply cannot breathe in situations of literal or symbolic confinement.

It is a fortunate illustrative irony that the inventor of modern air-conditioning, Willis Carrier, is a Sagittarian. Although not necessarily as prominent a name as some of the others on the Sagittarian list, Carrier not only made it possible for industry to reasonably function in the summer months, he essentially facilitated American population migration to the Sunbelt states. Carrier also, in the global orientation so characteristic of Sagittarius, presciently created a Japanese subsidiary for his products as early as 1930, and today Japan is certainly among the largest per-capita consumers of air-conditioning in the world.

Another icon of the Sagittarian spirit from a slightly earlier time is the railroad. The iron horse plays a prominent role in the stories of many Sagittarians, not just as a commercial entity but as a rugged metaphor for expansive ambition and far traveling dreams. Walt Disney (who built his own scale model railroad in his estate's backyard and made his wife sign a document yielding lifetime right of way for a tunnel under her garden) was asked by a conceptual artist to describe his early vision for Disneyland, and insisted that the essential thing was there had to be a train.

Somewhere along the endless tracks of an exploratory life, Sagittarius fully expects to encounter a worthy destiny. Their goal is not so much the depth of Scorpio but the pursuit of the diamond in an immense rough. Sagittarians almost always grow their businesses as big as possible, relentlessly plowing revenue into expansion rather than investor rewards, so that they don't fence out that thing, whatever it is, that is ultimately "it."

Walt Disney World was created in Florida, Disney once explained, because the land available to the enterprise conferred "the blessing of size." And if the financial risks seem enormous when the controls are almost always set to "Larger," there's the helpful observation of J. Paul Getty:

> If you owe the bank $100, that's your problem. If you owe the bank $100 million, that's the bank's problem.

Life Is a Battle Between Good and Evil; Success Depends on Acknowledging Both

Sagittarians sometimes embody an ethical paradox. Because they are so driven to explore life's possibilities and to become so fluidly and fully vested in the potential for real understanding, they are frequently far less available to the laudable qualities of loyalty, consistency, and tact. As a result, few souls are more capable of being simultaneously so good and so bad and so frustrating and so misapprehended.

Consider Andrew Carnegie, who is today perhaps as well known for his philanthropy as for his steel career. Carnegie gave away the vast portion of his wealth to peace causes and civic projects, observing that "the man who dies rich dies disgraced." Yet this same man, who idealized the steel-worker community and wrote with passion on the rights of labor unions and the virtue of labor, orchestrated one of the most horrific events in the history of labor relationships: The 1892 lock-out at the Homestead Mill resulted in deadly armed confrontation with Pinkerton and government troops and greatly contributed to the effective destruction of the American organized labor movement for fifty years.

Walt Disney, who arguably has brought more family entertainment joy into the world than any other individual in history, is less well known for his appearances in front of Senator Joseph McCarthy's House Un-American Activities Committee hearings, in which he identified specific artists who had struck the Disney Company as likely Communists. TLC Beatrice's Reginald Lewis, a great and modest philanthropist who at one time was the richest black man in America, received the funding that enabled his rise from Michael Milken's tainted junk bond dealings.

Now the point here is hardly to pick on Sagittarians, who in the long run are probably among the most delightful benefactors of mankind and the least likely to inflict pain without the repercussions of conscience. It's just that apparent contradictions of this sort are part and parcel of the nature of life that most Sagittarians are dedicated to exploring. A Sagittarian leader, it is well worth knowing if you must deal with one, is an experience omnivore who is hardly going to dismiss the negative (or classify it as such on someone else's say so) before he has sampled it and found it less valuable, practically and philosophically, than the positive.

What one mostly encounters with Sagittarians is behavior that is aptly classified as enlightened self-interest. Robert Woodruff was hardly going to refuse the government support that enabled him to sell transport trucks built from the blueprints he provided during WWI or that helped him to build an overseas network of Coca Cola bottling plants during World War II. Branch Rickey knew he was furthering the cause of society when he offered a baseball contract to Jackie Robinson, but he also well understood that breaking the color barrier meant getting access to the pick of the crop when it came to hiring other black ballplayers. Steven Spielberg's Indiana Jones was not going to duel a skilled swordsman when his own hand happened to be wrapped around a pistol.

To give them the benefit of the doubt that they deserve, Sagittarians most often recognize that understanding is not an easily won prize. Along the way they will take false paths and receive and deal pain. Most would agree with Walt Disney's observation that, "You may not realize it when it happens, but a kick in the teeth may be the best thing in the world for you."

Honor the Family of Man—As Best You Can

When it comes to their fellow man, Sagittarians find themselves caught between competing revelations. On the one hand, there is an honest appreciation of the fact that every living creature on the planet has inherent value and deserves a place in the choir (otherwise, why would the Creator have bothered?). On the other hand, life's primary rule seems to be that there is no realm on Earth where there is such a thing as absolute fairness or equality.

As a leader, Sagittarians often struggle to put these two items together in a coherent fashion. The generally open and empathic Sagittarius boss frequently has an enormously wide circle of friends, colleagues, advisors, and acquaintances, stretching across all demographic and cultural boundaries, each one contributing something to the Sagittarian's repository of useful wisdom. But this same individual can also be a hard-hearted son-of-a-gun when it comes to specific personal interaction or policy, always hunting for the greatest good of the enterprise and never shying away from the fact that it is the rare individual soul who is going to deserve or get everything they expect or want.

As described earlier regarding the conflicted employer/employee relationships of a Carnegie or a Disney, there is an ambiguous tendency to disregard history and foster the connection that seems on target right now. This quality most definitely seeps into family and personal relationships, with multiple spouses and family estrangements rarely being a surprise in Sagittarian histories. Serving the greater good, maintains Sagittarius, sometimes entails an unpremeditated and even unintended backhanding of those individuals closest by.

This relationship-oriented theme of the imperative of universality versus the difficulty of personal obligation is brilliantly explored in the work of Steven Spielberg. Among his films he explores the broad "collective" themes and contributions of the black experience, the Jewish experience, the Asian experience, the military experience, and the alien experience. It takes a Sagittarian, however, to simultaneously ask questions such as:

Should a man invited to meet aliens abandon his wife and children (*Close Encounters*)?
Do humans have a moral obligation to a robot programmed to love (*A.I.*)?
Is Peter Pan still entitled to be a Lost Boy when he grows up (*Hook*)?

In the works of Spielberg and Disney, for that matter, wisdom is often linked to the innocent idealism of the child. Only the pure-hearted Henry can save E.T., just as only Bambi can save his friends and become Prince of the Forest. Closer to the truth, though, is Disney's observation: "I don't believe in talking down to children, but I don't believe in talking down to any certain segment."

For all the demerits they can be dealt, Sagittarians do far better than most in managing to retain at least some of their idealism regarding the cooperative potential of mankind. Their dislike of inherited privilege and their considerable philanthropic commitments are part of their fabric for establishing universal connection. They generally hate for people to be excluded on the basis of class prejudice and will rise at their own peril to point out and correct an injustice.

"Ethnic prejudice has no place in sports," Branch Rickey once commented. Nor in the whole of global civilization, most Sagittarians would agree.

Wisdom First, Wisdom Lasts

Many of history's greatest Sagittarians are not exactly what you would call honor students. Although there have been some with academic proclivities, the average Sagittarian tends to view school as a form of incarceration. Why would anyone be so narrow-minded, their thinking goes, to believe that knowledge and understanding exist only, or even primarily, in a classroom?

And yet, there is really no group with a greater or purer ambition for wisdom. It's just that Sagittarians come to the game with eyes and minds wide open, congenitally unable to accept rote learning or schoolroom explanations along the line of, "That's the way it's always been done." That way, Sagittarians quickly come to understand, is only haphazardly the right way.

The mark of the Sagittarius leader is, ultimately, to guide us all to an understanding of a better way—one in which power is a servant to cultural improvement, and in which our better natures are not always ruled by our basest self-interests or prejudices. To this end the Sagittarian is the champion of the broad search, the honest inquiry, and the freedom of idea exchange. Disposed toward faith in the wisdom of the Creator and relying on the potential of clarity and grace, the uplink they can create between the masses and the Maker is sometimes profound.

"Almost nothing has real meaning anymore," Anchor Brewing's Fritz Maytag, the father of the craft beer movement, told Stett Holbrook of the *San Francisco Chronicle* in a 2004 article. "We're all looking for it. I find it very satisfying to put meaning into products."

Meaning! To a Sagittarian business leader, meaning is almost better than money.

✦ tips for dealing with sagittarius

- Sagittarians sometimes seem dreamy, but they are more appropriately characterized as relentlessly processing data and impressions from realms far beyond the immediate. They have a proclivity for inwardly making conceptual link-ups that involve greater breadth than the matter at hand. If you are speaking to one, especially about mundane matters and simple truths, make sure they are actually listening.

- To a Sagittarian, humor is the quality of being that lets the world know you are in on the paradox of human existence, its being simultaneous good and evil. They are sometimes prone to making jokes, even over painful subjects, expecting you to catch the sad irony beneath the brave laughing face. If you can respond with a laugh and cry at the same time, they will always find you a worthy audience.

- The term "painfully obvious" was doubtlessly invented by a Sagittarian. Look beyond the immediate, far beyond.

- *Hint*: Sagittarians often have a keen interest in food and wine that extends beyond the realm of snobbery to true gourmandism. These people will know their *foie gras* and wine varietals, but they will also be duly impressed by the best pizza in town. Prone to matters of personal expansion, the Sagittarian will always find "where to eat" worthy of discussion.

CHAPTER 15

ca P R I C O R N

The Value of Framework

Dear, never forget one little point: It's my business. You just work here.

—Elizabeth Arden, quoted in
Miss Elizabeth Arden: An Unretouched Portrait

DECEMBER 22 TO JANUARY 19

Asa Candler	December 30, 1851	Coca Cola
Sarah Breedlove Walker	December 23, 1867	Madame CJ Walker Co.
Helena Rubinstein	December 25, 1870	Helena Rubinstein, Inc.
Elizabeth Arden	December 31, 1878	Elizabeth Arden, Inc.
Ida Rosenthal	January 9, 1886	Maidenform
Conrad Hilton	December 25, 1887	Hilton Hotels
Howard Hughes	December 24, 1905	Hughes Aircraft, TWA, RKO
Alonzo Decker, Jr.	January 18, 1908	Black and Decker
Kemmons Wilson	January 5, 1913	Holiday Inns
Richard Nixon	January 9, 1913	U.S. president
Thomas J. Watson, Jr.	January 14, 1914	IBM
Generoso Pope, Jr.	January 13, 1927	*National Enquirer*
Vaughn Beals	January 2, 1928	Harley-Davidson
Gordon Moore	January 3, 1929	Intel
Earl Graves	January 9, 1935	*Black Enterprise* magazine
James Sinegal	January 1, 1936	Costco
Wayne Huizinga	December 29, 1937	Waste Management, Blockbuster
Henry Kravis	January 6, 1944	Kohlberg Kravis Roberts
Mel Gibson	January 3, 1956	Icon Productions
Jeff Bezos	January 12, 1964	Amazon

CapRicoRn SiGNatURes

Style: Conservative

Objective: Status

Strength: Perseverance

Weakness: Snobbery

Communication: Authoritative

Tactic: Leverage

Belief: Success

Reward: Heritage

as one turns from Sagittarius to Capricorn, one makes a leap from a generally open and optimistic cultural orientation to a generally guarded and pessimistic one. The Sagittarian leader tends to see the human menagerie as a sort of a stimulating and enlightening carnival, while Capricorn finds the endless diversity of human temperaments and predicaments—especially in the workforce—somewhat irritating and counterproductive to a useful parade. Yet insofar as success is the objective of any leader's life, one finds no less joy or fulfillment in Capricorn. Whereas Sagittarius believes that one's good fortune is eventually discovered as a result of broad and sometimes capricious exploration, Capricorn is inclined to the more conservative position that a happy destiny is the result of a hard, well-managed, socially-sanctioned climb.

In many ways the classic Capricorn value set represents what we have today come to accept as the indispensable toolkit of the success seeker. Horatio Alger, the famed nineteenth-century author, wrote over a hundred books in which a down-and-out protagonist employs his wits, pluck, a sound ethical disposition, a bit of luck, and an instinctive capacity for social climbing to break out of poverty's grasp. He was a Capricorn to his very soul. So was founding father Benjamin Franklin, whose wise and witty almanac aphorisms helped establish the virtues of hard work, time sensitivity, prudent resource management, and personal responsibility for a rebellious infant nation that was destined for greatness on the back of such notions.

Such themes receive "contemporary" treatment in the work of Mel Gibson, who may be appreciated as a cinematic icon of Capricorn values. Particularly in historical epics such as *Braveheart* and *The Patriot* one encounters the Capricorn passions for family honor, loyal duty to a worthy cause, cunning strategy, leadership as the authoritative herding of the flock's will to both tactics and principles and, ultimately, acceptance of the high standards of human attainment set by the heroes of history itself. Gibson's movies un-ironically advance the premise that even wearing the appropriate tribal costume is an essential part of the leadership art for Capricorn, along with recognizing the far more serious imperative of sometimes making terrible personal sacrifices to consummate collective goals.

Establishing the powerful sense of historical mythos that most Capricorn leaders possess helps clarify why the Capricorn is especially fulfilled when fully engaged in a leadership role. These are the individuals who feel the very existence of civilization, be it within a localized enterprise or a vast social institution, depends on their personal capacity for keeping chaos at bay, making hard choices, and aligning disciplined effort to the best interests of the majority *over the long run*. This dedication to being constantly on duty along with its companion exposure to stress sometimes extracts enormous tolls with regard to family life, personal health, event setbacks, and even psychological stability, but Capricorns are compelled to see their enterprises through to the end.

"A man is not finished when he is defeated," Capricorn U.S. president Richard Nixon once observed, with the historical poignancy of Watergate hanging over the remark. "He is finished when he quits."

capricorn Leaders: value statements

Father Knows Best

The leadership style of many Capricorns, both male and female, can be fairly characterized as paternalistic. On the plus side one encounters the provider, the protector, the defender of the faith, the master strategist, the authority, the mentor, and the essence of stability in the face of the dangerous unknown. On the negative side, one gets the ideologue, the punisher, the cold voice of reality, and the individual so transparently driven to have influence over others that even a well-intentioned remark can be experienced as a form of assault.

Capricorn leaders will generally describe themselves as passionately motivated by family concerns. But what one really tends to discover in a close look at these frequently family-absent workaholics are individuals who are working out their own complex feelings about the primal authority figure in their own lives. Many distinguished Capricorns will celebrate the sanctity of parenthood and place mom on a pedestal, but the real drive in business as well as personal life is often a fairly competitive urge to supplant and/or surpass dad in the roles of counselor, protector, and provider.

One gets the essence of this in the life of Thomas Watson, Jr., whose brilliant product-line strategies drove IBM to economic greatness far vaster than that attained by his famous founding father. Even so, the angst felt by Watson, Jr. at filling his father's shoes is the stuff of classic business lore. In his autobiography, most revealingly titled *Father, Son and Company* (New York: Bantam, 1991), Watson, Jr. writes: "I was so intimately entwined with my father, I had a compelling desire, maybe out of honor for the old gentleman, maybe out of sheer cussedness, to prove that I could excel in the same way that he did."

Rare is the Capricorn biography that doesn't reveal interesting insights about paternal relationships, sadly often including the early death of a parent. Much of the time these insights run toward the considerable influence that dad has in establishing a solid work ethic, but there are also plenty of relationships that speak toward more compelling adult motivations. Among these are the stories of:

Black and Decker's Alonzo Decker, Jr., who was fired by his
   father at the onset of the Depression and later hired back as
   a floor sweeper
The *National Enquirer's* Generoso Pope, Jr., whose father's
   mobster connections facilitated a business-starting loan from
   the notorious "godfather" Frank Costello
Mel Gibson, whose dad is a well-known Holocaust denier and
   who in Gibson's youth moved his American family to
   Australia in protest of U.S. government policy related to the
   Vietnam war.

The associates of Capricorn, regardless of their credulity in armchair psychology, should respect the fact that a father figure is bound to be a complex character, alternately capable of tendering the greatest empathy and encouragement and then demanding the most inflexible situational accountability.

"No subject occupies more executive time at IBM than the well-being of our employees and their families," Thomas Watson, Jr., once proclaimed. Upon another occasion he added, "I think my most important job in IBM is working with anybody who has a problem."

Yet be wary of the other side of the Capricorn boss, the one who has exercised his authority and then been defied too directly. As Wayne Huizinga has commented:

"I've never had a problem with terminating anyone, even family."

Run a Tight Ship

As has earlier been noted, the sign Virgo is most properly associated with the collection, analysis, and communication of data. The Virgo data emphasis tends, however, to emphasize data solutions, and yields its triumphs in such areas as financial analysis and in the measured flow of information, goods, and services. When it comes to rendering quantified fact into solid and profitable real-world business constructs, however, nobody tops the Capricorn.

The Capricorn advantage is that while Virgo occasionally falls in love with the process of measurement and the assemblage of the data itself, it is the Capricorn who worships only at the temple of tangible actions and results. There is a bedrock utilitarianism to Capricorn that has no patience at all for business chaff (e.g. wasted time, overly speculative insight or investment, and 99.9 percent of the stuff on the Internet) be it praised by humans or prompted by their computer surrogates. Capricorn's formula for success relies heavily upon the identification and stewardship of firm and fertile resources (frequently including real estate and other hard assets and always including key staff), which are brilliantly husbanded into business growth by a leader who never forgets a name or a number and rarely allows himself to be manipulated into the dark.

The examples of the Capricorn passions for conservancy and enlightened resource management are myriad and include:

- *Thomas Watson and IBM's System/360 Initiative.* In 1964, Watson insured the greatness of IBM by backing development of a new family of graded-capacity computers that could, for the first time in computer history, all efficiently run on the same software. His obsolescence-reducing product initiatives were backed by a corporate emphasis on lifetime career development and a customer-oriented business dependability commitment that Watson called "calendar integrity."

- *Kemmons Wilson and Holiday Inns' Standardization.* Wilson's innovations are legion. He was the first great hotelman to understand the economic wisdom of uniform building and operating specifications, and of making the manufacturing, menu development, purchasing, and training processes nationally centralized in-house functions. His national computerized Holidex reservation system that captured travelers already on the road was also decades ahead of its time.

- *Henry Kravis and KKR's LBO Strategy.* While excess eventually trashed much of the leveraged buy-out business, Kravis was originally hailed as a brilliant white knight for understanding that corporate assets were frequently undervalued by their owners and could fetch handsome profits as well as finance future growth when divorced from the corporate parent and sold independently.

- *James Sinegal and Costco's Retail Revolution.* Low overhead, minimal mark-up, and just-in-time inventory did not originate with Costco, but few companies have brought it to better fruition. Sinegal early understood that category breadth was more important than the number of items in a category, and that attractive price and quality could both be offered to the consumer if the company developed solid generics, remained flexible regarding branded merchandise, and sold in bulk. Well-paid employees and a passion for staying close to operations are also key ingredients in the mix. (Costco does not have a single

P.R. person; Sinegal makes regular store tours and personally scans hundreds of customer comment cards daily.)

- *Jeff Bezos and the Amazon Virtual Warehouse.* "Conserve money" is the mantra of Jeff Bezos, who defied a boatload of pundits by building an on-line virtual bookstore that has grown into a hugely successful general merchandise business. The Amazon model has thrived on a low corporate budget, central order taking, next-to-nothing build-out costs, and a virtually expense-free customer expansion model. While the investment community scratches its head over such policies as free shipping, third-party discount sellers, and running negative reviews on the website, Bezos adamantly maintains that these are the policies that will keep customers loyal ten years down the road.

Not to put too fine a point on it, but Capricorns insist that their organizations conserve the yarn, identify the most sensible pattern, and knit to demand. Capricorn leaders are people like:

Conrad Hilton, who broke apart large lobbies in the first hotels he purchased to create more revenue producing areas

Vaughn Beals, who reinvigorated Harley Davidson production with just-in-time inventory controls

Gordon Moore, who famously insisted that Intel executives use their air-mileage rewards for business trips

Wayne Huizinga, who busted apart his world champion Florida Marlins baseball team when the revenue numbers didn't add up

"Retail is detail," once commented James Sinegal by way of useful summary. "Show me a big-picture guy and I'll show you a guy who's out of the picture."

Take the Long Way Home

To fully understand Capricorn is to appreciate their prodigious respect for ample time filled with clear purpose. Unlike so many other individuals in contemporary society they refuse to worship the knee jerk reaction and the headlong speed that is never modulated to situational demands. While they certainly appreciate that sometimes a business success will depend on getting out of the blocks first, their overall course rewards endurance rather than velocity.

One simply does not outlast a motivated Capricorn. They rarely waver from a belief in their own eventual success and are among those rare creatures that respect that every obstacle may well be an opportunity. Whether it's Wayne Huizinga starting out with a single garbage truck, or Kemmons Wilson with one popcorn machine, or Conrad Hilton being forced to surrender all of his hotels but one during the Depression, the Capricorn march is a relentless one that always assumes there will be time enough to get to the top if one maintains a clear purpose and is always striving upwards.

One of the most inspiring Capricorn stories in this regard is that of Sarah Breedlove Walker. Born to former slaves, barely literate, orphaned at 7, married at 14, widowed at 20, Walker eventually managed to pull herself up from a life of domestic servitude by launching a line of hair and skin care products for black women. Madame CJ Walker, as she came to call herself, met her maker as the first black woman millionaire in the history of the United States.

Madame Walker once commented:

> There is no royal flower-strewn path to success. And if there is I have not found it. For if I have accomplished anything in life it is because I have been willing to work hard.

Capricorn does get worn out sometimes past the breaking point. It is hard to consider the lives of Howard Hughes or Richard Nixon or Mel Gibson, for example, without noting the occasionally dramatic effects of stress on grand ambitions. An underappreciated or professionally thwarted Capricorn is no stranger to moody depressions and will take pause to recuperate, although this too is part of an experience-based understanding that many problems left alone will take care of themselves.

So it is that a Capricorn leader will sometimes explore a vice or two, or let the hair *way* down as a brief pause for pressure relief. Yet for the truly long haul you will generally find Capricorn with a shoulder to the boulder, constantly and uncomplainingly churning uphill. Lodging magnates Conrad Hilton and Kemmons Wilson still had a strong hand in running their hotel chains at the ages of 91 and 90 respectively, and Maidenform founder Ida Rosenthal was still going to the office every day at the age of 87. In a more contemporary vein it is worth noting that of the four great Internet business startups of the 1990s—Amazon, Google, eBay, and Yahoo!—only one is still run by its founder, Amazon's Capricorn Jeff Bezos.

Thus, whether one sees the world in terms of days or lifetimes, the Capricorn universe is held together by sustained effort. "Work only half a day," Kemmons Wilson once advised, "it makes no difference which half—the first twelve hours or the last twelve hours." Or as Wayne Huizinga observed on another occasion: "Who says you can't go in at 4:30 or 5 in the morning? Why do you have to be home at 6 anyway?"

Status Is Next to Godliness

Let's come right out and say it. A Capricorn tends to be a bit of a snob. There is such a deep-seated longing for worldly success in the

Capricorn leaders, they can't help but place on a pedestal anyone who has attained it—inherited privilege, genetic good fortune, or dumb luck be damned.

Of course, the Capricorn leader prefers success predicated upon hard work, conscientiously developed talent, and worthy social contribution to success achieved by the latest youth cult hero or lottery winner. Success is serious business to the Capricorn leaders. Their own experience of it tends toward heavy lifting rather than lightning strike, and they are inherently mistrustful of the latest flash-in-the-pan celebrity who may capriciously mess up the cultural status quo and then sink out of sight tomorrow. But the top of the mountain is so exciting to those who spend their entire life climbing to attain it (the Capricorn animal icon is the mountain goat), that anyone who has managed to get "up there" is worthy of something closer to reverence than mere admiration.

With Capricorn there is a particular taste for contact with entertainment and sports celebrities (reflected glamour), with the stars of business (reflected competence), and with politicians (reflected power, not to mention their occasional usefulness in a zoning matter). Although space precludes a detailed analysis of this principle in operation in the lives of famous Capricorn leaders, it is impossible to consider Howard Hughes or Conrad Hilton or Helena Rubinstein or Earl Graves or Henry Kravis, etc., without appreciating the central role that the engagement of status contacts has played in their lives. Even more to the point are such enterprises as:

Elizabeth Arden's premium-priced cosmetic lines and Maine Chance Spa, unapologetically focused on the indulgence of an elite clientele

Generoso Pope's *National Enquirer* epiphany that celebrity news would sell far more tabloid newspapers than stories focused primarily on the bizarre

James Sinegal's awareness that his bare-bones Costco warehouses, if stocked with the right merchandise, would primarily appeal to the upscale shopper

What may also be usefully noted is how many of the Capricorn leaders are involved in some aspect of the hospitality industry. Kemmons Wilson (Holiday Inns) and Conrad Hilton (Hilton Hotels) are obvious, but Howard Hughes (Desert Inn plus other Las Vegas properties), Elizabeth Arden (Maine Chance Spas), Wayne Huizinga (Boca Resorts), and Henry Kravis (KSL Partners) have also made commitments, frequently quite upscale commitments, to the hotel and resorts industry. Surely many of these businesses made sense on the economic investment level, but one cannot avoid the image of the Capricorn host creating, controlling, and making a profit from a high-class clubhouse for the community's influentials, a Capricorn fantasy if ever there was one.

Appearances May Deceive, but That's the General Idea

As a final companion insight into the Capricorn value package, it's well worth recording how important appearances are to most of them. This isn't just a matter of good hygiene and neatness, although such concerns are certainly approved by the fundamentally conservative Capricorn. What we're getting at here is more toward the notion of a well-groomed appearance as tactical intent: first, to conceal vulnerability; second, to broadcast intent of success; and third, perhaps a bit magically, to actually become the thing that one first superficially projects oneself to be.

In this vein it is perfectly appropriate that it is a Capricorn, Elizabeth Arden, who is given credit for the concept of a "makeover," that is, the use of a beauty product regimen to enhance one's projected image and self-esteem. Prior to Arden, and her historical contemporary

Helena Rubinstein, it is recorded that cosmetics were largely the province of the underclass rather than appropriate aids for making oneself more "ladylike." Along these lines Sarah Breedlove Walker is to be cited for helping black women to feel better about their hair and skin appearance, and Maidenform's Ida Rosenthal must be given similar credit for designing and promoting a brassiere that simply made a woman feel and look better in a nice dress.

Close in intent is the work of Earl Graves, the founder of *Black Enterprise* magazine, who recognized that in coaching young black entrepreneurs and executives he had to emphasize appropriate style along with appropriate work behavior. "Work on developing a commanding presence," he advises his audience in his book, *How to Succeed in Business Without Being White* (New York: HarperBusiness, 1998). Although he has taken some liberal heat for the dress code he enforces in his business (dreadlocks and tattoos are just not going to cut it at *Black Enterprise)*, he vigorously maintains that young blacks must not give any external style cues that would inhibit someone else's desire for doing business with them.

Perhaps most revealing in this regard is the expressed viewpoint of Howard Hughes, whose appearance famously dissipated over the last years of his life. While he himself became a kind of dirty and disheveled creature infamous for the length of his beard and fingernails, he kept on top of his financial empire. Largely responsible for the end of the gangster era in Las Vegas and responsible for its era of nouveau elegance, Hughes late in his life reputedly observed:

> I like to think of Las Vegas in terms of a well-dressed man in a dinner jacket and a beautifully jeweled and furred female getting out of an expensive car.

One can bet that nobody who worked for him called Hughes on the discrepancy between behavior and belief. For as Hughes, every bit a king-of-the-hill Capricorn, is widely reported to have observed when called a "paranoid deranged millionaire" by a tabloid newspaper: "I'm not a paranoid deranged millionaire. Goddamit, I'm a billionaire."

✦ tips for dealing with capricorn

- You will be judged by your cover. Particularly in early encounters, dress conservatively.
- Never say anything that can be construed as criticism of family, theirs or your own.
- Never waste your time on their time. Find something useful to do.
- *Hint*: Capricorns can be reluctant to attend social events that are not well stocked with celebrity guests or of which they are not in control of themselves. Don't expect them to eagerly accept invitations to big hoop-de-doos, no matter how much "fun" you tell them it will be. What they really do like is to go to an event where they will be receiving some formal recognition of their own contributions to society.

aQUaRIUS

The Value of Friendship

Lots of people want to ride with you in the limo, but what you want is someone who will take the bus with you when the limo breaks down.

—Oprah Winfrey, O magazine

JANUARY 20 TO FEBRUARY 18

Abraham Lincoln	February 12, 1809	U.S. president
Horace Greeley	February 3, 1811	*The New York Tribune*
Thomas Edison	February 11, 1847	Edison Electric
John D. Rockefeller, Jr.	January 29, 1874	The Rockefeller Foundation
Thomas J. Watson, Sr.	February 17, 1874	IBM
Franklin D. Roosevelt	January 30, 1882	U.S. president
Frank Costello	January 26, 1891	The Genovese Crime Family
Christian Dior	January 21, 1905	Christian Dior
William Levitt	February 11, 1907	Levitt and Sons
Ronald Reagan	February 6, 1911	U.S. president
Bill Veeck	February 9, 1914	Baseball Executive
Walter A. Haas, Jr.	January 24, 1916	Levi-Strauss, Oakland A's
Samuel Lefrak	February 12, 1918	The Lefrak Organization
An Wang	February 2, 1920	Wang Labs
Paul Newman	January 26, 1925	Newman's Own
Steve Wynn	January 27, 1942	Mirage Resorts
Michael Bloomberg	February 14, 1942	Bloomberg, L.P.
Paul Allen	January 21, 1953	Microsoft, Seattle Seahawks
Oprah Winfrey	January 29, 1954	Harpo Productions
Matt Groening	February 15, 1954	Life In Hell Co. (*The Simpsons*)

aquarius signatures

Style: Idiosyncratic

Objective: Invention

Strength: Open-mindedness

Weakness: Memory

Communication: Enthusiastic

Tactic: Sincerity

Belief: Humanitarianism

Reward: Progress

With **Aquarius** one arrives at the apex of social consciousness.

So why is it that the Aquarians you know are among the most personally private, quirky, and socially inconsistent creatures on the planet? Many Aquarians appear totally absorbed by odd informational frequencies that only they seem to notice, and they are as likely to be as alien as they are accessible to their fellow Earthlings. Certainly the eccentric laboratory scientist and the absent-minded professor may come to mind.

For all their reflective detachment, however, it is their fellow Earthlings rather than themselves who most frequently captivate Aquarian attention and to whom they appear to owe their spiritual allegiance. Arising from a nearly unfathomable mixture of historical timing, broad-mindedness, and humanistic predilection, the great names in Aquarian leadership derive their greatness from selflessly rising to the collective needs and aspirations of community, generally during periods of crisis and cultural change. Determining cause and effect is not always easy with Aquarians, but they are often at their best when playing the roles—by accident or design—of: 1) popular champion/benefactor; and/or 2) progressive social engineer.

Although there are many examples of the Aquarian cultural champion throughout history (Babe Ruth, Michael Jordan, Charles Lindbergh, Jackie Robinson, and Rosa Parks are a few representative names on the list), surely the hardest to overlook from the leadership perspective is a remarkable set of U.S. presidents. Abraham Lincoln, Franklin Delano Roosevelt, and Ronald Reagan all took office during severe downturns in the nation's fortunes and all presided over very rocky initial years in office. The common gift and ultimate triumph of all these leaders, however, was an understanding of the psychological requirements of a suffering public, a suffering that demanded a strong and hopeful vision far more than it required stone-etched policy or vested rules, even when those rules were contained in the U.S. Constitution.

This last point is particularly germane to the subject of business leadership, for it is particularly difficult for the contemporary Aquarian executive to thrive amidst the exhausting conformity of today's share-price–driven, micromanaged, Sarbanes-Oxley world. The Aquarian business leader is quintessentially a free-wheeler, and will best excel in situations that tolerate a fair amount of seat-of-the-pants behavior (the sudden brainstorm, the unusual alliance, the quick reversal of plan) and, just as importantly, behavior that to some real extent places the common good before profits. Admirable enterprise efforts can and do happen in the sphere of an Aquarian, but even among the most business-gifted—including the likes of Paul Allen, Walter Haas Jr., Michael Bloomberg, and David Rockefeller—there is as much likelihood of encountering a passion for philanthropy and social service as there is for hitting the quarterly numbers.

Perhaps the essential business aspiration of the Aquarian is best captured in art by the great Aquarian novelist Charles Dickens. In *A Christmas Carol,* the ghost of his deceased business partner, Jacob Marley, confronts miserly old Ebenezer Scrooge:

"You always were a good man of business," Scrooge compliments the ghost.

"Business?" howls the tortured spirit. "Mankind was my business. The common welfare was my business; charity, mercy, forbearance, and benevolence were, all, my business. The dealings of my trade were but a drop of water in the comprehensive ocean of my business!"

It's a sentiment, for which we are all richer, and it plays great around the holidays and on daytime television but, alas, it's just not an easy message to carry to shareholders in the pages of an annual report. But an Aquarian will always gives it a try. Walter Haas, Jr., of Levi-Strauss, for example, a man who purchased the Oakland Athletics to keep the team in Oakland "because somebody had to do it," is absolutely revered in humanitarian circles for this unprecedented line in the 1971 stock–offering prospectus for Levi-Strauss:

Profits may be affected by Levi's commitment to socially responsible programs.

That's Aquarius in a nutshell. They are a bit idiosyncratic, perhaps, but eminently and demonstrably concerned about the family of man. If we are really heading into the Aquarian Age, well . . . there are worse fates.

aquarius leaders: value statements

Be Conscious of Community

"Public sentiment is everything. With public sentiment, nothing can fail; without it nothing can succeed," said Abraham Lincoln once upon a time. "A house divided against itself cannot stand," he famously observed upon another occasion. Lincoln was no average Aquarius or average anything, of course, but Aquarius he was to his very soul.

So was Franklin Delano Roosevelt, who took the highest office in the land under the dark cloud of the Depression and knew that the future of Democracy was in danger of perishing in the despair of the common man. "In our seeking for economic and political progress," he observed, "we all go up—or else we all go down." And he likely saved the future of our nation as we know it when he announced: "I pledge you, I pledge myself, to a new deal for the American people."

Aquarians are disposed towards a universal outlook that they temper with a hopeful search for functional common ground. Capable of mixing idealism and pragmatism, Aquarians are gifted in seeing all of life as a dynamic social network rather than a series of temporally enclosed and isolated personal events. At their best, as was true of famed Aquarian poet/philosopher Sir Thomas More in the sixteenth century, they have visions of perfect community that More was the first to call "Utopia."

Whereas it may be very hard to see the Utopia in projects as diverse (and real) as William Levitt's mass produced suburban village of Levittown, or Samuel Lefrak's vast Lefrak City apartment complex, or Steve Wynn's internationally-themed demographically-inclusive Las Vegas, they are all best understood as broad landmark conceptual responses to idealized community requirements at a particular moment in history, rather than simply as capital ventures.

Criticisms of any or all these projects aside, they all at least originally participated in the same optimistic spirit of community potential that has Microsoft cofounder Paul Allen so heavily invested in Seattle's South Lake Union "life science" center hub project. In a more strictly philanthropic vein, it is what prompted David Rockefeller to donate land for various national parks and for the buildings of the United Nations.

One gets a sense of the mindset here in a *Time* magazine comment by William Levitt, who in assessing the enhanced quality of life that he helped facilitate for tens of thousands of first-time home buyers notes, "In Levittown, 99 percent of the people pray for us." Similarly, speaking to a *San Diego Union-Tribune* reporter of his latest Las Vegas creation, the Wynn Resort, Steve Wynn enthuses, "We've built the most complex edifice on the planet Earth, interviewed 100,000 people, hired 9,000 of them, from electricians to executives, blackjack dealers to chefs, people of every description known to man."

It is the Aquarian nature to include rather than exclude. Aquarian entrepreneurs Horace Greeley, founder of the *New York Tribune,* and Michael Bloomberg, founder of the Bloomberg news empire, while separated by a century, share much commonality of purpose in their drive toward the broad democratization of "privileged" opinion and information, and in their eventual ambition for public office. Bloomberg, a multiterm mayor of New York City, was once described in a *Newsweek* article as being "far more passionate about giving money away than spending it." He is especially noteworthy in an Aquarian sense for being a Republican who atypically supports same-sex marriage laws, abortion rights, and the rights of illegal aliens, and for being a billionaire mayor who rides the subway to work every day.

Certainly when one has names like Abraham Lincoln and Jackie Robinson to call upon, the argument about the Aquarians' relationship to the universal advancement of human rights fairly writes itself. Susan B. Anthony, Anna Shaw, Rosa Parks, Betty Friedan, and Angela

Davis are just some of the additional names among the ranks of Aquarian rights activists. And of course there is Oprah Winfrey, who has demonstrated that a commitment to social caring can even turn a profit when the passion is sincere. Says Oprah instructively:

> I've been successful all these years because I do my show with the people in mind, not for the corporations or their money.

Help History Along

Famed designer Christian Dior made international fashion history when his voluptuous "New Look" apparel made a clear break with the severe fashions associated with the deprivations of the Depression and World War II eras. Michael Bloomberg changed a 190-year-old system when he had New York City Hall offices physically reconfigured into an open floor plan, an indication that the clandestine dealings of patronage politics needed to become a thing of the past. An Wang, founder of Wang Laboratories and very aware of his Chinese-American heritage, wryly commented that the driving purpose of his word-processor company was "to show that Chinese could excel at things other than running laundries and restaurants."

These may seem relatively minor footnotes in the broad sweep of leadership history, but they are all indicative of an Aquarian trait that is both the Achilles' heel and the ultimate source of their success. For while it is enough to drive the average Cancer or Capricorn mad, the simple truth is that Aquarius usually has a short and selective memory and very little reverence for "the way it has always been." This trait is sometimes the path to chaos, but it is amazingly useful when it comes to flexible, nonprejudicial problem solving and hopefully embracing the future.

Here again one must at least briefly mention Lincoln and Roosevelt, because while each certainly deserves credit for innovative problem solving on a grand scale, they are both frequently criticized for usurping authority not granted by the Constitution. Although certainly culpable of the charge, neither man thought the nation would survive the straitjacket of its own traditions, and they acted in ways that they would surely deem as historically necessary. Who is to argue?

"The dogmas of the quiet past are inadequate to the stormy present," Lincoln told Congress in the early days of the Civil War. "We must think anew and act anew."

And in a similarly dark hour, Roosevelt told the nation, "The only limit to our realization of tomorrow will be our doubts of today."

This stamp of a forward orientation liberated from the imperatives of history is a true Aquarian trademark. Even on the most personal level, the notion rings true to the type. As Oprah Winfrey once admonished her audience:

> Your job is not just to do what your parents say, what your teachers say, what society says, but to figure out what your heart's calling is and to be led by that.

The short and sweet of it is summarized in an oft-quoted comment made by a genuine Aquarian genius and eminently successful business leader, Thomas Edison, whose various companies were the collective genesis of General Electric. "Hell, there are no rules here," Edison once said about his business, "we're trying to accomplish something."

There's No Safe Port in a Brainstorm

Horace Greeley is best remembered for the quote "Go West young man, and grow up with the country." This alone is a fairly Aquarian sentiment in that its heart is firmly in the future. But Greeley's entire career as a distinguished journalist, editor, politician, and egalitarian reformer is worthy of the Aquarian mantle.

Greeley's *New York Tribune* grew to be the most influential newspaper in the thirty-year period leading up to and including the Civil War. Striking a thoughtful and socially considerate tone, the newspaper backed the populist issues of the day, vigorously opposed slavery, and avidly considered such topics as vegetarianism, Utopian society, and transcendentalism. It is no overstatement that Greeley was one of the most widely influential and respected citizens of his day, a source of truth and a national thought leader.

To fully appreciate Aquarius, however, is to understand how Greeley managed to lose it all in a relative eye blink. As a "Liberal Republican/Democrat" candidate for president right after the Civil War, Greeley took the audacious position that the war was over and all should be forgotten and forgiven, a position he backed by offering to personally put up bond for the incarcerated Confederate president, Jefferson Davis. The outrage was palpable as the *Tribune* lost half its subscribers and the war-weary Greeley was widely lampooned as an eccentric and a fool.

The unfortunate truth about many Aquarian leaders, even the great ones, is that in their enthusiasm for out-of-the-box ideas, and in their predilection toward being their own moral compasses, they are capable of grand lapses, moments of astoundingly bad judgment, and ruinous behavior. FDR almost lost his future political career when as assistant secretary of the Navy he authorized a sting operation that involved ordering non-homosexual enlisted men to perform oral sex on suspected enlisted homosexuals—a tactic he denied knowing about. But as Jonathan Alter points out in his book *The Defining Moment* (New York: Simon and Schuster, 2006), the best that could then be said of FDR was he was incompetent or a fool. Thomas Edison, in his desire to prove the efficacy of DC electricity over his rival George Westinghouse's alternating current, set up a series of demonstrations in which he electrocuted animals, and in one case he was involved in the public execution of an elephant!

There will be no apologies for this sort of thing offered here, but it is important to take in the Aquarian perspective. The shortness of memory that plagues many Aquarians is inversely proportional to their ability to come up with new ideas. And it is that quality of relentless idea generation that is most prized by the Aquarian leader, a few regrettable executive decisions and dead circus animals be damned.

"I have not failed," Edison famously remarked during his efforts to create the light bulb. "I've just found 10,000 ways that won't work." During the dark days of the Depression FDR told the nation:

> It is common sense to take a method and try it. If it fails, admit it frankly and try another. But above all, try something.

Another of the most successful leaders on the Aquarian list, the founder of IBM, Thomas Watson, preached the cannon of intellectual search and relentless experimentation. His comment, offered below, is particularly revealing. It states the Aquarian case plainly while also displaying an awareness of how the Aquarian is frequently perceived by more guarded souls. Said Watson:

> Follow the path of the unsafe, independent thinker. Expose your ideas to the danger of controversy. Speak your mind and fear less the label of "crackpot" than the stigma of conformity.

Predilections Are Personal but Virtue Is Universal

It may seem from all that has been written here that Aquarius is singularly unsuited for executive office. Idealism, eccentricity, and intellectual tempestuousness hardly comprise the sort of talent trifecta one is likely to find at the head of a vested organization. And in most cases this is just fine with Aquarians to whom, as it has already been pointed out, the imperative of incessant accountability is a straitjacket not worth the throne.

It would be an error to conclude, however, that there is no sense of social sacrifice in the Aquarian personality, especially given the number of famed generals born under this sign, including Stonewall Jackson, Douglas MacArthur, William Tecumseh Sherman, and Omar Bradley (in addition to William Henry Harrison, a war hero who was elected the ninth U.S. president, but died thirty days into his term). The broad tolerance Aquarians grant to personal outlook, their own and that of others, is only deemed sacrosanct insofar as it remains in the personal realm. Making the most exacting distinction between private and public life, they are fiercely stubborn about protecting autonomy in the former and in promoting the broadest possible social virtue in the latter.

On a number of levels the life of famed Aquarian actor and philanthropist Paul Newman is instructive in this regard. One of the most influential and respected actors of the entire second half of the twentieth century, Newman has remained scrupulously divorced from the Hollywood "scene," choosing to live his personal life privately in Connecticut with his wife of fifty-plus years, actress Joanne Woodward. Perhaps even more germane here is his retail food product company, Newman's Own, which donates all of its profits to charitable ventures and which operates under the Aquarian-themed slogan, "Shameless Exploitation in Pursuit of the Public Good."

Another good example of this split personal/public personality phenomenon can be found in the life of David Rockefeller, Jr., a life-long alcohol abstainer who argued influentially for ending Prohibition, which he did not feel was in the best interest of society as it increased disrespect for the law. Also relevant here are the social codes of suburbia developed by William Levitt, which guaranteed the private pursuit of happiness for the individual members of a nascent middle class but not at the expense of neighborhood fences or laundry hung out to dry in the front yard. The point is made a bit in the opposite direction by Microsoft cofounder Paul Allen who, while most publicly committed to his high-profile philanthropic projects, extracts a signed confidentiality pledge as the invitee price of admittance to his legendary private social affairs.

For Aquarian leaders, ultimately, a personal perspective is a bedrock right, but it is no trump to be played against a moral foundation. "Rules are not necessarily sacred," FDR once observed, "but principles are." And there's not much difference in Lincoln's directive, "Important principles may and must be inflexible."

It is fair to comment, however, that the mental flights of an Aquarian do tend to benefit from an occasional distance from the crowd. "Whatever you are, be a good one," Lincoln once commented in the full flush of open-minded Aquarian social commitment. But he is also said to have observed, in the full flush of Aquarian self-awareness, "Avoid popularity if you would have peace."

Friendship Is Life's Most Precious Gift and Noble Responsibility

At first glance, the oddest name in the list of Aquarian leaders at the top of this chapter is likely that of Mafia kingpin Frank Costello. His inclusion here does not mitigate the fact that he profited from a violent and immoral world, but the truth is that an ethically conflicted Costello was oddly a man of peace, who advocated negotiation over confrontation and who was widely respected as the man who could almost always come to an "honest" understanding with anyone of any station on either side of the law. He has been widely referenced as "the Prime Minister of the Underworld."

A Mafia boss may be an uncomfortable example, but the truth is that an Aquarian's ultimate triumph is the ability to bridge personal and public worlds via the virtues of what is best called friendship. While Aquarius experiences a dichotomy between public and private, there is yet a deep awareness that in either realm one is best served by such qualities as appreciation, empathy, good counsel, humor, generosity, and forbearance. If Aquarius has a magical quality, it is the ability to form what is experienced as a personal friendship with every member of a crowd.

The great contemporary exemplar of this principle is Oprah Winfrey, who has made the very word "girlfriend" an essential part of relationship vernacular. (In 2006, Budget Travel Online asked its users to name any celebrity they would like to take on a "girlfriend getaway," and Oprah scored more than twice as many votes as her nearest rival, Jennifer Aniston, who is also an Aquarian.) The quality of Oprah to get close to the multitude is well described by a fan quoted in a *Washington Post* article written by Eugene Robinson and titled "Church of Oprah":

> She just has the ability to connect on so many levels—your emotional needs, physical needs, psychological needs. It's her humanity. Everybody goes through the same things she goes through, but she has the willingness to share it.

Another famous resident of Chicago who had the gift of crowd empathy was legendary baseball mogul Bill Veeck. Famous for any number of outrageous fan-friendly promotions, including one in which he actually allowed fans to manage the game by raising placards in the stands (Veeck's team won), Veeck never forgot that it was the average grandstand guy who made the game of baseball both beautiful and profitable. Upon one occasion Veeck felt the fans' wrath when he attempted to trade away his team's most popular player, and he personally visited nearly every bar in town to apologize and explain. His most enduring contributions to the game are likely his early support for abolishing the reserve clause that made a player a piece of team property, and his creation of the "friendly confines" of Wrigley field, with its manual scoreboard, ivy-covered walls, and legendary party-hearty bleachers.

The key to the Aquarius spirit is contained in a comment Veeck once made about baseball fans. "I have discovered in twenty years of moving around a ballpark," said Veeck, "that the knowledge of the game is usually in inverse proportion to the price of the seats."

For all the personal reasons Aquarius may tend to avoid a leadership role, there is enormous identification with, and respect for, the needs, hopes, delights, and abilities of the masses. What makes Aquarians' leadership so memorable is their ability to fully embrace the concept of the collective.

As the French Aquarian author Antoine de Sainte-Exupery once remarked, "There is no hope of joy except in human relations."

✦ tips for dealing with aquarius

- At all costs avoid jokes or comments based upon ethnic, racial, or sexual bias.
- Try not to take offense at their forgetfulness, which may even include the names of long-term associates. They are easily distracted by their own bullet trains of thought.
- Aquarians are stubborn when they have made up their minds. Past a certain point, no matter how polite they seem, they are no longer listening to you.
- *Hint*: Aquarians like situations in which they can observe other people. If you take them to a sporting event or a concert they would rather sit where they can watch the crowd as well as the "professional" entertainment.

pisces

The Value of Fascination

Even if we counted beans for a living we secretly saw
ourselves as romantic poets.

—Steven Jobs, quoted in *The Journal of Popular Culture*

✦ FEBRUARY 19 TO MARCH 20 ✦

George Washington	February 22, 1732	U.S. president
"Buffalo Bill" Cody	February 26, 1846	Wild West Show
Alexander Graham Bell	March 3, 1847	Bell Telephones
David Sarnoff	February 27, 1891	RCA
Dorothy Schiff	March 11, 1903	*New York Post*
Benjamin "Bugsy" Siegel	February 28, 1906	Gangster, "Father of Las Vegas"
Walter Annenberg	March 13, 1908	Triangle Publications (*TV Guide*)
Edmund T. Pratt, Jr.	February 22, 1927	Pfizer
Rupert Murdoch	March 11, 1931	The News Corporation
Herb Kelleher	March 12, 1931	Southwest Airlines
Sanford Weill	March 16, 1933	Citigroup
Lawrence Bossidy	March 5, 1935	Allied Signal, Honeywell
Phil Knight	February 24, 1938	Nike
Thomas Burrell	March 18, 1939	Burrell Communications Group
Louis Gerstner	March 1, 1942	IBM
Michael Eisner	March 7, 1942	Walt Disney Company
David Geffen	February 21, 1943	Asylum Records, Dreamworks SKG

George Harrison	February 24, 1943	The Beatles, Handmade Films
Patricia Woertz	March 17, 1953	Archer Daniels Midland
Steven Jobs	February 24, 1955	Apple, Pixar
Michael Dell	February 23, 1965	Dell

pisces signatures

Style:	Empathic
Objective:	Art
Strength:	Vision
Weakness:	Emotional Vulnerability
Communication:	Caring
Tactic:	Acceptance
Belief:	Transcendence
Reward:	Joy

Pisces individuals, from the plainest to the most memorable, are best exemplified by the trait of coloring outside the lines, sometimes chaotically but often to trailblazing and magnificent effect. Although no strangers to a genius that is in part cerebral and rational (Albert Einstein, anyone?), the true Pisces are a spiritual and artistic adept, flowing through a life of transcendent feelings and irresistible emotions as natural to the Pisces as water to the fish. Prompted by heart rather than head, the Pisces may sometimes embrace practical consistency or the tried-and-true solution, but they tend to adapt to those only if they *feel* right, not primarily because they boast supporting empirical evidence and are somehow *provable*.

So very emotionally receptive and psychologically protean are Pisces that many seem to be possessed by the traits of their bordering signs, Aquarius and Aries, in which they tend to have a personal planet or two due to the astronomical scheme of things. Whatever the cause, one easily finds great Pisces leaders who, like Aquarius, are devoted in the broadest and most practical possible manner to the welfare of the society in which they find themselves—from George Washington (Mercury in Aquarius) to IBM's Lou Gerstner (Mercury and Venus in Aquarius) to Southwest Airlines' Herb Kelleher (Venus in Aquarius). Similarly there are other famously successful Pisces who, in addition to their great career achievements, will at least in part leave Aries-like legacies of self-serving ideologies and brutally frank temperaments in their wakes. This group includes Citicorp's Sandy Weill (Mercury and Uranus in Aries), Allied Signal's Lawrence Bossidy (Venus and Uranus in Aries), and Apple's Steven Jobs (Mars in Aries).

Nevertheless, for all that they may occasionally seem to inhabit the personalities of other astrological types, Pisces leaders do have a unique and profound niche in the affairs of the world. For while "visionary" is a term used liberally in this and other analyses of great business leaders, no sign has a greater or purer collective claim on the word than does Pisces. Bringing imagination and intuition to bear on the macro-culture, Pisces are the inspired people who almost literally wake up one day and just flat out "get" the *universal* implications and possibilities of telephones (Alexander Graham Bell); television (David Sarnoff); Las Vegas (Bugsy Siegel); popular entertainment (David Geffen); ethnic marketing (Thomas Burrell); sports infatuation (Phil Knight); and personal computing (Steven Jobs); not to mention the likes of America (Washington) or E=MC² (Einstein).

In the light of a business leadership study, where directed motivation and high-minded concepts are typically held in great regard, it's worth noting that the personal histories of even the most accomplished Pisces are often tales of outsider personalities and directionless career meandering in which the Pisces protagonist eventually manages to stumble across destiny and illumination. Hardly atypical is a comment by billionaire entertainment impresario David Geffen: "I never went to business school. I was just bumbling through a lot of my life. I was like the guy behind the curtain in the Wizard of Oz." Or as Disney head Michael Eisner says of himself: "I was just kind of interested in existing. I didn't have major goals."

Fortunately, though, a bit of real wizard often tends to emerge in Pisces. By being open to the light of revelation, by having the capacity to at least sometimes admit the ephemeral nature of ego, by reigning in the driven executive's standard-issue assuredness about the way things should be, Pisces becomes uniquely receptive to the tides of the human collective and a bellwether for the cultural direction things are going to take. "I'm good at deciding what people will like," says Geffen, explaining the fundamental art of Pisces. "I'm gifted at knowing what will be a success before it is a success."

So it is that the Pisces personality, largely driven by that which is beyond logic and data, is not an easy thing to explain or account for. But you'll know it when it heralds, and possibly even cashes in on, a real change in the world.

PISCES LEADERS: VALUE STATEMENTS

Go East, Young Man

Anyone who grew up during the times when the Beatles dominated popular culture remembers that their Pisces lead guitarist George Harrison, " the quiet Beatle," introduced the group, and by extension much of the youth culture of the Western world, to eastern philosophy and spiritual practice. "Everything else can wait, but the search for God," said Harrison, explaining his journey on a path to transcendent peace and loving ego surrender. The point here is that even the most materialistic Pisces, even one who was reportedly as interested in financial affairs and self-promotion as George, knows what the ex-Beatle was talking about.

It's assuredly not an easy leap from the quest for spiritual purpose and enlightenment to the rigorous hard-edged demands the competitive marketplace, but the ability to perform such acrobatics is essential to understanding the foundations of much great Piscean success. Steven Jobs took the first "real" money from his Atari days and applied it toward a lengthy and life-altering spiritual pilgrimage to India. Phil Knight, founder of Nike, also traveled East as a young man and famously found both the Japanese religious culture and their method of shoe manufacture essential to his personal peace and prosperity.

Of course, the cynical might brush these things off as typical philosophical fancies of the young. But the truth is that for Pisces, iconically represented by the fish, the sense of life's embrace by an oceanic consciousness rarely fades in importance. Southwest Airlines founder Herb Kelleher, certainly one of the most admired executives in the world, is frequently glorified as "egoless" for placing all of the people in his world on a level plateau of human worth. Ditto, if not always so laudably, for the painfully shy Michael Dell, whose "two in a box" shared-responsibility executive strategy is a testament to the elevation of enterprise over the stroked ego.

What one gets from the best Pisces leaders is an awareness of life's collective vastness and limitless creative potential, along with an ironic appreciation of its infinite petty ego-driven attachments. As abstract as this may sound, there really is no better way to appreciate Louis Gerstner's contribution at IBM. His "solutions for a small planet," as IBM's Gerstner-era ad slogan went, meant integrating systems, connecting disparate data sources, and embracing the needs of customers, rather than jealously guarding the IBM technology patents. Similarly, one can learn much about the Pisces personality from the title of Monica Langley's biography of Citicorp's Sandy Weill, *Tearing Down the Walls* (New York: Free Press, 2003).

The universal Pisces perspective is ably addressed by RCA's David Sarnoff, arguably radio and television culture's most influential pioneer, who started out life as a Talmudic scholar with the intent of becoming a rabbi. In an obituary, the *New York Times* described Sarnoff as "a man of astounding vision who was able to see with remarkable clarity the possibilities of harnessing the electron." *Time* magazine described him as "nearly clairvoyant."

"It is with a feeling of humbleness" said Sarnoff upon the introduction of television at the 1939 New York World's Fair, "that I come to this moment of announcing the birth in this country of a new art so important in its implications that it is bound to affect all society. It is an art which shines like a torch of hope in the troubled world. It is a creative force which we must learn to utilize for the benefit of all mankind."

We may live in a material world, as George Harrison once recorded, but Pisces knows that hardly means we are chained to mundane options or petty personal destinies.

I Feel for You

In some ways the Pisces worldview is close to that of Aquarius, particularly in its future orientation and broad humanitarian concerns. Where there is a departure between the two signs, however, is that in the Aquarian scheme of things the prevailing insights are derived from an intelligent empirical consideration of the rightness of democratic values and processes. For Pisces, on the other hand, the emphasis tends to be on a nondogmatic psychological and emotional connectedness that frequently bypasses the brain and heads straight for the gut.

What is unique to the Pisces personality, swimming in all that oceanic consciousness, is its ability to tune into true and unvarnished emotions—not just of other individuals but of crowds. The Pisces gift is that of the elite actor or artist who triumphs not so much on the force of personality but who is rather a master at reading the emotional temperature of the room. Whether dealing with the public or the workforce, the Pisces leader is actually not so much acting as empathizing at a very deep level.

That an urge to pluck the emotional strings of the masses has a strong pull on Pisces is evidenced in many Pisces histories, including the rather eccentric. Benjamin "Bugsy" Siegel, a gangland killer who wanted to be nothing so much as a film actor, settled for being the creator and host of Las Vegas' first upscale casino, playing to the risqué titillations of the American dream. William "Buffalo Bill" Cody was a much decorated frontier scout who found his calling on the stage as the impresario of "The Wild West Show," a theatrical rodeo of fact and fancy that played well in the American East and Europe to a collective yearning for an untamed West that was rapidly morphing into civilization.

It's not a far step from these examples to that of Walter Annenberg, one of many famed Pisces entertainment moguls. Annenberg's connection to broad public sentiment is clearly apparent in his massive philanthropic work on behalf of public education and in his professional stewardship of such magazines as *TV Guide, Seventeen,* and the *Daily Racing Form.* His self-avowed greatest glory, however, was serving as Richard Nixon's ambassador to England, a largely ceremonial role he played with such style and cultural sensitivity and to such popular acclaim that Queen Elizabeth eventually knighted him.

Pisces empathy plays well in-house, too. One of the more memorable features of Louis Gerstner's IBM turnaround was the inclusion of a program called "Operation Bear Hug," in which IBM managers were sent out into the field on a regular basis to simply have face time with customers and build actual human relationships. And again, an enormous part of Southwest Airlines success stems from Herb Kelleher's understanding that a service business must be built on the subjugation of one's own self-importance, that success is the residue of sincerely relating to and helping others.

"When we talk to other people about Southwest Airlines," says Kelleher, "I always tell them it's got to come from the heart, not the head."

"Go for the gut, go for the emotions," readily concurs Disney's Michael Eisner.

"When somebody gets mad in the workplace, or somebody yells at you, or blames you for something," says Eisner, "maybe they're dealing with their own frustrations, their own sense of failure. And I think understanding that makes you a better manager. Therefore, I put up with a lot. I go for the talent and put up with a lot of peculiar behavior, none of which I judge, as long as the people are basically ethical and moral."

Truth Is in the Eye of the Beholder

It's always worth remembering that with Pisces one is dealing with people who tend to esteem the truths of the heart way over those of the head.

Certainly one great example of this in business is the rise of Nike under Phil Knight, the man reputed to have made more money from sports than anyone else in history. What Knight recognized far sooner than most was that sports was in the process of becoming an international obsession facilitated by modern communications technology, and that its champions were capable of inhabiting larger-than-life, wish-fulfillment personas that were far more mythic than mundane.

Michael Jordan and Tiger Woods may have some human shortcomings and merely mortal powers, for example, but you would never know that from a Nike commercial.

"Sports is like rock 'n roll," Knight once famously observed. "Both are dominant cultural forces, both speak an international language, and both are all about emotions."

One gets a similar sense of fact's embrace of fancy in the professional lives of the great populist media giants of Pisces heritage. Dorothy Schiff, Rupert Murdoch (curiously, Murdoch bought the *New York Post* from Schiff and both celebrate the same birthday), and Walter Annenberg all very much accepted the notion that a media outlet is every bit as much an extension of one's own belief system and a rallying post for general cultural undercurrents, as it is an organ for dispensing the unvarnished truth. The examples of emotion-fueled publishing decisions in the lives of the aforementioned are legion, but perhaps the neatest historical fact from an astrological perspective is that Walter Annenberg turned his fortune into one of the world's most important collections of Impressionist art.

"If it moved me that was enough," once said Annenberg about his collection."

It is a similar feeling that underlies much Pisces commentary about business in general. In the Pisces universe it is often the MBA rather than the artist who is most suspect. Truth to a Pisces is rarely as easy as summoning facts.

"I believe in the emotional and psychological side of life," says David Geffen, adding, "I think I'd rather have an English major than an economics major."

And even Lawrence Bossidy, famous for his edge and a near-brutal approach to cost containment during his years at Allied Signal and Honeywell, is on the record with the following advice for business aspirants: "Take at least some liberal arts courses."

Sometimes You Need to Be (or Hire) the Angel of Death

Lawrence Bossidy is just one of the Pisces names that tends to call forth feelings that are a bit short in the touchy-feely department. It's well and good to extol the Pisces connections to art, empathy, and universal consciousness, but with Bossidy you have an individual who unflinchingly chopped 20 percent of the Allied Signal workforce, fired any department head who fell short of goals two quarters in a row and, not without some irony, entitled his book of business wisdom *Execution* (New York: Crown Business, 2002). This is not to pick on Bossidy, because other Pisces leaders—for example Michael Dell, Louis Gerstner, Sandy Weill, Steve Jobs, David Geffen, and Rupert Murdoch—are also at least occasionally on the list of hard-hearted realists, who will attack and slash as necessary, and sometimes it would seem just for spite.

As has already been noted, some of the astrological explanation for this state of affairs is that the neighboring sign of Aries often has an influence on Pisces, and much of the peaceful Pisces sun sign nature can be overshadowed by the martial influence of close-by personal planets under the war god's influence. Additionally, empathy and sensitivity do not just confine themselves to the good vibrations, and one must not overlook the fact that a Pisces can be a conduit for a negative flow as easily as a positive one. Perhaps most importantly of all, however, sensitivity is a far cry from senselessness, and sometimes a CEO has got to do what a CEO has got to do.

Although some Pisces business leaders seem to take a perverse pleasure in planting the hatchet themselves, it is somewhat more typical for the Pisces leader to hold on to creative ideation functions for themselves and to hire "protection" when it comes to a broad sense of business accountability. While he could be rough and intimidating himself, Steve Jobs' Apple was sometimes referred to as "Camp

Runamok" until John Sculley came aboard to provide professional operations management. Similarly, Michael Dell has his Kevin Rollins, and Rupert Murdoch has his Fox chief, Roger Ailes.

About running a business generally, Murdoch has commented:

> You can't build a strong corporation with a lot of committees and a board that has to be consulted at every turn. You have to be able to make decisions on your own.

He also has observed that "too often you get a group of very brilliant Harvard MBAs in a company that are set up to study strategy or whatever, and it tends to slow things down." But then he turns his attention to the other side of the coin.

"When you say someone is a micromanager," Murdoch once commented about Ailes, "it sounds like a bad thing. But in Roger's case there is no limit to how much he can micromanage. The way he handles talent, the way he watches the costs, and the advertising and so on. He's really an outstanding executive."

It might be overstating things to brand Pisces as realists. What they do tend to be, at least regarding the big picture, are fatalists. With their enormous perspective they simply are inclined to understand that boundless freedom and assiduous control will inevitably take alternative (or even simultaneous) turns at the wheel, and also that things flourish for a while and then either undergo transformation or replacement, as is true for all things in creation. Patricia Woertz, the CEO of Archer Daniels Midland, speaks a true Pisces perspective when she observes, "Nothing is created without something being destroyed."

Similarly, as the late George Harrison noted in 1970 upon the breakup of the Beatles, on the best-selling solo album ever released by one of the Fab Four: "All things must pass." No matter how closely it is monitored or counted.

All You Need Is LUV

To the Pisces leader it is the vision that is sacred. Even if it is Michael Dell talking about efficiencies in the manufacturing process, or Edmund Pratt stressing the importance of an R&D pipeline, or Lawrence Bossidy hammering ruthlessly at the details that lead to a succession of enhanced quarterly reports, it is the battle to realize and perfect something conceived in the spirit that almost takes precedence over the results.

"I'm not doing this because I need or want to make another billion," said David Geffen upon the formation of Dreamworks SKG, "that would have no value. It's all in the doing, all in the journey."

"Believe me," RCA's David Sarnoff once observed, "the thrill is as much in the battle as in the victory."

The Pisces visionary spirit is in Steve Jobs, when he is as concerned with the design aesthetics of the latest Apple computer or the iPod as he is with their functions. It's in the understanding that, for the consumer, ease of use and the creative results of computation far outweigh the importance of the technology. It's embedded in Jobs' not-so-simple but all-encompassing observation, "I want to put a ding in the universe."

The visionary spirit is in Thomas Burrell, who fought his way up from the mailroom and helped a reluctant Madison Avenue understand that a black consumer is not the same as a white consumer. Burrell's vision resulted in a series of commercials for the likes of McDonald's and Coca-Cola that are just as popular with whites as they are with blacks. "Whites are easier to reach through Black advertising than vice versa," observes Burrell, and everyone wonders why they didn't think of that before.

Certainly the visionary spirit is in Herb Kelleher, who has set the airlines community on its ear by somewhat magically combining the pricing virtues of no-frills travel with a strong sense of human consideration and service. Kelleher likes to remind people that fiscal responsibility trumps flamboyance at his Southwest Airlines, but any of his employees will tell you that the true vision extends far beyond that.

"A company is stronger if it is bound by love rather than by fear," says Kelleher. And that's a pure Pisces perception.

✦ tips for dealing with pisces

- Always present a Pisces with an opportunity to empathize with your concerns. They are not necessarily bleeding hearts, but they do trust emotional connection.

- Understand that a Pisces is not faking heightened sensitivity. When this individual retreats, it is to seek peace. Do not follow them into the cave.

- Pisces place highest value on creativity and have high tolerance for an imaginative presentation of facts. But if they pay you to keep the books, errors will be counted as personal betrayals.

- *Hint*: Pisces tend to have very deep connections with their families, particularly with their mothers, who are often singled out as the sources of early inspiration and wisdom. If you ever have the opportunity to do something nice for a Pisces' mom, grasp the opportunity. It's more appreciated than if you did something nice for the Pisces themselves.

 part THREE

BUSINESS BEYOND
SUN SIGNS

 It is theory that decides what we can observe.

—Albert Einstein, quoted in *Physics and Beyond*

tHe LanɡuaɡE
of tHe staRs

I don't believe in astrology. I'm a Sagittarius and we're skeptical.

—Arthur C. Clarke, broadly attributed
and quoted on the Southern Methodist
University Department of Physics website

Now that you have had the chance to spend a few pages deep within your archetypal sun self, we have arrived at the point where an astrological education might begin in earnest. Ample resources are at one's disposal for such an undertaking, with Google hits numbering over a million each for "astrology classes" and "astrology teachers," and with "astrology books" clocking in at 2 million-plus. Suffice it to say, if it has not already been amply indicated in earlier chapters, a full instructional rendering of this complex topic would easily embrace a manuscript well longer than the one in hand, and is beyond the scope of this introduction. (Discretion here shall be along the lines of not providing too impossibly elaborate watch-making instructions for a busy individual who has simply stopped by to inquire the time.)

Even so it would seem perfunctory not to provide at least some sort of cosmic crib sheet for those who are tempted to ponder astrology further or are at least desirous of carrying on the orientation a bit longer. In this spirit Chapters 18 and 19 are intended to provide the business executive with a rudimentary business astrology lexicon and some basic interpretive factors that provide some of the conceptual basis of business astrology. If you are the type of leader who, having learned about sun signs, now wants to delve more deeply into this field, you might want to check out such excellent introductory books and terminology compendiums as Stephen Arroyo's *Chart Interpretation Handbook* (Sebastopol, Calif.: CRCS Publications, 1989) and Debbi Kempton-Smith's delightful *Secrets From A Stargazer's Notebook* (New York: Bantam Books, 1982), along with the reasonably accessible business-focused material in Madeline Gerwick's *Good Timing Guide* (Fulton, Calif.: Elite Books, 2007) and the helpfully titled *Business Astrology 101* (Pleasant Hill, Calif.: StarCycles Publishing, 2001) written by Georgia Anna Stathis.

Before proceeding, note that I have made a conscious decision not to include any diagrams, charts, symbols, or technical astrological notations in this work. Although they are all in fact vital to the efficient and comprehensive practice of the craft, they can easily be as distracting as they are helpful in what is meant to be a big picture conceptual overview. I can only ask forgiveness from the Virgos for not being overly rigorous about drilling down into the detritus and in not honoring their beloved chart fetish, and from everyone else for the inescapable whiff of credulity (guilty!) that must seep in over the next few sections.

So what is the easiest way to "get" the nomenclature and technique of astrological chart reading? Well, have you ever played the Parker Brothers board game *Clue*? Astrology readings are largely variations on the theme of Miss Scarlet, with the candlestick, in the ballroom.

Now it must be offered once again that astrology can be very, very complicated and we are only addressing its most basic techniques and principles here. As already alluded to throughout this book, business horoscope reading on the expert level can be like assembling a 50,000 piece jigsaw puzzle, with no guiding picture on the box, from double-sided pieces that need to be manipulated by tweezers, and that refuse to stay put once you've moved them. Yet while it is easy to disappear in an avalanche of tenuously interlocking temporal data and generous definitions, the essence of solving an astrological mystery really does boil down to a basic *Clue*-like matter of suspects (the Planets), weapons (the Signs) and crime scenes (the Houses).

tHe pLaNets

Planets are the essence of astrology, although by "planets" most astronomers categorically mean 'anything up there,' from moons to suns to asteroids to vast galactic nebulae, each with their own energy configuration and mythological status. (The deeper we see into space and the better our powers of computation become, incidentally, the more grist there is for the astrology mills.) Ultimately, though, it is the heavenly population of our good old solar system and its relational movements to Earth that drives the key insights of astrology.

Astrological interpretation establishes the planets as energies, or in a language sense as verbs. Without getting too far into linguistic weeds, it's useful to acknowledge that all things are ultimately made of energy, so that planets may also be seen as embodiments (nouns), whether of abstract concepts or actual things. Thus, in business the planets stand for any concrete or conceptually coherent expressions of commerce-oriented energy.

With Venus, for example, the principles of beauty, harmony, and value might literally mean money in the bank, or it could represent pleasing office aesthetics or the value of good team interaction. Venus can mean lots of other things, too, but the general principle surrounding the energy of Venus will be of some objectified action or principle that is pleasing and valuable to the business. In any chart, including a business chart,* Venus will identify the people, processes, and products that originate from the desires of the heart.

As indicated in Part One of this book, any astrological chart, or horoscope, is best understood as a snapshot of space at a particular instant in time from a specific point on Earth. In this snapshot, one records the astronomical position of the planets and any other astronomical bodies—most certainly including the Sun and Moon—that are deemed to have an energy influence by the chart interpreter. The exact placement of planets (energies) in signs (filters) and houses (domains of actions) is a bit trickier as these may be determined either by empirical observation of the sky, by mathematical averaging, or by various complex formulae that take in the irregularities of astronomical motion. By tradition, though, there will always be twelve signs and twelve houses in a traditional consecutive order, starting at a random point in the consecutive cycle dependent upon the portion of the sky on the eastern horizon, or ascendant, at the moment the "photograph" is taken. The placement of planets in particular signs or houses can be managed to one's business advantage, as has been suggested in Chapter 2, through the creation of "electional" charts that try to capture auspiciously placed planetary positions for the matter at hand.

---

*The term "business chart" may still be vague to some readers at this point. It may help to keep in mind that astrology is the study of time and the portents ingrained within any specific moment. Thus while a business chart is frequently created for the moment when a business is incorporated (given legal status) or when it completes its first sales transaction, there is technically nothing that cannot be timed or given significant temporal status. The moment of an important new hire, the media launch of an ad campaign, the opening of a new unit, the purchase of a competitor, the redecoration of the lobby, or a name change are just some of the events for which a business chart would be instructive.

Along these lines, and very generally, the business principles represented by the Sun, Moon, and eight planets are:

- *Sun:* Anything of primary importance to the business existence (Identity)
- *Moon:* Anything that's an investment in people, either material or emotional (Security)
- *Mercury:* Anything that is dependent upon interpersonal communications (Process)
- *Venus:* Anything that is generally pleasing and enhances value (Heart)
- *Mars:* Anything that there is a great inherent drive to do (Action)
- *Jupiter:* Anything that expands fortune beyond previously assumed boundaries (Vision)
- *Saturn:* Anything emphasizing principle and policy in the aid of long-term success (Time)
- *Uranus:* Anything built upon event-driven adaptation for the greater good (Change)
- *Neptune:* Anything that is intuitive rather than fact-based, for good or bad (Spirit)
- *Pluto:* Anything predicated on the principle of transformational power (Will)

In addition to the above, perhaps the greatest appreciation of the planets in business horoscopes comes as a result of embodying the planetary energies in the form of iconic personalities, and here we mean anyone in the organization chart from the CEO to the stock clerk. Whether in an electional chart for a new business in which various key roles may be assigned, or in the charts of vested companies where roles may be identified on the basis of ongoing influence and practice, the iconic identification of staff is a human resources bonanza. What one encounters is a useful articulation of roles that, for better or worse, tend to be embraced by players independent of job descriptions. So it is that in any work situation there may be:

- *Sun:* **The Monarch** (usually the CEO, unless weak or absent)
- *Moon:* **The Caregiver** (anyone who makes the welfare of others—often their superiors—their prime directive; also pertains to those who feel they are protecting the company from heresy)
- *Mercury:* **The Thinker** (data processors and communicators, technical types, and sales talkers)
- *Venus:* **The Peacemaker** (consensus seeker looking for harmony and value; sometimes places peace above action)
- *Mars:* **The Warrior** (irritating but indefatigable and invaluable, the action taker)
- *Jupiter:* **The Sage** (the big idea person, tends to both spend and to attract luck)
- *Saturn:* **The General** (traditional authority; often associated with senior executives and anyone with real long-term experience who counsels a vested approach)
- *Uranus:* **The Wizard** (the genius, sometimes found in R&D but most always likely to be a surprise; a change maker)
- *Neptune:* **The Dreamer** (inspired, sometimes out of it and sometimes all-knowing; often very useful as a bellwether)
- *Pluto:* **The Executioner** (pure passion; can make anything happen but is often difficult to supervise)

Actually, for symbolic reasons that may now be apparent, it is somewhat traditional to identify the Sun or Saturn in a business chart as the CEO, but it's not really that simple. From the boss's perspective, all these planets may be extensions or requirements of a single leadership personality. From the perspective of the organization, though, any planetary placement may represent an individual who is in *de facto* control—for example, the totally informed executive assistant (Mercury) who really runs the show, or the ad agency creative dreamer (Neptune) who gets it right almost all of the time and whose work really does drive sales.

the signs

Behavioral clarification comes by taking the personalities and cosmically assigning them weapons or, more benignly, values-based tools and tactics (signs). It may help to note that astrology tends to see the signs as lenses that modify the planetary energies that pass through them. Whatever the semantics, whether The General (Saturn), for example, is inclined to lead through logical tactics and efficient systems (Virgo) or through massive epiphanies (Sagittarius), he always remains The General.

As this may be more than you care or need to know, let's just stipulate that there are weapons/tools/tactics (signs) wielded by the personalities (planets). The key business characteristics of the signs are:

- *Aries:* Direct action
- *Taurus:* Resource allocation
- *Gemini:* Information flow
- *Cancer:* Emotional manipulation
- *Leo:* Creative charisma
- *Virgo:* Systems integrity
- *Libra:* Consensus building
- *Scorpio:* Power plays
- *Sagittarius:* Epic epiphanies
- *Capricorn:* Traditional hierarchies

- *Aquarius:* Cultural invention
- *Pisces:* Oceanic consciousness

the houses

Houses speak to the Earth's rotation, and the constantly changing orientation of any spot on Earth to the belt of zodiac signs in the sky. With the 1st house calculated from the eastern horizon (or ascendant) at the instant of an event, the houses are a construct of twelve contiguous background slices of sky that are best understood as the screens on which the energy of the planets and the filtering qualities of the signs are projected. They are extremely valuable in business chart interpretations as they indicate "where" in the enterprise the embodied energies (planets) and the tactics (signs) are primarily being brought to bear.

At this point, as an example, we can calculate that a business chart with the planet Pluto (powerful transformational intent) in the sign of Gemini (information flow) will likely be indicative of a business marked by strong-willed, likely confrontational communications. Add a house—say the 7th house, which traditionally stands for partnership matters—and one can easily imagine a situation in which business partners are very confrontational in their interpersonal communications, with each constantly attempting to argue the other into a submissive position.

Rather disconcertingly, exact house placements can be affected by a difference of just a few minutes in some houses' systems, and astrologers are even more widely divided over the calculation of houses than they are of signs. Although some of their differences are arcane and minute, others can have a very meaningful impact on chart placements. A few of the most influential astrologers even go so far as to do without a strong commitment to houses, relying on the cardinal points (these are marginally akin to true north, south, east and west but are more celestially oriented) for all the interpretive orientation they require.

Most astrologers do use houses, though, whatever the precise system for their calculation. Although they won't necessarily agree on the houses in which the planets will fall, there is reasonably consistent agreement on what the houses signify. Some of the key business interpretations of the houses are:

- *1st House:* Owners/stockholders, public face of the company, name and general reputation
- *2nd House:* Liquid assets, investments, developable talent
- *3rd House:* Communication functions, training materials, office milieu, local transactions
- *4th House:* Base of operations, real estate and capital facilities, heritage policies
- *5th House:* Creative departments, meetings and conventions, celebrations, and amusements
- *6th House:* General workforce issues and conditions, human resources, the daily grind
- *7th House:* All relationship activities, including partners, competitors, and customers
- *8th House:* Situations dependent upon the assets of others (loans, credit, competitor strategy and vulnerability, sales)
- *9th House:* Philosophy, brand building and marketing, long-distance transactions
- *10th House:* Internal and external leadership activities and conditions, public rank
- *11th House:* Group alliances, role in society, innovative capacity, intangible value
- *12th House:* Proprietary information and trade secrets, unsuspected conditions

As all the planets, all the signs, and all the houses appear in every chart, one begins to apprehend both the beguilement and the difficulty of the interpretive task. Even at this point, however, key components are missing. For it is virtually impossible to determine the essence of a chart without considering the relationship of the points in the chart to one another and, just as significantly, factoring in the ongoing passage of time.

aspects and transits

So let's assume that we are looking at a business chart of a small retail company, calculated for the moment of its first merchandise sale. In this hypothetical chart the planet Uranus (The Wizard) is in the sign of Capricorn (hierarchical imperatives) in the 9th house (marketing). In this company one might expect to encounter a brilliant marketing plan, given considerable organizational prominence, at least by those involved with its execution.

Now consider that this same company chart may also have its Moon (The Caregiver) in the sign of Libra (consensus building) in the 6th house (the general workforce). In such a company, one might easily encounter an emotional argument that fairness depends on considering everyone's opinion. This, as I hardly need to point out, is likely to create some conflict with the marketing department geniuses, who have assumed a fair amount of authority and aren't really inclined to put their brilliance up to some sort of popular vote.

The tension between the two energies in this hypothetical chart is described in astrology as an *aspect*, in this case one called a *square*. While there are many possible aspects in a chart, and many rules about distance and direction pertaining to them, most astrologers classify the following as "major" aspects:

- *Conjunctions.* Planets are at the same point in the chart. Energies are combined.
- *Sextiles.* Planets are 60 degrees apart. Energies create opportunities. (This aspect incidentally shows up with remarkable frequency in landmark business events, some of which are explored in depth in this book's appendix.)
- *Squares.* Planets are 90 degrees apart. Energies operate at cross-purposes.
- *Trines.* Planets are 120 degrees apart. Energies flow easily.
- *Oppositions.* Planets are 180 degrees apart. Energies are in direct conflict.

Aspect interplay gives the chart a sense of dynamism. What considerably enhances this sense of energy flow is the fact that the planets in the sky are constantly moving on in their merry orbits, thereby going into and out of aspect with the planets in the original chart. When a planet moving in the sky forms an aspect with the position of any planet in the original chart, this describes a *transit*.

To return to our original example, let's postulate that the planet Jupiter (which represents expansiveness and, often, good fortune) passes over the Moon position in the company chart, forming a conjunction to the Moon and a square to Uranus. Under such a circumstance one might foresee a situation in which general workforce "feelings" regarding the marketing strategy, although a considerable irritant to the aristocratic marketing geniuses, actually result in a beneficial contribution to the marketing effort. Saturn (representing tradition and authority) passing over that same Moon position, on the other hand, could indicate a severe executive admonition to the Caregiver personality to mind her own departmental business. This allows The Wizard a victory but at the price of emotional estrangement from the individual, who is, astrologically speaking on the basis of energy type and house position, likely the company's very popular HR director.

Chapter 19 takes the principles introduced in this chapter and somewhat rigorously applies them to the specific tasks of brand building and marketing, concluding with some actual historical examples of the astrological process in action. This is done, quite admittedly, because people involved with marketing are far more likely to be openminded about astrological analysis than, say, those involved with accounting. This, by the way, is an observation not a judgment, and even an astrologer can recognize why the financial temperament bias towards cold hard numbers and away from mythological archetypes is probably a darn good thing.

In this light, what is rightfully remarked upon and reiterated here is that astrology, for all the technical expertise and exacting detail that must be employed in its practice, is ultimately a storyteller's medium. Sound detection and deductive processes help, but mastery is in large part a matter of imagination and intuition.

Have you ever played the Parker Brothers board game *Clue?*

seLLiNG BY tHe staRs
Astrology and Marketing

> *Your brand personality should be an accurate representation*
> *of your company; otherwise you're creating a brand*
> *relationship that's based on someone else's personality.*
>
> —Mike Moser, *United We Brand*

The marketing function is in turmoil at this point in business history. Competition is unprecedented, consumers refuse to coalesce into large easily identifiable categories, and every human being with a battery pack is now an empowered media maven. The industry wrings its hands over dead marketing models and increasingly turns to the consumer via customer-generated content and buzz marketing to do the work that was once done by professionals.

In the midst of this scenario, which desperately calls for brilliance and true outside-the-box thinking, the marketing function is increasingly laced into the straitjacket of metrics. Never mind that the marketing function—when allowed to operate on its natural principles of curiosity, courage, creativity, capaciousness, and joy (yes, joy)—may bring an overarching, if only vaguely measurable, wisdom to the relationship between seller and buyer. A marketer who today doesn't come up with a precise and pedantic measurement of contribution to profit is a marketer out of a job.

Astrology, of course, has an explanation for this. It is "simply" that everyone born in the years between 1958 and 1971 was born while the planet Pluto (despite its recent astronomical downgrade, still the symbol of all irresistible power and a remarkably useful generational marker) was passing through the astrological sign of Virgo. Thus, this entire cohort group, today increasingly in control of things, has a passion for tasks and data and precise formulas and engineered solutions and measurement, with little predilection for embracing the fact that life is quite often just one big screwball comedy.

As capricious as this analysis may sound, there's little denying that it is the Pluto-in-Virgo generation that has burrowed and bunkered deeply into The Age of Information. Deep inside they just *know* that inspiration and personal charisma and a desire to be entertained and emotionally fulfilled—the hallmarks of the Pluto-in-Leo generation that preceded them—are untrustworthy attributes at best and represent a perverse form of personality idolatry at worst. Pluto-in-Virgo people do not often set goals on the basis of what they feel in their gut, and are hardly above sarcastically categorizing those that do as doddering or stupid.

The problem for business in this scenario is that marketing is being directed to find the consumer's soul with a microscope and a scalpel. The contention here is that it may be far more productive to search for that soul with a toy magnifying glass and a rubber knife. Or maybe even with astrology.

As addressed in Chapter 18, the basic tools of astrological analysis are planets, signs, and houses. In the case of the marketing function, these can be broadly summarized as *product, pitch,* and *target,* all to be explored via astrological terminology in this chapter. As is relentlessly the case with astrology, these categories and the particulars within are hardly chiseled to didactic perfection, but even a Pluto-in-Virgo soul might accept that there is at least the appearance of a comprehensive and rigorous framework to guide even the vaguest and flightiest of astrological assertions.

Again, as in all practical applications of astrology, the central artifact is the chart representation of planet, sign, and house placements calculated at the moment of "birth." Whether one is analyzing a chart for the marketing particulars of a company or campaign already in existence or selecting an auspicious moment to create an electional chart for a launch, there is legitimate debate over the appropriate "birth" moment. The general business milestones already cited—i.e., incorporation, business opening, and first sale—are always useful, but in the case of marketing one may also gain considerable interpretive utility out of the first public announcement of a new product or service and/or the first media appearance of a new campaign. These last two factors are additionally attractive for the relative flexibility they allow in the creation of an electional chart.

Specific interpretive factors will be explored at considerable length throughout the rest of the chapter, but a brief hypothetical example may be of some use:

John is an auto mechanic (auto mechanics are primarily under the energy influence of Mercury, so it becomes the key planetary symbol in John's marketing chart) who plans to first advertise his business when the planet Mercury (which also represents communication) is transiting the sign of Leo (messages having to do with personal satisfaction) in the 8th House (markets comprising people who tend to approach everything as a battle and test of wills). A kindly astrologer, sensing the difficulty that John might have selling personal satisfaction in auto maintenance to people who love to fight, points John to a slightly later alternative first advertising date, when Mercury is passing through Virgo (messages having to do with error-free and efficient service) in the 4th House (markets in which family concerns, such as the family car, are a top emotional priority). John has been given a meaningful message and context, and has probably been spared a lot of grief, so he cheerfully pays his astrologer.

Some complex examples of high profile, real-world product launches are included at the end of this chapter, but that's really all there is to it in a nutshell. It's okay to think of it as a game, as the gift of the stars to marketing is in the contemplation of meaning rather than the proof. And if you remain a Pluto-in-Virgo person who is offended by the mere mention of all of this, I hope you have at least been persuaded to come after the author with only a rubber knife.

pLanets: pRoDucts anD seRvices

The planetary energies represent the products or services being sold, on both the concrete and the abstract core-characteristics levels. If one markets cosmetics, for example, one would pay particular attention to the planet Venus as the principle of beauty and as the so-called ruler of beauty products, and to Neptune as the principle of glamour and as the "ruler" of products dependent upon creating illusions. By the same token, however, one would look to Venus and Neptune in the chart of any product or service, to discover *how* (the sign) and *where* (the house) the factors of beauty and glamour are most likely to be communicated and reflected. For example, a high performance car might be essentially a Mars object, but its aesthetic appeal will still be reflected by Venus and Neptune and the signs and houses in which they are located at the moment of first marketing.

Sun
- Things that make an individual feel *important, individuated,* and *alive.*
- Activities concerned with vitality, personal flattery, individuality, and ambition.

- Personal recognition services and events, talent competitions, risk pursuits such as gambling and competitive sports, adventure excursions, high-visibility luxury goods and services, diamonds and gold (bling).

Moon
- Things that make an individual feel *nurtured, safe,* and *included.*
- Activities concerned with domesticity, care taking, clan connections, child rearing, emotional fulfillment, traditional motherhood roles.
- Personal insurance, kitchens, comfort food, housing and home-care products, patriotic products, vested membership groups and related paraphernalia, family dramas, and sitcoms.

Mercury
- Things that make an individual feel *informed, involved, amused,* and *helped.*
- Activities involving opt-in communication and instruction, "bulletin board" material, neighborhood buzz, getting around town, and community-based goods and services.
- Local and personal-interest periodicals, telephones, instant and text messaging, local schools and learning centers, automobiles as local transportation, the neighborhood bar and grill, local shops, artisans, and amusements.

Venus
- Things that make an individual feel *comfortable, beautiful, and loved.*
- Activities involving romance, partnership, happy social gather-ings, personal and environmental decoration, pleasure pursuits, and attractive hard-asset investments.
- Products and services generally classified as "feminine," partnership-oriented recreation and travel, the arts and

architecture, relaxation products and destinations, friendly-competition venues, valuable collections, and almost anything having to do with fashion.

Mars

- Things that make an individual feel *vigorous, daring,* and *potent.*
- Activities involving confrontation and competition, stamina and strength, the principle of aggression.
- Products and services generally classified as masculine, high-performance vehicles, martial organizations and activities, contact sports and paraphernalia, things made of iron and steel, spicy foods, and most modern video games.

Jupiter

- Things that make an individual feel *satiated, happy*, and *wise.*
- Activities involving joy and abundance, philosophical and social truths, valuable manifestations that are "foreign" or "lucky" in origin, the twin principles of heartfelt charity and guiltless personal indulgence.
- Products and services characterized by representation to enlightened subscribers, idea-based institutions, superior products and services deriving from international experiences and sources; long-distance travel, cheerful indulgences, and anything predicated upon an open mind, honesty, and humor.

Saturn

- Things that make an individual feel *mature, responsible,* and *enduring.*
- Activities involving long-term goals and ambitions, anything related to work and career management; the principles of stability, patience, and sacrifice; and traditional fatherhood roles.

- Products and services that emphasize making good use of time and resources, all things related to a mature audience, career counseling and materials, conservative long-term insurance and investments, retirement planning, utilities, and serious status objects.

Uranus

- Things that make an individual feel *inventive, iconic,* and *wired.*
- Activities involving the sudden expression of originality within a vested cultural context, the broad-based transmission of entertainment and ideas, and the principles of cultural benefaction and behavioral inventiveness.
- The products and services of the computer age, major media platforms, large populist-targeted political-social-cultural organizations and events, all "new and improved" advances and breakthroughs, and radical and counter-culture products and enterprises that develop mass appeal.

Neptune

- Things that make an individual feel *mysterious, glamorous,* and *illuminated.*
- Activities involved with artistic and spiritual expression, the operation of faith and belief in one's life, the capacity for producing and experiencing the inexplicable, the creation of powerful illusions.
- Faith-based institutions, metaphysical products and services, drugs and alcoholic beverages, escapist entertainment, fantasy retreats, and anything capitalizing upon the lure of the mysterious and the unknown.

Pluto

- Things that make an individual feel *torqued, terrified,* and *transformed.*
- Activities involved with the pursuit and expression of absolute power, matters and methodologies that rise above a consideration of society's rules and consequences, matters of life and death, and the principle of domination that verges on destruction.
- Anything capable of transforming the world without the world's express cooperation or permission: cancer, poison, terrorists, WMDs, war, HIV, gangbangers, corrupt politicians, global warming, tsunamis, sexual predators, meth labs, werewolves, the living dead, nuclear weapons. (A little Pluto goes a long way, even though more sanguine astrologers like to invoke the principle that death inevitably comes before rebirth. In any event, Pluto will frequently be "active" in the charts of "games" and "entertainments" dealing with the aforementioned matters, and in the nightmare charts of everyone else. Maybe the astronomical demotion of Pluto to dwarf planet is a blessing, unless we've really ticked it off in the process.)

SIGNS: PITCH AND PERCEPTION

The keywords encapsulated by the signs may prove valuable in two regards. First, they are useful as a set of descriptors that can provide a values-based context to the perception of products and services, again either by chance or design. Second, these descriptors can also have value in indicating an effective tone for engaging customers of the various sun signs. This is particularly true for those companies that do extensive CRM projects that include birthday recognition, and for those sales and counseling professionals engaged in one-on-one selling situations who can get a peak at the client's date of birth.

In either case we are in the area of the communication of brand attributes. Marketing luminary Mike Moser, in his essential work *United We Brand* (Cambridge, Mass.: Harvard Business Press, 2003), speaks of *brand personality,* which he describes as "the tone and attitude your organization is going to use to deliver your core brand message." The signs can be most helpful as a concept and tactics catalyst in this regard.

Here follows a list of keywords encapsulated by each of the twelve signs:

Aries

- *Tone:* Energetic, lively, spicy
- *Selling Point:* Trend setting, brand new, fast and powerful, youthful
- *Pitch Phrase:* "Act today . . ."
- *Hint:* The early bird gets the worm
- *Avoid:* Understatement

Taurus

- *Tone:* Concrete, calm, discretely sensuous
- *Selling Point:* Luxurious, dependable, enduring, stable
- *Pitch Phrase:* "Its value will only increase . . ."
- *Hint:* You *can* judge a book by its cover if it's covered in leather
- *Avoid:* Verbosity

Gemini

- *Tone:* Clever, neighborly, wryly amusing
- *Selling Point:* Interesting, multi-purpose, convenient
- *Pitch Phrase:* "And that's not all . . ."

- *Hint:* Might trade Manhattan for $24-worth of genuinely amusing trinkets
- *Avoid:* Certainty

Cancer

- *Tone:* Nurturing, emotionally connected, concerned
- *Selling Point:* Safe, secure, affordable
- *Pitch Phrase:* "The whole family will love it . . ."
- *Hint:* Smiles are really no substitutes for umbrellas
- *Avoid:* Aloofness

Leo

- *Tone:* Dramatic, flirty, flattering
- *Selling Point:* Essential, exciting, complete
- *Pitch Phrase:* "Satisfaction guaranteed . . ."
- *Hint:* This is a cat we're talking about: think scratching posts and satin pillows
- *Avoid:* Seller self-importance

Virgo

- *Tone:* Detailed, pragmatic, smart, natural
- *Selling Point:* Time-saving, error-free, customizable features
- *Pitch Phrase:* "Leading experts agree . . ."
- *Hint:* "All things being equal" is not an acceptable premise
- *Avoid:* Superficiality

Libra

- *Tone:* Charming, fair-minded, socially inclusive
- *Selling Point:* Peer popularity, stylishness, attractiveness
- *Pitch Phrase:* "Well-balanced . . ."
- *Hint:* If three choices are good, two are better
- *Avoid:* Vulgarity

Scorpio

- *Tone:* Sexy, edgy, dark
- *Selling Point:* Dangerous, deep, power-enhancing
- *Pitch Phrase:* "If you dare . . ."
- *Hint:* If you can't offer up a blood sacrifice, a discount will also be appealing
- *Avoid:* Confrontation

Sagittarius

- *Tone:* Upbeat, broad-minded, insightful
- *Selling Point:* Variety, scope, growth potential
- *Pitch Phrase:* "Universally acknowledged as . . ."
- *Hint:* Life is an international buffet, but tonight's dinner may come from a box
- *Avoid:* Provincialism

Capricorn

- *Tone:* Cool, competent, classy
- *Selling Point:* Well-crafted, status-conferring, classic
- *Pitch Phrase:* "Previously successful clients . . ."
- *Hint:* Go to the head of the class
- *Avoid:* Informality

Aquarius

- *Tone:* Media-friendly, bright, inventive
- *Selling Point:* State-of-the-art, brilliant features, socially responsible
- *Pitch Phrase:* "Timely as tomorrow . . ."
- *Hint:* You can't fool all of the people all of the time, especially Aquarians
- *Avoid:* Predictability

Pisces

- *Tone:* Soft-core, empathic, inspirational
- *Selling Point:* Artistic, intoxicating, sanctuary-like
- *Pitch Phrase:* "It will make your spirit soar . . . "
- *Hint:* Whose reality are we talking about?
- *Avoid:* Sharp edges

HOUSES: market targets

As has already been noted, it is necessary to know the exact time that an action is initiated in order to know where the planets are situated in the twelve houses. Although this is not so much a problem in building an electional chart (house positions change completely every two hours) it does effect the analysis of already existing events in which only the date, and not the specific time of initiation is known. Rectification of charts, the calculation of a chart based on past events and manifest personality factors rather than knowledge of a specific date or time, is an activity that astrologers sometimes take on behalf of clients in order to clarify planetary house placements.

With regard to marketing, houses can actually or symbolically signify the cohort group being marketed to, as well as the primary sphere of product or service usage. Broad demographic formatting is the more challenging of the two, but most astrologers are in agreement that the houses at least represent progressive age/life-stage phases. Again, keep in mind that astrology is a language of esoteric symbols; it's not likely that fixed annuities (Saturn) are going to be easily sold in the 3rd House (early childhood), or that the latest shooter video game (Mars) will be happily represented in the 4th House (family connections). However, the gift of astrological perception is being able to comprehend that sometimes such ill-fitting unions are the very nature of the thing that must be ascertained, addressed, and/or accomplished.

Here are the consumer attributes and interest areas one may find represented by each of the houses:

1st House

- *Principle*: The projection of one's inherent nature
- *Life-stage*: Birth, including all lifelong natal characteristics
- *Spheres:* The body (especially face and head), the personality, one's self-opinion
- *Where:* Exteriors, high impact areas, early morning

2nd House

- *Principle*: Developable talents and resources
- *Life-stage*: Infancy, including all natural aptitudes and material advantages
- *Spheres*: The ears and throat, material possessions, earning power
- *Where:* Treasure troves, indulgent environments, authentic displays and collections

3rd House

- *Principle*: Thought and communication
- *Life-stage*: Early childhood, including speech development and first schooling/socialization
- *Spheres:* The chest and lungs, the neighborhood universe, affordable transportation
- *Where:* Community clubs and hang-outs, biking and walking places, public schools and bookstores

4th House

- *Principle*: Emotional connectedness
- *Life-stage*: Childhood, including recognition of family role and dynamics
- *Spheres:* The stomach and breasts, the home, one's received (vs. free will) associations
- *Where*: The family kitchen, safes and safe places, restricted communities

5th House

- *Principle*: Creativity, fun, and adventure
- *Life-stage*: Late adolescence and the teen years, including first independence
- *Spheres:* The heart, the high school stage, the playing fields of youth
- *Where*: Neon nightlife scenes, high adrenalin venues, romantic escape destinations

6th House

- *Principle*: Purification, service, and self-improvement
- *Life-stage*: Child-adult transition, including first mature work responsibility
- *Spheres:* The lower digestive tract, natural settings, workshops
- *Where*: Health-oriented venues, jobs at staff level, service organizations

7th House

- *Principle*: Discretionary personal relationships, cooperation, and competition
- *Life-stage*: Early adulthood, including traditional engagement period

- *Spheres:* The flanks and lower back, arbitration and alliance enterprises, peace activism
- *Where:* Attractive social venues, restorative exercise and retreat venues, late afternoon larks and gatherings

8th House

- *Principle*: Life and death confrontations, profound tests of will
- *Life-stage*: The late-twenties, including (male) physical peak
- *Spheres:* The genitalia, bloody battlegrounds, transformative and regenerative enterprises
- *Where*: "The street," operating rooms, places where savings and souls are at risk

9th House

- *Principle*: Broad experience and wisdom
- *Life-stage*: Early maturity, including recognition of life philosophy
- *Spheres:* Leg muscles, where deep understanding is experienced, global enterprise
- *Where*: Courts, colleges, spiritual centers, places of cultural exchange
  (Note: This is where astrologers most often locate *marketing* itself.)

10th House

- *Principle*: Status and leadership
- *Life-stage*: Adulthood, including child-rearing and career activity peak
- *Spheres:* The leg joints, the place of authority, self-directed success or failure
- *Where*: The boss's office, upscale facilities, subordinate counseling environments

11th House

- *Principle*: Valued associations and group fulfillment
- *Life-stage*: "Middle age," including awareness of broad social purpose
- *Spheres:* The nervous system, the (social) laboratory, networks
- *Where*: Mass media, mass gatherings, public spirited clubs and campaigns

12th House

- *Principle*: Culmination and self-undoing
- *Life-stage*: Old age, including surrender to the beyond
- *Spheres:* Feet and toes, the unseen and the unconscious, any realm defined as oceanic
- *Where*: Places of remove and retirement, places of spiritual or alien contact, mysterious places of personal completion

HISTORICAL examples

The following actual marketplace events are astrologically interesting, although they are all admittedly analyzed after the fact. The dates are verified by at least two sources, but it is not always easy to determine the exact moment of "birth;" therefore, in a number of cases the discussion of House placements is kept to a minimum or dispensed with altogether. Also, while each of these events is obviously considered on more than the "beginner" level of astrology, each is also actually open to much deeper and alternative analysis. The aim here is mainly to offer some representative chart dynamics that may help illustrate the kind of conceptual thinking that astrology may bring to the marketing discussion.

Chanel No. 5—Introduction: May 5, 1921, time unknown—Paris, France

■ Venus (perfume as beauty) is in Aries (something new). Neptune (perfume as glamorous illusion) is in Leo (self-esteem). Coco Chanel launched an entirely new era in perfume with this first major synthetically enhanced perfume designed to "reflect personality" by contrasting a woman's natural beauty with something artificial and abstract rather than something authentically and entirely floral.

■ Jupiter (wisdom) is in Virgo (pragmatic expression) and is in opposition (conflict and change) to Uranus (mass appeal) in Pisces (intoxication). Both of these are square (dynamic differences) to Pluto (sexuality) in Cancer (deep emotions). Again, the crafting of the first major perfume to rely on synthetic aldehydes and animal gland fixatives pitted the classic understanding of perfume against its popular conception as floral intoxication. The double square to Pluto, called a T-square, indicates that the conflict between Jupiter (a new concept) and Uranus (mass appeal) is resolved by a product that is, in essence, an emotionally intense (Cancer) aphrodisiac (Pluto).

Note: The original formula of the perfume contained natural civet gland excretions, which are no longer used. Marilyn Monroe, who was also born with Venus in Aries and Neptune in Leo, is given much credit for Chanel No. 5's popularity, on one occasion declaring it was "the only thing" she wore to bed.

Crest Toothpaste—American Dental Association Endorsement: August 1, 1960, 9 A.M. CDT (est.)—Chicago, IL

■ Venus (toothpaste as a cosmetic) is conjunct (power combination) Uranus (mass appeal and technical advancement) in Leo (self-satisfaction) in the 12th House (hidden undoing, e.g., microscopic bacteria). Clearly here is a credible astrological signature of a technically enhanced popular cosmetic product that makes people feel good about their personal image while combating tooth decay.

▪ Moon (mother) in Scorpio (threatening) is in the 3rd House (early childhood) trine (harmonious flow). Mercury (communication) is in Cancer (protection) in the 11th House (valuable allies). Crest corporate parent P&G could simply not have come up with a more astrologically on-target campaign than the Norman Rockwell, kid-centric, "Look, Mom—No Cavities!" Interestingly, the ad copy speaks of its effectiveness for all members of the family, "including children of all ages."

Note: Crest was the #4 toothpaste brand prior to the ADA action. Afterwards, Crest sales more than tripled in the next two years, securing a leading 37-percent market share.

ESPN, *SportsCenter*—First Broadcast Day: September 7, 1979, 6 P.M. EDT—Bristol, CT

▪ Mars (sports) is in Cancer (emotional fan connection—think "home team") in the 5th House (fun), and is trine (harmonious flow) Uranus (mass appeal) in Scorpio (heavy confrontation) in the 9th House (universal principles). Here an enjoyable rooting connection to sports is successfully morphed into universal life and death significance by popular mass media.

▪ Sun (life force), Venus (social and aesthetic principles), and Saturn (authority/longevity) are conjunct (power combination) in Virgo (efficiently-rendered detail) in the 7th House (competition). All three of these Planets are also sextile (opportunity) both Mars (action) and Uranus (television). The sports/mass appeal connection is opportunistically affected by a data-intense message embodying strong identity, social connectivity, pleasing aesthetics, action, and authority.

Note: At 30,000-plus unique episodes, *SportsCenter* is the most prolific show in the history of television. There has never been a day since its inception, including 9/11, that at least one edition of the show has not aired.

Apple iPod—Introduction: October 23, 2001, 9 A.M. PST (est.)—Cupertino, Calif.

- Mercury (opt-in communication device) is conjunct (power combination) Venus (popular music) in Libra (social and aesthetic attractiveness). Mercury and Venus form a trine (harmonious flow) to Saturn (status object and management) in Gemini (clever amusements) and also form a sextile (opportunity) to Pluto (transformation) in Sagittarius (broad scope). Again the stars give a pretty decent product description. The three developmental principles of iPod are fast downloads, easy music organization and aesthetic appeal—all amply reflected in the introduction chart. The opportunistic relation to Pluto suggests the device's "world changing" potential.

- The iPod's signature Mercury and Venus are square (dynamic differences) to Jupiter (breadth) in Cancer (the clan). This may indicate that at its introduction the iPod could only download music from an Apple computer, thereby excluding 95 percent of the potential market.

Note: The iPod is immediately popular but sales don't skyrocket until the iPod mini is introduced on January 6, 2004. There are numerous exact interactions between the iPod chart and the launch chart of the iPod Mini. The Mini chart has Venus (enhancement) in Aquarius (a popular technological breakthrough) exactly on the Uranus (technology) of the iPod chart. At the same time, however, the Mini sun (expression of purpose) is closely square (dynamic differences) with the signature iPod Mercury and Venus conjunction.

One of the criticisms leveled at the new Mini is that its relatively high price and smaller storage capacity make it hard to come to a satisfactory purchasing decision.

McDonald's—Opening Day: April 15, 1955, 10:30 A.M. CST (est.)—Des Plaines, Ill.

■ The McDonald's chart, here taken out of temporal order, boasts an astonishing number of complex and compelling multiplanetary aspects, as one might expect from an enormously influential agent of cultural change. Many concepts barely rumored in this book (grand trines, grand crosses, mutual receptions, midpoint trees) are relevant in this instance; frankly, to pick only a few observations seems to give short shrift to all that is available here. Themes most definitely indicated are the birth of a food system for an automobile culture (Sun and Mercury in Aries, as well as Mars in Gemini), the challenge to a traditional idealized type of dining (Neptune in Libra), and the emergence of a radically new and globally popular family dining surrogate (Jupiter and Uranus conjunct in Cancer); all of this in vital aspect interaction, all linked to a host of other business considerations from cash flow to clowns to charity contributions, and all imbued with rare and statistically anomalous cosmic power.

■ It's hard to explain. As it should be.

"And as I sat there, I couldn't help but wonder where the doers in our industry had gone? The crazy ones? The curious? And the misfits? The ones who make change not follow trends."

—Noelle Weaver, *Advertising Age*, March 21, 2007

CHAPTER 20

CONCLUSION
The Future of Astrology Is Looking Up

 In this world nothing is certain but death and taxes.

—Benjamin Franklin, personal correspondence

As the preparation of this manuscript neared its completion, I had the good fortune to attend a first-rate professional astrology conference. Now please banish any thoughts of crystal balls and wizard hats. Most of the PowerPoint presentations were as good as any I've seen on the legitimate business circuit, and in most cases the speakers were agreeably passionate and prepared, and genuinely thought provoking.

The conference, named The Blast, was held in the enchanted red rock setting of Sedona, Arizona. It was the brainchild of a young astrological entrepreneur by the name of Moses Siregar, III. Attracting close to 300 serious devotees of the craft, Moses's conference may have single-handedly changed the face of astrology for the next several decades.

As some of the vested astrological luminaries who spoke at the event took care to note, astrology has been searching for a sea change. The issue is that modern Western astrology has for the past half-century served primarily as the slightly demented handmaiden of psychology. It has become a widely embraced practice over the last decade or so for leading astrologers, most now in their fifties and sixties, to wonder out loud when and whether a new generation of astrologers would ever make themselves known.

Siregar III's chief accomplishment was to at last put that new generation up on the stage, right next to their wondering predecessors. The new breed's names—Chris Brennan, Nick Dagan Best, Rebecca Crane, Adam Gainsburg, Maria Mateus, Kenneth Miller, Jonathan Pearl, Kelly Lee Phipps, Sherene Schostak, Bill Street, and others whom I may have most regrettably but unintentionally failed to mention—are not yet well known through the length and breadth of the astrology kingdom, but they will be. For while apparently well versed in traditional astrological knowledge that has been passed along for millennia, these younger astrologers also bring a unique message that, as an internationally-respected astrologer by the name of Robert Blaschke pointed out, represents a clear "new wave" passing of the generational torch.

These new astrologers, in terms of Blaschke's cogent analysis, are unique in that they are questing for synthesis. The Western psychological tradition is great in these young minds, but no less so is the far more karma-connected fatalistic practice of the Eastern astrologers. And in both Eastern and Western traditions, these young astrologers are pointing out, there remains so much in historical concept and technique waiting to be rediscovered, developed, contemporaneously applied, and integrated with an eye to specific situational applications.

This is excellent news for any business enterprise that might be tempted to dabble in astrological insight. Abetted by the power and versatility of computer and communications technology, astrologers can now be individually responsive in ways that even monarchs of ancient times couldn't possibly expect or even define. Of course there will always be "good" and "bad" astrologers, but it definitely now seems that the flexibility and functionality of the craft has every chance of increasing.

As for the rest of it as wrestled with in this manuscript, it seems there really is only one good objection to the consideration and use of astrology, and that is related neither to the issue of its rationality nor its spiritual propriety. The real problem is one of prejudice, and not the world's prejudice against astrology but astrology's against the individual. Because it must be asked, if you accept that someone is a Virgo, even if it's just for the impressionistic value of such a classification, are you really entitled to make assumptions about that individual's values, character, and fate?

The fervent hope here is that you have been brought to the point at which the only possible answer to such a question is "yes and no."

Fortunately it is part of the sublime nature of things that people will sometimes fool you, and will always represent something of a mystery. A reasonable astrologer will admit that simply knowing someone's sun sign is akin to knowing their name—an interesting, resonant, potentially valuable, and maybe even motivational piece of information, but far from a complex personal profile. And yet a lot of the common wisdom of astrology is just knowing someone's sun sign and expecting them to act in accordance with the astrology texts.

Because of the richness of personality and the subjective fallibility of the observer, this sort of easy analysis doesn't always work. That it does seem to work a fair portion of the time is entirely remarkable, however, and when it does the conceptual resonance can be astonishing. It really does make the spirit soar.

Perhaps it may even be fairly said that the experience of accurate astrological revelation, even in something as simple as a sun sign, may create a fostering of tolerance rather than a lessening. As so eloquently observed by Kenny Moore, there is a cheerful half-faux fatalism most people allow themselves when accepting astrological judgment. Truth can be mined, but at the same time the subject doesn't have to be taken too seriously or dogmatically. It's a nicer and arguably more creative and constructive space than business generally allows.

As also explored briefly in this book, there are potentially rich applications of astrology related to timing and trends and team building, and these, if managed rightly, are truly wondrous windfalls. But it may really be more than enough to note that your Virgo boss really doesn't want any fancy tap dancing in your report, or that the Libra department head is going to go to fairly great lengths to avoid head butting. Even if it doesn't make you richer or right, it just might open your mind to some powerful and accessible principles of the universe, which forever afterwards may sparkle a little more brightly and inspiringly if, admittedly, not any more scientifically or spiritually correct.

Landmark business events, astrologically timed

Astrology is more than a little intriguing as a time-specific indicator of major business history events. The following examples consider at least one significant planetary *aspect* (described in Chapter 18) in effect at some of these significant business occasions. They are particularly remarkable for the fact that *in every case the aspects are exact*, with a variance of one degree or less from geometrical precision.

The examples given here also include at least one *transit* aspect (also described in Chapter 18) being made from the event chart planets to the planets in the natal chart of the leader most engaged in the event. Here, too, one-degree or less "orb" is adhered to. Please note that there are many other methods for event timing and interpretation that might be employed here, but even this most rudimentary of astrological techniques is likely to give an open-minded individual ample pause for wonder, especially considering the precision of the timing.

Admittedly, the need to rely on astrology's jargon here challenges easy comprehension. Yet these are the "facts" as astrology records them, and they are spoken in the language of this art-craft. Those who can find the spirit to admit these and similar manifestations of cosmic clock reading into their arsenal of applied concepts will likely be the richer for it—not to mention enlightened and entertained.

Leader: J. P. Morgan (Aries)

Event: Incorporation of U.S. Steel, then the largest business enterprise ever launched

Date: February 25, 1901

Event Chart Aspects: Pluto in Gemini is in opposition to Uranus in Sagittarius. This indicates the power of a transformative perception challenging the vested organizational principles of society.

Aspects to Leader Chart: Event Pluto in Gemini is sextile Morgan's Pluto in Aries. This indicates the opportunity to successfully exert one's personal will in a situation involving profoundly transformative news. Also exact is a sextile from the event Jupiter in Capricorn to Morgan's Uranus in Pisces that would indicate an opportunity for considerable long-term business profit from a brilliant "collective unconscious" (or secretly manipulated) inspiration.

Leader: Donald Douglas (Aries)

Event: The first flight of the DC-3 airplane, the craft that popularized public air transportation

Date: December 17, 1935

Event Chart Aspects: Mars in Aquarius is sextile Jupiter in Sagittarius. The movement of groups of people is in an opportunistic relationship to fortunate long-distance travel.

Aspects to Leader Chart: The event Saturn in Pisces is trine Douglas's Uranus in Scorpio. A business development whose cultural time has come is in smooth-flowing relationship to a transformative expression of technological advancement.

Leader: Edwin Land (Taurus)

Event: First sale of a Polaroid Land camera, the first to develop photographs "instantly"

Date: November 26, 1948

Event Chart Aspects: Mars in Sagittarius is in opposition to Uranus in Gemini. This aspect speaks to a new concept of action facing off against existing popular expression. At its birth, instant photography is a truly revolutionary notion.

Aspects to Leader Chart: The event Saturn in Virgo is conjunct Land's Jupiter in Virgo. The time has come to reap the rewards of a good concept in engineering.

Leader: Queen Elizabeth II (Taurus)

Event: Coronation as Queen of England

Date: June 2, 1953

Event Chart Aspects: The coronation chart of Elizabeth II has an inordinate amount of powerful aspects. In the case of this chart the planets Mercury, Mars, Uranus, Neptune, and Pluto are all in exact and favorable aspects to one another. Although not a powerful or rare aspect in itself, it's interesting to note that Mercury and Mars in Gemini are exact to the same minute of orbital arc, presenting a strong image of news (Mercury) about leadership (Mars). The power and positive effect of this news is underscored by the Mercury/Mars sextile to Pluto in Leo.

Aspects to Leader Chart: As with the event chart itself, there are many exact aspects from the event to the individual. One that is notable is that the event chart's Mercury/Mars conjunction is exactly trine Elizabeth's Jupiter in Aquarius, which would make the new Queen's ascendancy very popular news throughout the breadth of her kingdom.

Leader: Cyrus Curtis (Gemini)

Event: Ladies Home Journal delivers America's first ever million–copy magazine issue

Date: February 1, 1904

Event Chart Aspects: Saturn is conjunct the Sun in Aquarius, which may be generally indicative of a popular idea whose time has come. Just as interesting, though, is a Venus in Capricorn opposition to Neptune in Cancer, which addresses the pragmatic side of female-role responsibility in opposition to the nebulous romantic characterization of motherhood.

Aspects to Leader Chart: Any astrologer would immediately note an exact conjunction between Pluto and Uranus in Aries in Curtis' natal chart, giving him great promise as a popular trendsetter. In the event chart here, however, Pluto in Gemini is sextile (and is at the midpoint) of an exact trine between Saturn in Aries and Mars in Leo in Curtis' chart. The aggressive enthusiasm for an enormously influential and reader–flattering periodical is amply indicated by this combination.

Leader: Robert Maxwell (Gemini)

Event: Death under mysterious circumstances

Date: November 5, 1991

Event Chart Aspects: Mars is conjunct the Sun in Scorpio and, if reports of Maxwell's fall from his yacht that place the event just before dawn are correct, this conjunction takes place in the first house of the physical self and identity. Those who view the death as somehow nefarious rather than accidental are supported by this chart combination in Scorpio, especially as this conjunction is sextile Neptune in Capricorn, which might certainly indicate the opportunistic carrying out of secret plans.

Aspects to Leader Chart: There are many intriguing connections here. One is drawn to the event Uranus in Capricorn in opposition to Maxwell's Pluto in Cancer, which might broadly indicate a timely surprise and death at sea. What truly fascinates, however, is the very prominent and exact connections between the event Jupiter in Virgo and its sextile (and midpoint) relationships to Maxwell's own Jupiter in Scorpio and his Pluto in Cancer. These combinations sometimes can refer to expanded understanding and spiritual regeneration, and may speak to psychological and material circumstances of which we will never know. In any event it speaks to the difficulty of considering Jupiter simply as the planet of "good fortune."

Leader: John D. Rockefeller (Cancer)

Event: Takes first salaried job as a clerk/assistant bookkeeper

Date: September 26, 1855

Event Chart Aspects: The seemingly odd selection of this date is derived from the fact that Rockefeller is said to have annually celebrated this occasion with more passion than his birthday. A pleasant aspect in the event chart is Mercury in Libra trine Jupiter in Aquarius, which at the very least indicates a sound idea with prosperous social implications.

Aspects to Leader Chart: It may have been a somewhat ordinary day to others, but it was no mild passing to Rockefeller. Here the Venus in the event chart is exactly conjunct Rockefeller's Jupiter in Libra, which definitely could indicate finding the love of one's life. The event's Neptune is also exactly conjunct Rockefeller's Uranus in Pisces, which speaks to the most extraordinary sort of world-changing inspiration.

Leader: Leona Helmsley (Cancer)

Event: The opening of the Helmsley Palace hotel in New York City

Date: September 15, 1980

Event Chart Aspects: The sextile between Mercury in Libra and Venus in Leo, although hardly rare, still suggests a fortuitous link between beautifully balanced perception and the role of a deeply heartfelt personal vision. The simultaneous conjunction between Jupiter and Sun in Virgo would indicate both an enormous attention to detail and the likely good financial fortune of the project.

Aspects to Leader Chart: Although it has not been mentioned until this very late moment, most modern astrologers tend to pay a fair amount of attention to a planetary object orbiting between Saturn and Uranus called Chiron, variously identified as an asteroid or as a comet nucleus or as the leading representative of a class of celestial objects called centaurs. Although astrologers are still refining its symbolic meaning, they most often tend to associate Chiron with personal sacrifice that ultimately benefits both the individual and mankind. In this particular event, Chiron in Taurus is exactly square Helmsley's Jupiter in Leo, indicating an energy conflict between material self-sacrifice for the collective good and the self-glorification requirements of a copious ego.

Leader: Lucille Ball (Leo)

Event: First telecast of *I Love Lucy*

Date: October 15, 1951

Event Chart Aspects: Pluto in Leo exactly sextile Sun in Libra is an enormously favorable aspect for the emergence of a powerful celebrity creation that has the opportunity to project unique and inescapable charm. This is greatly compounded by the fact that the Sun is closely conjunct (less than two degrees in both cases) on its respective sides by Neptune and Mercury in Libra.

Aspects to Leader Chart: Lucy's chart was as lit up as her personality on the night of her first telecast. The event's Mars in Virgo sextile Lucy's Jupiter in Scorpio hails a good business decision, but perhaps the most engaging aspect is the sextile from the event's Uranus in Cancer to Lucy's Mars in Taurus, indicating that on this newfangled home appliance called the television, the *I Love Lucy* show was likely in for a good long run.

Leader: Frederick W. Smith (Leo)

Event: FedEx goes operational

Date: April 17, 1973

Event Chart Aspects: Although it slightly violates the parameters of this exercise (the planets involved are less than two degrees apart, rather than the specified one degree), it's hard not to notice the "almost" exact trine from Saturn in Gemini to Mars in Aquarius. Here is a symbolically explicit example of business information flowing rapidly among the general population as a result of a breakthrough idea.

Aspects to Leader Chart: Pluto in the event chart is in exact conjunction to Smith's Neptune in Libra. While this is a major rather than a personal aspect, it can still signify the power of inspiration in the field of one-to-one human connectivity. (Note that some astrologers consider Neptune as the planet representing flight in terms of its "magical" quality.)

Leader: J. Willard Marriott (Virgo)

Event: Opens his first A&W root beer stand, the first step on a path to the Marriott Hotel empire

Date: May 20, 1927

Event Chart Aspects: Sun and Mercury are conjunct in Taurus, and both are sextile to Neptune in Pisces. Thoughts of endurance are signified here, in opportunistic configuration to great dreams. (It is noteworthy that this is also the day that Charles Lindbergh left on his flight to Paris.)

Aspects to Leader Chart: The concept of the moon's nodes has been lightly touched upon in this book, primarily as a concept too rigorous to explain in an introductory text about astrology. Without going on about the astronomy here, it is worth noting that astrologers invariably consider the moon's nodes in matters of destiny and life purpose. In this instance the key aspect is the event's Saturn in Sagittarius conjunction with the Jupiter and North Node conjunction in Marriott's chart. Here is an individual who has come upon an unparalleled moment to embark upon a fortunate personal destiny.

Leader: Muriel Siebert (Virgo)

Event: Becomes first woman to own a seat on the NYSE

Date: December 28, 1967

Event Chart Aspects: An exact conjunction between Mercury and the Sun in Capricorn is exactly trine Jupiter in Virgo. There is good news of a business personality in a positive relationship to an expanded rules-intensive paradigm. Interestingly, astrology marks this primarily as a business event rather than as a feminist event, although it was certainly both.

Aspects to Leader Chart: There is a nice bit of synchronicity as the event Jupiter conjuncts Siebert's Mercury/Jupiter conjunction in Virgo. Considering that her application was met with much resistance by the old-boy network, such well-aspected approval represented extremely fortunate news for Siebert.

Leader: Henry Ford II (Virgo) and Lee Iacocca (Libra)

Event: Ford fires Iacocca as President of Ford Motors

Date: July 13, 1978

Event Chart Aspects: The perplexing nature of the act, considering Iacocca's success at Ford, is revealed in a pair of exact aspects to Neptune, the planet of illusions. Mercury in Leo trine Neptune in Sagittarius would indicate that a willful decision was made that was easily executed, even if it was not clearly understood in the broad culture. Mars in Virgo exactly square Neptune, however, indicates that the act was officious and abrupt, with the authoritative Virgo (Ford) severing ties to the glamorous icon (Iacocca) despite any clear regard for the deeper cultural consequences.

Aspects to Leader Chart: The aspects from the event to Ford's charts are somewhat subtle; an exact *inconjunct* (a 150-degree angle that represents disharmony) from Sun in Cancer to Uranus in Aquarius speaks compellingly of the conflict of a family business owner at difficult ends with a popular icon. Iacocca's chart, on the other hand, could not be more compelling: The event Saturn in Leo in exact opposition to Iacocca's Mars in Aquarius is a "firing" aspect extraordinaire, and the perfectly exact event Pluto conjunct Iacocca's Mercury, in this context, fairly screams of a beheading.

Leader: Ray Kroc (Libra)

Event: Formation of McDonald's System, Inc. (buys concept rights from McDonald brothers)

Date: March 2, 1955

Event Chart Aspects: Jupiter in Cancer trine Saturn in Scorpio is an excellent business aspect, and in these particular signs speaks symbolically about food (Cancer) and business profit (Scorpio). Also interesting is the exact square from Venus in Capricorn to Neptune in Libra that suggests one party truly does not grasp the business value of the deal.

Aspects to Leader Chart: An exact sextile from the event's Saturn in Scorpio to Kroc's Saturn in Capricorn is a powerful indicator of a solid long-term business opportunity. The trine from the event Venus in Capricorn to Kroc's Venus in Virgo indicates that this will be a thoroughly delightful development to Kroc, extremely gratifying and rewarding. (Note that the sign of Capricorn speaks to business in general, and the sign of Virgo to systems.)

Leader: Jack Welch (Scorpio)

Event: GE announces purchase of RCA, then the largest non-oil merger in American history

Date: December 12, 1985

Event Chart Aspects: There are few extremely sharp aspects for this date, although it might be fairly mentioned that the deal was cut a few days ahead of the announcement. Two days earlier the Sun had passed over Uranus in Sagittarius, which could easily have an ascribed meaning of creating a single strong identity for an expanding technology and media business.

Aspects to Leader Chart: Neptune in Capricorn in the event chart forms a sextile to Welch's Saturn in Pisces. Neptune in Capricorn speaks of inspired or legendary business, while the aspect speaks of an opportunistic energy flow to a very similar configuration in Welch's chart (Saturn and Capricorn bear a close values relationship, as do Neptune and Pisces). The event chart Neptune also forms a very precise trine to Welch's Uranus in Taurus, signifying the fortuitous link between the inspired nature of the business event and Welch's inherent appreciation of popular electronic media (Uranus) and its value (Taurus).

Leader: Bill Gates (Scorpio)

Event: Announces intention to retire from the daily business affairs of Microsoft

Date: June 16, 2006

Event Chart Aspects: There are a number of tight aspects in this chart, including Sun in Gemini in opposition to Pluto in Sagittarius, Mercury in Cancer inconjunct to Neptune in Aquarius, and Mars in Leo conjunct Saturn in Leo. The first indicates a nimble individual consciousness coming up against broad cultural imperatives; the second involves an emotional decision in difficult aspect to a spiritual calling; and the third clearly represents the ending of one form of self-identification and the beginning of another.

Aspects to Leader Chart: Neptune in Aquarius in the event chart is square to Gates's Venus conjunct Saturn in Scorpio. This configuration paints a conflict between the "cosmic" obligation of a humanitarian calling and a powerful executive who has a unique gift for competing and making money in the business realm. Squares, it may well be noted, are almost always experienced as difficulties at first, but also have enormous power when they are resolved.

Leader: Walt Disney (Sagittarius)

Event: Steamboat Willie premiere, the first synchronized sound cartoon and introduction of Mickey Mouse

Date: November 18, 1928

Event Chart Aspects: This chart boasts a remarkable exact Grand Trine (a powerful aspect in which three planets all form trines with one another), here including Venus in Capricorn, Neptune in Virgo, and Jupiter in Taurus. Without too much equivocation one can see these three elements as Mickey Mouse himself (Venus in Capricorn captures both his cuteness and his sense of earnest authority), the magic of engineering that can produce talking cartoon characters (Neptune in Virgo), and the pile of money that's going to be made from all of this over the long-haul (Jupiter in Taurus).

Aspects to Leader Chart: The aspect that leaps out is the event chart's Mars in Cancer in direct opposition to Disney's own Mars in Capricorn. This will frequently signify a struggle for dominance, but in this case one may simply recall Disney's reflections on Mickey and see the birth of a true alter ego. The event chart also has Neptune exactly sextile to Disney's Neptune, signifying an opportunistic relationship between the magic and the magician.

Leader: Walt Disney (Sagittarius)

Event: The opening of Disneyland

Date: July 17, 1955

Event Chart Aspects: Pluto in Leo is exactly sextile Neptune in Libra, which in part serves as description of a fun-seeking generation (Pluto in Leo) in relationship to magical creativity (Neptune in Libra). The cross-generational iconic power of Disneyland is even more apparent in the fact that the midpoint of the event's Sun in Cancer and Jupiter in Leo, as well as its Uranus in Cancer and Mars in Leo is at the point of zero degrees of Leo, a so-called fated degree that connects the baby boomers to the previous generation.

Aspects to Leader Chart: As with the McDonald's/Ray Kroc chart discussed earlier, the event chart Saturn in Scorpio is sextile Disney's Saturn in Virgo, indicating a stable long-term business opportunity—in this instance greatly enhanced by Disney's natal Saturn and Jupiter conjunction. Also noteworthy is the event's Uranus in Cancer trine Disney's Mercury in Scorpio, indicating the easy energy flow between the family television and Disney as the all-powerful host in the nationally broadcast opening and in subsequent Disney themed television.

Leader: Asa Candler (Capricorn)

Event: Publishes ad in Atlanta newspaper declaring sole ownership of Coca Cola™

Date: May 1, 1889

Event Chart Aspects: The event is perfectly encapsulated in the chart's one major aspect, Sun conjunct Venus in Taurus. This is easily translated as "I have something of value."

Aspects to Leader Chart: The cosmic clock agreeably chimes in with the event Jupiter directly conjunct Candler's sun in Capricorn. "Yes," says the universe, "your chances of business success have considerably increased."

Leader: Jeff Bezos (Capricorn)

Event: Named by *Time* magazine as 1999's "Man of the Year"

Date: December 27, 1999

Event Chart Aspects: The key planet here is Jupiter in Aries, which is sextile Mars in Aquarius and trine Mercury in Sagittarius. The Jupiter and Mercury combination proclaims " big news," and the (midpoint) Mars in Aquarius would seem to represent a mover in the field of technology.

Aspects to Leader Chart: Pluto in Sagittarius in the event chart is trine Bezos's Jupiter in Aries, which establishes the power of the event to beneficially expand the personal reputation of the recipient. The most exact aspect, though, is a precisely exact trine between the event Mercury in Sagittarius and Bezos's Venus in Aquarius, enhanced by an almost equally exact conjunction between the event Mars in Aquarius and Bezos's Venus. *Time* may rest assured that Jeff Bezos was truly thrilled by this honor. Frankly, given the precision of all the Venus and Jupiter aspects at this particular moment, it's hard to see how *Time* could have picked anyone else.

Leader: Thomas Edison (Aquarius)

Event: First electrical power distribution system switched on in New York City

Date: September 4, 1882

Event Chart Aspects: The event is elegantly described by a single planet, Pluto in zero degrees of Gemini, a spot-on symbolic rendering of power coming to the neighborhood for the first time. Aspect-wise, Uranus in Virgo—a clear representation of electrical engineering—is trine Neptune in Taurus, which can be read as a magical event transpiring in New York (Taurus is a sign often identified with New York City by astrologers).

Aspects to Leader Chart: This is a complex and intriguing set of charts with quite a few challenging aspects, including a square from the event Neptune in Taurus to Edison's Mercury in Aquarius, and an opposition from the event's Mars in Libra to Edison's Uranus in Aries. While this could be parsed down some, the aspects basically indicate that the work was probably not easy and the results perhaps not exactly what Edison expected—although the combinations do suggest considerable power. On the positive side, though, there's a strong trine from Jupiter in Gemini to Edison's Neptune in Aquarius, adding up to the successfully flowing miracle of neighborhood illumination.

Leader: Oprah Winfrey (Aquarius)

Event: Oprah's first episode of *AM Chicago*

Date: January 2, 1984

Event Chart Aspects: Jupiter in Sagittarius sextile Mars in Libra speaks directly to the opportunity for a hugely successful beginning for a powerful feminine personality.

Aspects to Leader Chart: The fact that the Mars referenced above directly conjuncts Oprah's Neptune and is therefore also sextiled by Jupiter indicates the immense potential for Oprah's dreams to be fulfilled. The same event Mars just a few minutes past one-degree-wide of Oprah's Pluto in Leo, symbolizes an enormous amount of power available for personal realization.

Leader: David Sarnoff (Pisces)

Event: RCA broadcast of Dempsey–Carpentier heavyweight fight, a turning point in radio history

Date: July 2, 1921

Event Chart Aspects: Sometimes astrology seems too accurate to be true. This heavyweight championship fight, notable as the first major entertainment-based national radio broadcast in American history, took place during a precisely exact trine from Mars in Cancer to Uranus in Pisces. That Mars was also conjunct by less than one degree to the Sun and to Pluto clearly indicates a prominent battle (this was a heavyweight championship fight) in a free-flowing energy relationship to the magic of technology.

Aspects to Leader Chart: The profundity of this event in the life of a man who is arguably electronic media's greatest historical visionary is represented by a host of amazing aspects involving Pluto, the planet of transformation. All within one-tenth of a degree or less, the event Pluto makes a trine to the Sun, a square to Jupiter, a square to Saturn and an exact conjunction to Sarnoff's north node, previously cited as the indicator of personal destiny.

Leader: Dorothy Schiff (Pisces) and Rupert Murdoch (Pisces)

Event: Schiff sells the *New York Post* to Murdoch

Date: November 19, 1976

Event Chart Aspects: The compelling aspect in this chart, more than one degree apart but less than two, is a Sun conjunction to Mars in Scorpio in opposition to Jupiter in Taurus. Oppositions will frequently appear in event charts related to sales, as they represent the two sides of a negotiation. Here one has a willful competitor with a fierce survival instinct facing off against extremely deep pockets.

Aspects to Leader Chart: There are many remarkable factors involving the relationship of this event to the respective natal charts of Schiff and Murdoch. First, though, one is inclined to consider the enormously compelling relationship between the birth charts of the two individuals themselves. Born 28 years apart on the same day—March 11—the two charts have identical Pisces sun signs, but they are also linked by *exact* conjunctions of Murdoch's Saturn to Schiff's Venus in Aquarius, Murdoch's Venus to Schiff's Uranus in Aries, Murdoch's Chiron to Schiff's Saturn in Capricorn, and Murdoch's Mars to Schiff's south node in Libra. This is way too much to go into here, but suffice it to say that the branch of astrology that dabbles in past lives and reincarnation would have an absolute field day with this particular pairing of personalities!

Regarding the relationship of the event chart to the respective personalities there are many exact contacts, but one is particularly drawn to an exact conjuction of the event's Pluto in Libra to Mars in Schiff's chart, and to Pluto conjunct the south node and in opposition to Uranus conjunct the north node in Aries in Murdoch's chart. This would seem to be a most fated deal but one that left both participants more than a little spiritually and emotionally bloodied.

INDEX

aBOUt tHe autHOR

Steven Mark Weiss is an award-winning business author, trade journalist, professional speaker, and consultant. His specialization is the research into the identification of demographics-based cultural trends, which he links to the vested long-term values rather than the transitory behaviors of cohort groups. This thesis is fully explored in a previous work, *The Consistent Consumer.*

Audiences for Weiss's highly regarded insights have included a diverse group of professional associations and companies, including: California Closets; the National Basketball Association; the National Restaurant Association; the National Association of Convenience Stores; the Food Service & Packaging Institute; Beringer Blass Wine Estates; and the heretofore McDonald's-owned Chipotle Fresh Mexican Grill. It was a Chipotle executive who described Weiss as "one of the smartest people I've ever met in the *mind* business."

In *Signs of Success*, Weiss takes a thirty-year astrological avocation and explores the broad utility of astrology in business contexts. Frankly, it seems to us that he had way too much fun writing this truly engaging and potentially quite valuable book. For more information, visit Steve's website at www.stevenmarkweiss.com.